A History of
IRONCLADS

Sink before Surrender

A History of

Ironclads

The Power of Iron Over Wood

John V. Quarstein

In partnership with The Mariners' Museum,
Newport News, Virginia.

Charleston · London

History
PRESS

Published by The History Press
Charleston, SC 29403
www.historypress.net

Cover image: "Battle of Hampton Roads," chromolithograph, ca. 1880. *Courtesy of John Moran Quarstein.*

First published 2006

Manufactured in the United Kingdom

ISBN-10 1.59629.118.4
ISBN-13 978.1.59629.118.8

Library of Congress Cataloging-in-Publication Data

Quarstein, John V.
  A history of ironclads : the power of iron over wood / John V. Quarstein.
      p. cm.
  "First published 2006."
  ISBN-13: 978-1-59629-118-8 (alk. paper)
  ISBN-10: 1-59629-118-4 (alk. paper)
  1. Hampton Roads, Battle of, Va., 1862. 2. Armored vessels--History. 3.
Monitor (Ironclad) 4. Merrimack (Frigate) 5. Virginia (Ironclad) 6.
United States--History--Civil War, 1861-1865--Naval operations. 7.
Virginia--History--Civil War, 1861-1865--Naval operations. I. Title.
  E473.2.Q37 2006
  973.7'52--dc22
                                  2006028257

CONTENTS

List of Maps   6

Acknowledgements   7

Introduction   9

Chapter 1: Oar to Sail   15

Chapter 2: Sail to Steam   24

Chapter 3: Shot to Shell   42

Chapter 4: Wood to Iron   58

Chapter 5: The Power of Iron Over Wood   85

Chapter 6: Iron Fever   153

Chapter 7: Questions of Iron and Time   177

Chapter 8: Sink Before Surrender   210

Chapter 9: Victory and Vision   222

Appendix 1: Ironclad Recovery   255

Appendix 2: Union Ironclads   259

Appendix 3: Confederate Ironclads   262

Select Bibliography   265

Index   269

LIST OF MAPS

Battle of Lepanto	23
Battle of the Capes	33
The Glorious First of June	36
Attack on San Juan d'Ulua	50
Battle of Hampton Roads	104, 105
Battle of New Orleans—Passing of the Mississippi Forts	124
Battle of Drewry's Bluff	133
Battle of Mobile Bay	197, 198
Battle of Lissa	231
Battle of Santiago Bay	239

ACKNOWLEDGEMENTS

I embarked upon this chronology as a result of my work supporting The Mariners' Museum's *Monitor* Center. One of my early tasks was the creation of a simple timeline. This chronology was designed to guide the creation of the *Monitor* Center's exhibit, explaining the historical and technological background to the March 8–9, 1862 Battle of Hampton Roads. As the timeline kept expanding, my friend and *Monitor* Center curator, Anna Gibson Holloway, advocated that the information be expanded into a chronology that presented an evolution of technology and tactics that influenced the construction of the USS *Monitor* and the CSS *Virginia* (*Merrimack*). We quickly realized that the story did not and could not end with just the ironclads that fought in Hampton Roads. So, the volume was expanded to detail all ironclad actions during the Civil War and how these events influenced warship design.

I am indebted to so many people for helping me create *A History of Ironclads*. I must thank John Hightower, president of The Mariners' Museum, for supporting my work on this effort as well as his wonderful assistant Marge Shelton for her encouragement on this project. I could not have gathered all of the great photographs without the assistance of Claudia Jew, director of Photographic Services and Licensing at the Mariners' Museum, and the photography staff: Jason Copes, Megan Evans and Sidney Moore. Their support provided the book with the extra interpretation needed to place this technological and tactical chronology in focus. Furthermore, I have to thank Sara Kiddey of the Mariners' Museum. Sara created the maps that accompany the book as well as transcribed and prepared the text for publication. She was very supportive in keeping everything on track and organized.

Several of my coworkers and volunteers at Lee Hall Mansion greatly assisted in this endeavor. Michael Moore and Tim Smith assisted with the photographic collection and documentation. Michael and a former employee at Lee Hall Mansion, Sarah Goldberger, edited the text. I would be most remiss not to thank my son, John Moran Quarstein, for his assuming the task of researching twentieth-century monitors. His marvelous mother, Martha, also helped prepare part of the text for publication.

Everyone associated with this project has my deepest appreciation and gratitude. Without their help, I could not have embarked upon this volume. *A History of Ironclads* is a better book thanks to all the tasks they completed on my behalf.

INTRODUCTION

THE MARCH 8–9, 1862 BATTLE of Hampton Roads introduced a new style of naval warfare that influenced ship design and tactics for seventy years thereafter. This indecisive engagement between two quickly produced experimental warships sounded the death knell for sailing wooden warships and marked the rise of steam-powered armored battleships. Few events in naval history brought forth onto the battlefield an amalgamation of so many old and new technologies that left behind such a powerful legacy.

The CSS *Virginia* (*Merrimack*) and USS *Monitor* did not just appear out of thin air. Each vessel was the combination of several old and new technologies. The Southern integration of ram, rifled cannon, sloped armor and steam power only met its match with the North's union of rotating armored turret, screw propeller, heavy smoothbore iron guns and shot-proof below-waterline ship operations. This clash of armor produced instant results. Wooden sailing ships no longer ruled the seas. The age of the heavy gunned iron warship was born.

Over 25,000 people watched the Battle of Hampton Roads. They witnessed the unbelievable as traditional naval vessels were rapidly destroyed by an iron monster that appeared from the depths of Dante's *Inferno*. The next day's scene was even more awe inspiring. The CSS *Virginia* and USS *Monitor* steamed about belching fire and smoke in an inconclusive duel that eventually decided the fate of all of the navies then floating throughout the world. Even though both ships did not survive 1862, their impact can still be seen throughout Hampton Roads. Many of the same spectators and a few of the battle's participants were able to clearly see this legacy forty-five years later when President Theodore Roosevelt's "Great White Fleet" returned to Hampton Roads from its triumphant voyage around the world.

The age of the steel battleship was nearing its high point. The comparison between the design of Civil War ironclads and the integration of the lessons learned since the *Monitor* and *Virginia* engagement could clearly be visualized by the few who noticed the old monitor, USS *Canonicus*, floating in the harbor. Although this venerable relic would soon be scrapped, her detail to the 1907 Jamestown Exposition was a symbolic link to the Battle of Hampton Roads.

Naval warfare totally changed over the next one hundred years. By the twenty-first century, few sailors from 1900 could recognize the ships and weapons. Many of these new types of warships were built within a musket-shot away from where the CSS *Virginia*'s first victim lay at the bottom of the James River. History's correlations were confirmed by those who witnessed the return of the USS *Monitor* to Hampton Roads on August 9, 2002.

A little over 140 years from the day she fought her epic battle with the CSS *Virginia*, the *Monitor*'s turret floated on a barge up the James River to The Mariners' Museum. When I saw the turret come into the harbor from my house I declared that it was the closest sight that I would ever see of a *real* monitor in action. I was thrilled particularly by the fact that as I looked

INTRODUCTION

"Sinking of the Rebel Steamer *Florida*" near Fortress Monroe, November 28, engraving, dated 1864. *Courtesy of John Moran Quarstein.*

out at the turret, behind it, across Hampton Roads at Sewell's Point, were three modern U.S. Navy *Nimitz*-class aircraft carriers. Technology had moved full circle once again.

I have been studying Civil War ironclad development and its impact on naval warfare virtually my entire life. The Battle of Hampton Roads influenced so many events. Major General George B. McClellan's 1862 Peninsula Campaign was altered and eventually failed in many ways because of the March 8–9, 1862 Battle of Hampton Roads. More importantly is the engagement's place in the evolution of naval warfare. The CSS *Virginia*–USS *Monitor* duel is one of the most revolutionary naval battles in history. As a "Top Ten Battle," the question remains why it is so important. We must also consider how the battle relates to events before and after it occurred. Finally, what does it mean to us today? The last question is so relevant because now people can actually come face to face with the *Monitor*'s turret. When visitors touch this iconic object or interact with artifacts like a sailor's shoe from the *Monitor*'s sinking, they can see and feel all of the events and emotions wrapped up in this dramatic story. This experience becomes even more meaningful if all of this history has been placed into context and interpreted.

Historians have been talking, studying and writing about the Battle of Hampton Roads since 1862. The *Monitor*–*Virginia* duel is perhaps the most discussed Civil War naval battle. Accordingly, when I began considering how to identify this engagement's proper place within the course of history, I decided that it would be best to do so in a chronological format so as not to produce yet another narrative. Therefore, this timeline has been conceived to highlight all of the changes in naval technology and tactics throughout history that influenced the development, use and impact of Civil War ironclads.

Date selection was based on the relevance of events, inventions and people to the development of ironclad warfare. Each entry is thoroughly explained and placed in its historical context. Since this chronology is primarily a Civil War history, I have sought to detail the revolutionary naval events of 1861 to 1865 in a more comprehensive manner. Therefore, critical battles such as Head of the Passes, Drewry's Bluff, Wassau Sound and Mobile Bay are detailed minute by minute to provide the reader with greater insights in an engagement's influence. Although most chronologies are just lists of dates, I sought to illustrate these events

USS *Atlanta*. View of the former Confederate ironclad serving as a Union warship in the James River below Richmond, Virginia, ca. 1864. *Courtesy of The Mariners' Museum.*

to intensify reader interpretation. The result is a useful guide to the evolution of ship design, ordnance and propulsion system associated with the Battle of Hampton Roads and the entire Civil War. *A History of Ironclads* is in essence the history of the rise of technology building up to the Civil War and the subsequent development of ironclad warships, which would dominate the seas for the next sixty years.

CHAPTER 1

OAR TO SAIL

RAMSES III OF EGYPT IS credited with creating the first warship. Around 1200 BC Egypt was threatened by a seaborne invasion and the pharaoh ordered the construction of narrow-beam coastal vessels powered by a single sail and oars. Designed primarily to use oar-power in battle, these ships featured a ram protruding from the bow. The warship was the weapon. Besides being destructive forces themselves, these vessels also served as platforms or delivery systems for warriors. Galleys would dominate naval warfare throughout the Mediterranean Sea for the next 2,800 years. Modifications to hull design and motive powered to enhance the ram's impact continued throughout this age.

During the Persian Wars, the Greeks used triremes to defeat several invasion fleets. This vessel featured three banks of oars, which gave this galley design great speed, mobility and ram impact. In the great Greek victory of Salamis, the Greeks were able to out-maneuver their stronger opponent with speed and destroyed two hundred Persian ships with their rams. Triremes were soon outmoded by quadriremes and quinqueremes (four or five banks of oars); however, the tactics remained the same. These warships would either directly ram the enemy's vessel or would glide close by the side of an opposing ship to break off their oars. In either case, the enemy was disabled or sinking and could then be dispatched in combat between warriors.

Although primarily noted for its prowess on land, Rome was forced to develop a navy during the Punic Wars. The Romans raised a fleet of quinqueremes to challenge Carthage's control of the Mediterranean Sea. They devised new tools to compensate for their poor seamanship. While the ram still was the decisive weapon, the Romans sought to close with their enemy and used land-based infantry tactics to overwhelm them. The legendary success of the Roman legion on land was transferred onto the sea. A boarding ramp (corvus) transformed engagements into an infantry melee. A tower, painted to appear as if made of stone, was added to provide a protected fighting platform. Nevertheless, their greatest victory during the First Punic War, the Battle of Ecnomus, was won by ramming. Once the Romans defeated Carthage in the Second Punic War, they were able to extend their power into the Aegean Sea. By the Battle of Myonnesus, Rome gained complete naval supremacy throughout the Mediterranean region. Julius Caesar's conquest of Gaul resulted in the first combat between galleys and sailing ships. At Quiberon Bay, Caesar's galleys were successful because the Gallic venetes were becalmed. The Romans developed several new naval fighting techniques during their civil wars. The Octavian fleet was commanded by Marcus Agrippa. Agrippa strengthened his ships with strong wooden beams around the waterline as protection against ramming. He won the Battle of Cumae with the first use of "belted armor." Agrippa used two additional new weapons to win the battles of Naulochus and Actium. The fire-arrow proved to be extremely destructive. However, the Roman land-based tactics were given a boost with a grapple projectile known as harpax or harpago. The harpax

"Battle Between
Spanish and
Barbary Pirates,"
Sebastian D. Castro,
oil painting on
board, ca. 1625–75.
*Courtesy of The
Mariners' Museum.*

was fired at enemy ships on the end of a line. This act allowed the Romans to drag two ships together to seek a decisive engagement. The victory at Actium left the Roman fleet supreme for the next four hundred years.

Roman rule was first threatened by the Barbarian invasions. The eastern empire, Byzantium, survived this onslaught, but its naval supremacy would eventually be threatened by the followers of Islam. Although the Battle of the Masts was a major Arab victory, the Arabs were overwhelmed by the superior tactics and maneuverability of the Byzantines. In an effort to prevent the capture of their flagship, the Arabs chained their vessels together and became a "floating fortress" and destroyed Byzantine ships with boarding parties. The Arab conquest of the eastern Mediterranean continued to their first attack on Constantinople, AD 717–718. This naval assault was repulsed by the Byzantine use of "Greek fire." This substance was invented by the Syrian engineer Callinicus. Greek fire was a mixture of saltpeter, pitch, sulfur and oil. Once ignited and hurled onto an enemy's ship, it could not be extinguished. Emperor Leo II's use of this new weapon destroyed the Arab fleet in two decisive actions.

The Viking expansion and colonization throughout Western Europe was made possible by a new ship design. While powered by sail and oars, these ships were sturdy and intended for sailing in open waters. The reinforced hulls featured keels, which enabled larger masts (hence, larger sails), thereby providing greater speed and stability. This design enabled the Norsemen to create kingdoms in Normandy, Sicily and the British Isles. As galleys continued to dominate naval actions in the Mediterranean, warships in Northern Europe eschewed oars and relied solely on sail power. Merchant ships evolved from the "knorr." In times of war, these vessels were modified with two high "castles" fore and aft shaped like land fortresses. The mast's top was fortified with a "topcastle." The increase of waterborne trade during the thirteenth century caused the construction of broad-beamed ships with rigging. These vessels evolved from the Norse longboats and the various Mediterranean sail-powered vessels. The fore and after castles became part of the hull, resulting in the Northern "cog" and the Mediterranean "caravel." These larger sailing ships were fitted with up to four masts, generally carrying square sails, an arrangement that much improved their sailing qualities. By the fourteenth century the stern rudder made its appearance. As the tiller-rudder system improved steering, improved instruments, like the compass and astrolabe, enabled long-distance oceanic voyages to be undertaken.

Ship armaments become more powerful during the fifteenth century. The cannon had greater destructive power than catapults. Ships were enlarged and modified to safely mount more guns.

The sail and cannon combined to end the age of galleys and rams. The 1571 Battle of Lepanto was the last major engagement fought by galleys. Don Juan of Austria's victory was achieved by outstanding leadership, superior tactics and a reliance on cannons and muskets instead of rams and bows.

1190 BC	Ramses III defeated an invasion of "Sea People" using warships powered by oar and sail with a bow ram.
480 BC	Battle of Salamis. The Greeks, commanded by Themistocles, defeated a much larger Persian fleet led by Xerxes. Themistocles selected a narrow channel, the entrance to which was covered by the small island of Psyttaleia. The Persian attack was unable to take advantage of its numerical superiority and the Greeks surrounded their opponents' left wing and forced it back upon the right wing. The fierce attack of the Spartan triremes settled the day. The Greek trireme with its ram proved decisive: two hundred Persian ships were destroyed to the loss of twenty Greek vessels.
256 BC	Battle of Ecnomus. A Roman fleet of 330 ships attacked a similar sized Carthaginian fleet commanded by Hanno and Hanikar Barca off Sicily's Cape Ecnomus. The Carthaginians were arrayed in a broad front formation, whereas the Romans advanced in a v-shaped van with one squadron following with transports. The Carthaginian center feigned retreat, drawing the Roman squadron into a trap. The Punic fleets attacked the transports, but were soon enveloped by Roman squadrons. Even though the Carthaginians used superior tactics, they were unable to counter the Roman boarding ramp during close action. The Carthaginians lost 90 ships and were forced to sue for peace.
190 BC October	Battle of Myonnesus. Romans gained control of the Aegean Sea.
73 BC	Battle of Lemnos. Romans destroyed the fleet of Mithridates III of Syria and attained naval supremacy throughout the Mediterranean.
56 BC	Battle of Quiberon Bay. Julius Caesar's galleys defeated the Gallic venetes. Caesar was able to destroy his enemy's becalmed sailing ships.

36 BC

Battle of Mylae. Following the Battle of Cumae, Octavian gave command of his fleet to his boyhood friend Marcus Agrippa. Agrippa constructed his ships with beams along the waterline as protection against ramming. This first use of "belted armor" made Agrippa's ships larger and stronger than the faster and more maneuverable ships of Sextus Pompey. The extra armor made Agrippa's ships immune to ramming and sank thirty of his enemy's ships.

Battle of Naulochus. Agrippa employed two new weapons, fire-arrows and a grapple projectile (harpax), during this engagement. Consequently, Agrippa was able to damage enemy ships before they closed in or escaped. The fleet of Sextus Pompey was organized in a close formation along the coast, preventing his smaller ships from taking advantage of their speed and maneuverability. Agrippa outflanked his enemy's fleet by the seaside and forced them onto the coast. The result was a complete defeat for Sextus Pompey with twenty-eight of his ships either sunk or burnt.

31 BC
2 September

Battle of Actium. The Roman Civil Wars ended in an epic showdown between Octavian and Anthony at Actium on the Ionian Sea. Agrippa moved against the fleet of Anthony and Cleopatra at the entrance to the Gulf of Ambracia. With a rising wind, Anthony attempted to break out. However, Agrippa's superior numbers and use of fire-arrows resulted in an overwhelming victory.

AD 323

Battle of the Hellespont. During a conflict for control of the Roman Empire between Licinius and Constantine, Constantine's son Crispus attacked Licinius's fleet at Byzantium using two ranks in loose formation. Licinius's fleet, commanded by Amandus, was held in a close battle order. Crispus's first rank hit and opened the enemy line, thereby allowing the second rank to exploit the gaps and achieve victory.

AD 655

Battle of the Masts (Dhatal-Sawari). After the death of Mohammed in 632, his followers endeavored to establish an Islamic world order. The Arab forces spread throughout the eastern Mediterranean Sea, which resulted in an advance against Constantinople. A five-hundred-strong Byzantine fleet under the personal command of Emperor Constans II fought a two-hundred-ship Arab fleet commanded by Abdallah ibn Sa'd. The superior tactics and maneuverability of the Byzantine fleet nearly resulted in victory. However, the Arabs chained their ships together to form a floating fortress and destroyed the Byzantine fleet ship by ship with boarding parties.

AD 678

First Attack on Constantinople. The Arabs blockaded Constantinople for four years striving to wear down the city's defenses. The city was finally saved by the introduction of a new weapon, Greek fire. This mixture of saltpeter, pitch, sulfur and oil was ignited and projected at enemy ships by a "siphon." This weapon decimated the Arab fleet and the siege was broken.

AD 718
Spring

Second Attack on Constantinople. The Arabs were repulsed again by Greek fire.

AD 838

Capture of Dublin. Norsemen introduced a sturdy vessel with a keel, which enabled a stronger and more stable hull, thereby allowing for larger sails. Propelled by oar and sail, the long-ships were able to cross large bodies of open water and allow the Norsemen to strike throughout Europe. When rowing, they lined their wood and iron shields along the sides of their ships. This action provided them with additional protection against enemy missiles similar to armor plating.

"Viking Knarr—
ca. AD 1000,"
Daniel Pariser,
model, dated
1991, Brooklyn,
New York.
*Courtesy of The
Mariners' Museum.*

AD 874

Vikings discover Iceland.

AD 899

Alfred the Great of Wessex defeated a Danish fleet. His ships were larger than those of the Danes.

AD 1066

Battle of Hastings. William of Normandy, a descendant of the Norsemen who conquered Normandy, completed the last successful invasion of England.

AD 1217
August

Battle of Dover. The English thwart a French invasion when an eighty-strong French fleet was attacked by forty Cinque Port vessels commanded by Hubert de Burgh. The English vessels passed the French fleet as the English fleet sailed northeast, turned and attacked the French from the rear. The French ships were captured one by one as English archers kept the French crews beneath the main deck and then captured the vessel. Only fifteen French ships escaped. This battle was the first to employ sailing tactics.

AD 1304

24 June — Battle of Sluys. Edward III of England prepared to reclaim his hereditary lands in France. He organized a large naval force and moved against the French fleet positioned in the western Scheldt near Sluys. The French were divided into three squadrons: two sailing and one Genoese galleys. The sailing vessels were anchored and chained together, with the galleys held in reserve. The English, with their greater mobility, were able to attack this defensive position and the French ships were captured one by one.

18 August — Battle of Zierikzee. A French fleet consisting of sailing vessels from Normandy and Spain along with galleys from Genoa attacked the Count of Flanders's fleet in the Scheldt estuary. The Flemish were defeated because galleys still proved superior to sailing vessels in narrow waterways. The battle witnessed the first recorded use of "fire ships." A fire ship could be a boater raft that had been filled with combustibles set on fire and then floated toward enemy ships. Fire ships were feared by wooden sailing ships, especially when at anchor or operating in narrow waterways.

1492 — Christopher Columbus, on a westerly voyage in the caravels *Santa Maria*, *Nina* and *Pinta*, discovered the New World for the Spanish crown.

1501 — Frenchman Decharges invented gun ports. This concept enabled the heavy guns to be carried lower in the ship, with a resulting improvement in stability.

1519–21 — First circumnavigation of the globe by Ferdinand Magellan and Sebastian del Cano.

"Venetian State Galley," John Hood, drawing, wash, ca. 1758. *Courtesy of The Mariners' Museum.*

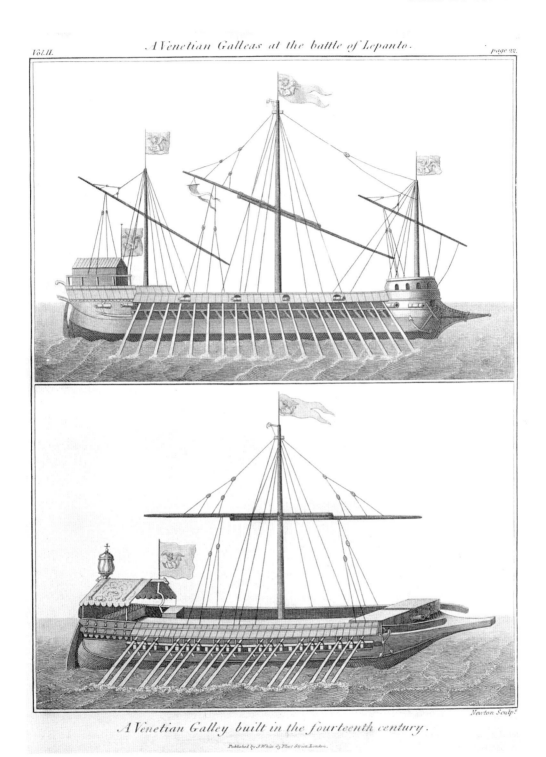

Vol. II.   A Venetian Galleas at the battle of Lepanto.   page 22.

Newton Sculp.

A Venetian Galley built in the fourteenth century.

Published by J. White & Fleet Street, London.

"Venetian Galleys," Newton (engraver), J. White (publisher), engraving, London, England, ca. 1700. *Courtesy of The Mariners' Museum.*

1571

7 October

<u>Battle of Lepanto</u>. Pope Pius V organized a Christian coalition of Spanish, Venetian and Genoese under the command of Don Juan of Austria. The coalition assembled over 200 vessels and 80,000 men to check the advance of the Ottoman Turks. The Turks conquered most of the eastern Mediterranean, including the islands of Cyprus and Rhodes. They tried to expand their control of the Adriatic and Western Mediterranean. The Turks assembled 240 ships and 80,000 men under the command of Ali Pasha. Ali Pasha's fleet consisted mainly of galleys with few cannons. In turn, Don Juan's fleet had galleys armed with cannon as well as six large Venetian galleass (galliots). These warships were oversized galleys with four masts, lateen sails and fifty cannons. A galleass featured an enclosed forward platform fitted with swivel guns and could be considered a forerunner to the modern armored turret. These ships had a ram instead of an ornamental stern and below the waterline a cutwater served as another offensive weapon. The galleasses were the heaviest ships afloat. Despite his artillery assets, Don Juan recognized that the battle would be a close action. He believed he had another advantage in his armored Spanish soldiers with their arquebuses. Don Juan also removed the iron rams from many of his ships to enhance their maneuverability in a close action. Don Juan advised his men that they should not fire "until near enough to be splashed with the blood of an enemy."

At dawn on October 7 the two most powerful fleets ever assembled advanced against each other in the Gulf of Patras. Both fleets were organized in three squadrons and approached their foe in a crescent formation. The galleasses, four of which were operating in front of the main Allied line, opened the battle with their heavy cannon. Several Turkish vessels were damaged or sunk. The fleets closed by midday. The Turkish exploited a gap between the Allied right squadron and center only to be eventually destroyed by the intervention of the reserve containing two galleasses. The Allied left wing was outflanked by the Turks and the situation became critical. Don Juan's center captured the Turkish flagship and Ali Pasha was killed. The Turks retreated, leaving behind over 150 ships and 30,000 casualties. Lepanto was a resounding Christian victory and the last major engagement involving galleys. Don Juan's fleet was victorious because of his use of musket and cannon over ram and crossbow.

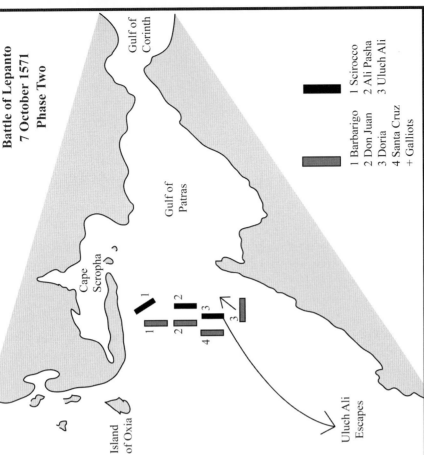

Battle of Lepanto
7 October 1571 Phase Two

Gulf of Corinth

Cape Scropha

Gulf of Patras

Island of Oxia

Uluch Ali Escapes

1 Scirocco
2 Ali Pasha
3 Uluch Ali

1 Barbarigo
2 Don Juan
3 Doria
4 Santa Cruz
+ Galliots

Illustration by Sara Kiddey

Don Juan's strategic intent was to use his cannon to weaken the Turkish fleet before closing into combat range. His three forward squadrons approached in a crescent-shaped formation headed by four galliots. Likewise the Turks held themselves in a crescent with their flanks close to the coasts. While a gap formed between Don Juan's and Doria's squadrons, it was partially filled by the Santa Cruz's squadron. When Don Juan crushed the Turkish center and captured Ali Pasha's flagship, Uluch Ali's squadron was able to escape. The cannons and muskets of the Allies overwhelmed the Turkish ram and crossbow.

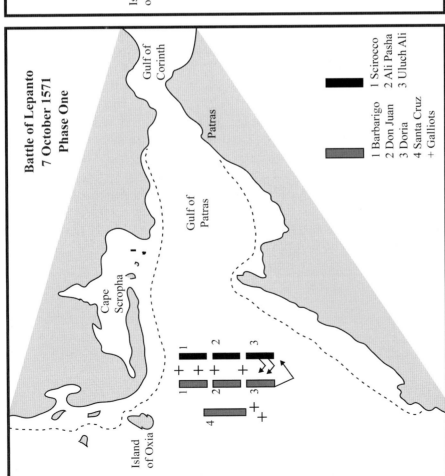

Battle of Lepanto
7 October 1571 Phase One

Gulf of Corinth

Patras

Cape Scropha

Gulf of Patras

Island of Oxia

1 Scirocco
2 Ali Pasha
3 Uluch Ali

1 Barbarigo
2 Don Juan
3 Doria
4 Santa Cruz
+ Galliots

Illustration by Sara Kiddey

Don Juan of Austria assembled an Allied fleet of 200 Spanish and Venetian ships with eighty thousand men. The Allies divided their command into four squadrons. The key to Don Juan's strategy was the use of the Venetian galliots. Each galliot was armed with fifty cannons. These ships were the most powerful vessels employed during the engagement. The Turkish fleet was commanded by Ali Pasha, and he divided his forces into three squadrons guarding the entrance to the Gulf of Patras. Ali Pasha had 220 ships and over eighty thousand men.

CHAPTER 2

SAIL TO STEAM

A MAJOR SHIFT IN POWER TO the north and west was already underway by the Battle of Lepanto. The Mediterranean powers, their energies somewhat sapped by constant conflict with Islamic forces, gave way to the rise of the Atlantic-based powers. Several factors prompted this evolution. The Ottoman Turks had disrupted the ancient trade routes used by Europeans to obtain spices and other goods from the Far East. How to regain this trade was solved by a new understanding of geography and by the development of new ship types capable of carrying considerable cargo while weathering heavy seas. This situation gave rise to the Age of Exploration. Once the sea captains of Portuguese Prince Henry the Navigator opened the trade route around the Cape of Good Hope and across the Indian Ocean and Christopher Columbus discovered the New World, a struggle arose for the control of sea routes and resources. The Age of Exploration gave way to the Age of Imperialism when new ships were armed with new weapons as Western European nations sought economic power and political supremacy. As Sir Walter Raleigh noted: "Whosoever commands the sea commands trade; whosoever commands the trade of the world commands the riches of the world, and consequently the world itself."

While the Europeans experimented with artillery and larger wooden ship designs, a new style of warship was being developed in the Far East. In 1592, the Japanese launched a massive invasion of Korea using 800 ships and 140,000 men. Korea had but 80 ships in its fleet; however, many of these galleys were iron plated. The introduction of this new technology gave the Koreans an overwhelming series of victories at sea.

Iron plating was a foreign concept to European shipbuilders. European maritime powers sought to build bigger, faster ships with more and more armament. Since control of the seas meant world power, various nations sought to maintain professional navies. No longer could merchant ships be transformed into warships when danger loomed. Naval power in the pre-Industrial Age required dynamic leadership, superior warship design and improved firepower. Shipyards built stronger and highly specialized vessels. Improvements, such as copper sheathing, increased speed. Ships of the line (fifty to ninety or more guns), frigates (thirty-eight to fifty guns), sloops (eighteen to thirty-eight guns) and corvettes (eighteen guns or less) were ship types that enabled navies to enforce blockades, protect convoys, complete reconnaissance and force decisive fleet actions. While sail power had its limitations, there were only a few technical changes to ordnance. Nevertheless, each proved to be significant. The short-range carronade (also called the smasher) was introduced and it had an immediate effect during close, ship-to-ship, broadside-to-broadside actions. Cannons were fitted by the late eighteenth century with flintlock mechanisms increasing firing safety, speed and aim.

Battle tactics changed as a result of these improvements. Cannons proved to be a decisive factor when the English fleet defeated the Spanish Armada. Single ship actions witnessed vessels

"The Glorious Defeat of the Invincible Spanish Armada," London, England, ca. 1784. *Courtesy of The Mariners' Museum.*

pounding each other with shot to de-mast or hull the enemy. Specialized shot, such as chain, bar and grape, decimated the opposing warship's crew. The ships would eventually close with victory being achieved by boarding. Large fleet actions evolved during this era. Limited mobility was counter-balanced by artillery improvements. Nevertheless, navies often maintained a more technical approach to combat. The English combat experience during the First Anglo-Dutch War resulted in formal instructions of the *Fleet In Fighting*. This 1653 concept advocated line ahead formation and attack from the weather gage. While these instructions gave the British a clear victory over the Dutch during the Battle of Gabbard Bank, the short range of cannon often resulted in uncontrolled melees. The three Anglo-Dutch Wars proved the power of active blockades and prompted greater control over fleet actions. The Duke of York's 1673 *Fighting Instructions* ordered captains to conform to a rigid battle line when engaging the enemy's fleet.

Once the Dutch had been overwhelmed, England faced France as its newest competitor and would struggle for almost 125 years for economic supremacy. The War of Spanish Succession witnessed the first time that fleets were not placed in ordinary during the winter months so as to maintain a constant blockade. This war resulted in the ruin of French trade and immense profits for the English. This cycle continued throughout most of the eighteenth century. During the worldwide conflict known as the Seven Years' War (French and Indian War), the British sought a decisive naval action to destroy the French fleet. Despite fears of a French invasion of the

British Isles in 1759, British Secretary of State William Pitt recognized an offensive was the best defense. Striking at French overseas possessions and trade, the British were able to secure a series of tremendous victories in 1759. Along the French coast, Sir George Rodney was able to destroy invading barges in Le Havre, while Edward Boscawen defeated a French squadron from Toulon. However, it was Sir Edward Hawke who broke with convention and pursued the French fleet into Quiberon Bay in a gale and humbled the French navy. Hawke had moved away from the rigidity of formal tactics and achieved victory through his boldness and decisive attacks.

Unfortunately, the British did not effectively maintain their fleet following their great victories of 1759. The French, seeking revenge, allied themselves with the rebellious American colonies. Perhaps one of the most important contributions made by the French was Rear Admiral Francois Joseph Paul, Comte de Grasse's victory during the Battle of the Capes. A failure in naval leadership cost the British greatly. Rear Admiral Thomas Graves was far too cautious and relied on inconclusive tactical formations during the Battle of the Capes. Nevertheless, Vice Admiral Sir George Rodney was able to defeat de Grasse on April 12, 1782, during the Battle of the Saintes. Rodney achieved victory by penetrating the French line.

The Battle of the Saintes is significant for several reasons. The British ships were faster because of coppered bottoms and many of their ships had flintlock-firing mechanisms, which enhanced English gunnery. Leadership and aggressive tactics were also the keys to victory. John Clerk of Eldin wrote his celebrated *Essay on Naval Tactics* in 1787. The volume criticized the line ahead instructions and individual ship duels during fleet actions. Instead, Clerk advocated the concentration of force against one part of an enemy's fleet so as to destroy it with superior numbers. He believed that maintaining flexible control of ships within a squadron during combat would enable elements to seize upon opportunities to pierce or envelop the enemy's line. The commander who took these concepts to the forefront was Horatio Nelson. Nelson's determination to achieve complete annihilation of an enemy can be witnessed in his three great victories: the Nile, Copenhagen and Trafalgar. Yet it was far more than just Nelson's combat tactics and relentless pursuit of his enemy that gave Great Britain control of the seas for the rest of the nineteenth century. Nelson's leadership and personal bravery set a standard for naval officers throughout the world.

British efforts to wage economic warfare and impressment were some of the key factors causing the War of 1812. This war about "Free Trade and Sailors' Rights" pitted the small U.S. Navy against the Royal Navy, which was already deeply occupied with France. While early single ship-to-ship encounters boosted American morale, it was major naval victories on Lake Erie and Lake Champlain that saved the United States from an invasion from Canada. The War of 1812 also introduced a new style of warship when Robert Fulton constructed the first steam-powered warship, the *Demologos*. Renamed the *Fulton* after the inventor's death, this steamship was launched in June 1815. The *Fulton* was primarily a harbor defense vessel. The *Karteria* was the first purpose-built steam-powered warship to actually participate in combat. Built in Great Britain for the Greek Navy, the *Karteria* served with distinction under the command of former Royal Navy officer Frank Hastings during the Greek War of Independence. As this conflict introduced steam power to naval warfare, the war truly marked the end of the Age of Sail. An Allied English, French and Russian fleet fighting for Greek independence defeated the Turks on October 20, 1827, at Navarino Bay. It was the last battle fought wholly undersail.

1588

<u>The Spanish Armada</u>. Commanded by Duke of Medina Sidonia, the fleet included six squadrons of sail, one of galleys (including four large galliots) and a supply squadron. The 130 ships had 10,000 sailors and 20,000 soldiers on board. The Spanish regarded artillery as a secondary weapon, and cannons were primarily small-caliber guns mounted on the high castles of the galleons. The Spanish relied on boarding to achieve victory. The English fleet was commanded by Lord High Admiral Lord Howard. He was supported by the dynamic "sea dogs" Sir Francis Drake, Sir Richard Hawkins and Sir Martin Frobisher. The fleet contained 200 ships, mostly small-armed merchantman vessels. These sailing ships featured heavy-caliber broadside guns.

31 July

When the Armada was sighted, the English set sail from Plymouth. The Spanish fleet entered the English Channel in a crescent formation. The English engaged the rear of the Spanish fleet using their superior sailing abilities and artillery to inflict heavy damage on their enemy's ships.

1 August

Two large Spanish galleons, *Senora de Rosaria* and *Nuestra Senora de Rosa*, were captured.

4 August

Spanish ship *Santa Anna* ran aground at Le Havre and was destroyed.

6 August

The Spanish fleet reached Calais.

7 August

The English sent eight fire ships into the Spanish anchorage. The Spanish ships cut their cables to escape; however, several vessels ran aground and were lost.

8 August

The Spanish fleet was scattered from Dunkirk to Gravelines. Drake attacked the disorganized command and drove the Spanish onto the Flanders coast, inflicting heavy damage by grounding and cannon fire. Medina Sidonia, realizing that he had lost twenty ships and over five thousand men, decided

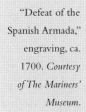

"Defeat of the Spanish Armada," engraving, ca. 1700. *Courtesy of The Mariners' Museum.*

Defeat of the Spanish Armada.

to return to Spain by sailing around the British Isles. The Armada returned to Spain a failure with only sixty-five ships and ten thousand men. This naval campaign was the first decided by artillery.

1592

May

Battle of Okpo. A unified Japan, led by Shogun Hideyoshi, attempted to conquer the Korean peninsula. An army of 140,000 men in 800 ships was assembled. The Korean fleet only had 80 warships; however, many of these were "turtleships" (Kohbakson) developed by Admiral Yi Sun-sin. Turtleships were the first iron-plated warships. A typical turtleship averaged from 90 to 110 feet in length with a 25- to 30-foot beam. The bulwarks were extended to support a roof, which was covered with three-eighths-inch iron plate. The iron was affixed with knives and spearheads to repel boarders. The turtleships were armed with several cannons and a barbed ram. These warships were fitted with one sail; however, propulsion was primarily achieved by oars.

Admiral Yi Sun-sin was able to thwart a Japanese supply squadron and sink 29 ships in two days.

August

Battle of Pusan. Admiral Yi Sun-sin destroyed 130 Japanese ships without loss to his own fleet. The Japanese were forced to evacuate northern and central Korea.

1597

September

Battle of Chin Do Island. Yi Sun-sin, with only 12 ships, defeated a 130-strong Japanese squadron.

1598

November

Battle of Noryang. Yi Sun-sin attacked two Japanese squadrons using turtleships and fire-arrows. One squadron lost fifty ships. The other was virtually destroyed. Admiral Yi Sun-sin was killed by a musket ball entering a port.

"Yi-Soon-Sin, Korean Admiral and Image of Turtle Ship," engraving. *Courtesy of The Mariners' Museum.*

1637

The English launched the *Sovereign of the Seas*. The *Sovereign of the Seas* was the first three-decker warship and mounted 100 guns. She was the largest vessel of her kind with dimensions of 127-foot length, 48-foot beam and 23.6-foot draft.

1652

8 October

Battle of Kentist Knock. General at Sea Robert Blake attacked the Dutch fleet commanded by Witte deWith. The fleets were evenly matched; however, the engagement evolved into a series of irregular combats between individual ships and groups of ships. The Dutch fleet retreated.

1653

Fleet in Fighting Instructions issued, advocating concentration of force, line ahead formation and attack from the weather gage.

12–13 June

Battle of Gabbard Bank. The English concentrated its fleet and held off the Dutch with their stronger artillery. The English lost one ship, the Dutch seventy. All Dutch sea trade ceased.

"Admiral Blake,"
J. Mollison,
engraving, Society
for the Diffusion
of Useful
Knowledge.
*Courtesy of The
Mariners' Museum.*

1657

20 April   <u>Raid on Santa Cruz</u>. The English strove to capture the Spanish silver fleet and attacked the harbor fortifications. The Spanish arranged their defenses so that the entrance was heavily defended by artillery, and the twenty-two galleons were protected by batteries along the beach. The aggressive Admiral Robert Blake divided his command into two groups, one of which attacked the Spanish galleons and the other contents with the land-based artillery. Within six hours, the Spanish ships were destroyed and the batteries were silenced. The English did not lose any ships. However, they failed to capture the silver. This engagement was one of the few during the Age of Sail when sailing ships successfully fought fixed fortifications without land support.

1676

2 June   <u>Battle of Palermo</u>. During the Franco-Dutch War (1672–1680), the French attacked the anchored Dutch-Spanish fleet. Under covering fire from nine ships of the line, the French sent six fire ships in the harbor, which virtually destroyed the Allied fleet. Because of the new line ahead battle formations, the Battle of Palermo was one of the last major uses of fire ships. The future of this weapon was relegated to attacking anchored vessels.

1682

French naval hero Abraham DuQuesne introduced a new weapon and new ship type. Mortars were mounted in specially designed vessels called ketches. These ships were a broad beamed vessel with the foremast removed to make room for the heavy mortars, which could fire two-hundred-pound bombs. A "bomb ketch" needed to be strongly constructed to support the deck from below and to handle the recoil shock. With these vessels, the French executed the first mortar bombardment from sea against the pirate town of Algiers.

1719

21–26 July   <u>Attack on Marstrand</u>. Danes and Swedes collided during the Great Northern War. The Danes, allied with Russia, endeavored to gain control of the Baltic. Danish Admiral Tordenskjold struck at the Swedish anchorage by first landing an artillery battery to bombard the anchored vessels. With seven ships of the line, two frigates, twelve galleys and seven gun "punts," the Danes attacked and destroyed the Swedish fleet. Victory was achieved because of the land-based artillery and the use of ships propelled by oars in shallow waters.

1756

20 May   <u>Battle of Minorca</u>. Admiral John Byng attacked the French squadron off Port Mahon, but he was unable to bring his entire command into effective action. Byng fell back to Gibraltar, leaving the British garrison to be captured by the French. Admiral Byng was recalled and court-martialed. He was convicted and shot. His guilt was not that he lost the battle, or that he was a coward; rather, Byng failed to follow the *Fighting Instructions*. His execution was a lesson to all other English naval commanders that they must follow the rigid guideline, which limited the opportunity for decisive action.

"George Byng, Lord Torrington," Sir Godrey Kneller (artist), J. Houbraken (engraver), engraving, dated 1749. *Courtesy of The Mariners' Museum.*

1759
20 November   Battle of Quiberon Bay. During a heavy gale, the British blockading squadron of twenty-seven ships of the line commanded by Sir Edward Hawke attacked the French fleet of twenty-one ships of the line commanded by Admiral Conflans as it tried to escape into Quiberon Bay. With a rising west-northwest wind, Hawke overtook Conflans at the treacherous entrance to Quiberon Bay. The French rearguard was overwhelmed: the *Formidable* was captured, *Superbe* and *Thesee* capsized and *Heros* struck its colors and ran aground. Since three other French ships ran aground and were burnt, Quiberon Bay was an overwhelming victory for the English. Hawke was able to deviate from the *Fighting Instructions* and to aggressively attack his retreating foe.

1765   HMS *Victory* was commissioned. This 104-gun ship of the line would stay in active service for over fifty years.

1767   Andrew Sprowle established Gosport Shipyard on the Elizabeth River near Portsmouth, Virginia.

1769   James Watt patented the steam engine.

1770   Great Britain began copper sheathing hulls below the waterline. "Coppering" slowed the buildup of marine growth that had lessened a warship's speed.

1776   Production of the first carronade. This short-barreled, large-bore cannon created for ship-to-ship broadside action was first made by the Carron Company of Scotland. The carronade was economic in weight, powder requirements, space, crew and reloading time. Carronades were very destructive at close range, using heavy solid shot to smash enemy timbers and masts or chain shot to decimate an enemy's crew.

1778   Captain Sir Charles Douglas of the HMS *Duke* installed musket locks on all cannon aboard his ship. The flintlocks proved to be a more reliable and faster rate of fire. Furthermore, it gave greater control over the timing of the fire.

1779
23 September   John Paul Jones of the USS *Bonhomme Richard* attacked and captured the HMS *Serapis* off Flamborough Head, England. This engagement was one of the bloodiest single-ship actions of the Age of Sail.

1781
5 September   Battle of the Chesapeake Capes. Comte de Grasse's fleet of twenty-four ships of the line had blockaded the entrance to the Chesapeake Bay. Rear Admiral Thomas Graves sailed from New York to open the bay to maintain communication with Lord Cornwallis's army at Yorktown, Virginia. As Graves approached the Capes, de Grasse raised anchor from Lynnhaven Roads and

"Battle of the Virginia Capes," print, process. *Courtesy of The Mariners' Museum.*

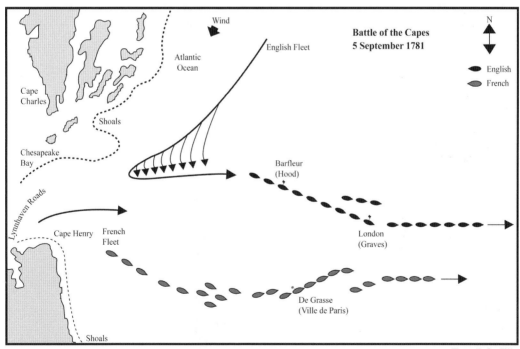

Illustrated by Sara Kiddey

Admiral Sir Samuel Graves approached the Chesapeake Capes with nineteen ships of the line. His had the weather gage; however, he allowed Comte de Grasse's fleet of twenty-four ships of the line to organize out of Lynnhaven Roads. The two fleets followed a parallel course out into the Atlantic. Only the English van maintained combat range with the French.

endeavored to organize his battle line as his fleet entered the Atlantic Ocean. Graves failed to engage the French while de Grasse was forming his line of battle. Instead, Graves gave up the weather gage and formed a line ahead to come down on the French from the north. The wind shifted and part of the English fleet was becalmed. Only Graves's van came within artillery range of the French. Graves broke off the attack and returned to New York. The battle itself was inconclusive; however, the result was decisive, as it resulted in Cornwallis's surrender at Yorktown, Virginia, to General George Washington's Franco-American army six weeks later.

1782

12 April   Battle of the Saintes. Lord Rodney with thirty-six ships of the line attacked Comte de Grasse's thirty-one-ship command near Guadeloupe. The two fleets approached each other in a line ahead, but the wind shifted, causing gaps in the French line. Rodney seized this advantage and penetrated the French line in three places. The French fell into confusion and retreated. Rodney captured five French ships, including de Grasse's flagship *Ville de Paris*. After numerous inconclusive naval engagements following *Fighting Instructions* that limited the opportunity to win complete victories, Rodney's victory by penetration opened a new phase in naval warfare.

1783   Marquis de Jouffroy constructed the small stern wheel steamship *Pyroscaphe*.

1787   Thomas Blomefield introduced a new pattern cannon that had a stronger breech to lessen the chance of an iron gun breaking apart during discharge. Blomefield pattern guns used more powerful gunpowder, thereby increasing the destructive power of solid shot.

1788   Patrick Miller and William Symington constructed steamboat *Charlotte Dumas*. Lieutenant Colonel Sir Samuel Bentham demonstrated the effects of explosive and incendiary shells. Bentham organized a flotilla of galleys armed with thirty-two- and forty-two-pounder cannon as well as eight- and thirteen-inch howitzers.

27 June   Russian Rear Admiral John Paul Jones used Bentham's galleys and a few larger ships to destroy a Turkish Black Sea fleet at Liman.

1790   Admiral Lord Richard Howe issued Royal Navy's first *Signal Book for the Ships of War*, which was based on ten flags, numbered zero to nine.

1794   Gosport shipyard was leased by the U.S. government and Captain Richard Dale was named superintendent.

1 June   Also known as the Battle of Ushant, the Glorious First of June was the first clash at sea between France and Great Britain during the Napoleonic Wars. Admiral Lord Richard Howe was able to defeat the French fleet commanded

"Lord Rodney," Sir Joshua Reynolds (artist), Edward Scriven (engraver), engraving, ca. 1780. *Courtesy of The Mariners' Museum.*

"Victory Over the French Fleet," Thomas Waller (artist), J. Wells (engraver), engraving, ca. 1782. *Courtesy of The Mariners' Museum.*

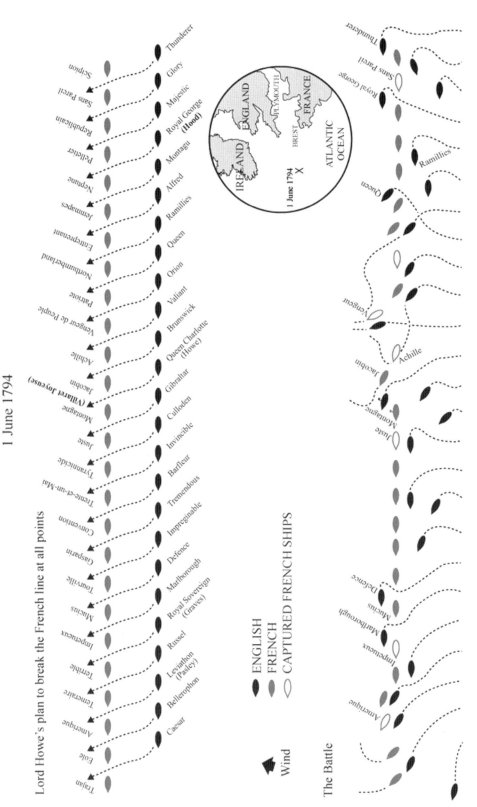

The Glorious First of June
(Battle of Ushant)
1 June 1794

Lord Howe's plan to break the French line at all points

ENGLISH
FRENCH
CAPTURED FRENCH SHIPS

Wind

The Battle

The French Brest squadron commanded by Rear Admiral Villaret de Joyeuse endeavored to protect the American grain convoy and engaged the British blockading squadron of twenty-six ships of the line four hundred miles west of Ushant in the Atlantic Ocean. The British fleet, commanded by Lord Howe, deviated from the usual withdrawing tactic employed by a fleet when fighting to leeward. Instead, Howe ordered to break through the French line with bows-on to achieve a decision. The French fleet was soundly defeated with the loss of seven ships of the line and seven thousand casualties. Despite their tactical defeat, the grain convoy was not intercepted by the British.

by Rear Admiral Villaret de Joyeuse. The engagement, however, did not stop the American grain convoy from reaching France to end a famine.

1798

The U.S. Navy was formally established and Gosport Navy Yard became one of the navy's primary bases. The French Directory received a "floating circular citadel" concept.

1–2 August

<u>Battle of the Nile</u>. Nelson won his first great victory when the British fleet of fourteen ships of the line attacked a French fleet of thirteen ships of the line commanded by Admiral Brueys. The French were anchored off Aboukir Island. Nelson attacked the French van from both sides and battered the five leading French ships into submission. The battle's high point was reached when Bruey's flagship, *L'Orient*, exploded. The entire French fleet was overwhelmed and the French army in Egypt was cut off from France.

"Admiral Lord Nelson," John Hoppner (artist), Charles Turner (engraver), Mezzotint, ca. 1806. *Courtesy of The Mariners' Museum.*

1800	Discovery of fulminate of mercury.
1801	The U.S. Navy purchased the Gosport Navy Yard from the Commonwealth of Virginia and Captain Samuel Barron served as the first superintendent.
2 April	Battle of Copenhagen. Lord Horatio Nelson won a resounding victory and forced Denmark to maintain its neutrality. During the first phase of the battle, Nelson's commander, Sir Hyde Parker, ordered Nelson to break off action. Nelson turned a blind eye to Parker's signal and continued the attack. The Danish fleet surrendered two hours later and Nelson won another victory.
1803	Captain Home Popham published *Telegraphic Signals or Marine Vocabulary*, which recommended an improved signaling system.
1805	Andrew Gillespie devised an impregnable and moveable turret to "take sure aim at any object."

"Battle of Trafalgar," Thomas Luny, oil painting, dated 1806. *Courtesy of The Mariners' Museum.*

21 October	Battle of Trafalgar. Admiral Lord Horatio Nelson destroyed a combined Franco-Spanish fleet. Nelson achieved complete penetration and envelopment of the Allied fleet.
11:00 a.m.	The Spanish-French (Allies) fleet sailed north in a latterly disorganized formation. Nelson learned about this situation and ordered an attack based on a plan he had previously and thoroughly discussed with his captains. Nelson headed into the Allied fleet from the west in two columns. Nelson's column was to pierce the enemy line at the point of the Allied flagship, whereas the second column, commanded by Vice Admiral Cuthbert Collingwood in the *Royal Sovereign*, was to strike the Allied rear.
12:00 p.m.	*Royal Sovereign* broke through the enemy's line. Nelson's *Victory* did the same shortly thereafter.

1:30 p.m.	*Victory* engaged the *Redoubtable*. Nelson was mortally wounded by a marksman in the rigging. Aided by the *Temeraire*, the *Redoubtable* was taken and soon after, so was the *Fougeaux*. The Allied ships *Bucentaure* and *Santissima Trinidad* (a four-decker, mounting 130 guns) were overwhelmed and the Allied commander, Admiral Pierre Charles de Villeneuve, was captured.
4:00 p.m.	English captured fifteen ships of the line.
4:30 p.m.	Nelson learned of his victory just before he died.
5:30 p.m.	Allied vessel *Achille* exploded and basically ended the battle. The British won a complete victory; Nelson's fleet captured seventeen Allied ships and destroyed another.

The five French ships that escaped from the battle were blockaded in Cadiz. The British attained total command of the seas, thereby thwarting any possible invasion of Great Britain by Napoleon.

1806

Sir William Congreve developed rockets as a tactical weapon.

8 October

First successful use of Congreve's rockets. The port of Boulogne, France, was burned when bombarded by two hundred rockets.

1807

Albert Bloodgood conceived a floating, revolving turret with guns ranged through its interior so that as the turret turned, each cannon could fire successively, thereby maintaining a constant barrage.

Scottish Presbyterian minister Alexander Forsyth patented the use of mercuric fulminates as a primer for firearms. Placed over the fire hole, the fulminates would detonate the charge by being struck. The percussion cap became the safest and most dependable ignition system for muzzle-loading weapons.

American inventor Robert Fulton built the *Clermont*, which was the first commercially successful steamboat to carry passengers on the Hudson River from New York to Albany at five knots.

2–4 September

Bombardment of Copenhagen. The British used incendiary projectiles, including Congreve rockets, to bombard and subdue the Danish capital.

1813

1 June

Chesapeake-Shannon Duel. Gunnery training decided the bloodiest single frigate-to-frigate action of the War of 1812. The impetuous Captain James Lawrence, after only commanding the *Chesapeake* for two weeks, agreed to a duel with the HMS *Shannon* near Boston Harbor. The *Shannon*'s crew had been trained by its commander, Captain Sir Philip Broke, in concentrated fire with all guns laid on the principle of converging lines. Frequent drill and technique resulted in a resounding victory. Lieutenant George Bomford developed the first American shellgun, known as the columbiad. The columbiad combined features of the gun, howitzer and mortar. The weapon could fire either shot or shell.

"Shannon and Chesapeake," Provo William Perry Wallis, oil painting, dated 1813. *Courtesy of The Mariners' Museum.*

"Robert Fulton," Alonzo Chappel, engraving, dated 1874.
Courtesy of The Mariners' Museum.

1814	Sir William Congreve invented the twenty-four-pounder Congreve gun, which was capable of firing shot and shell. The gun's smooth exterior and curved breech influenced later gun designs.
11 September	Battle of Lake Champlain. Lieutenant Thomas Macdonough's flotilla thwarted a British invasion with its defeat of a British squadron. Macdonough achieved victory by reversing his anchored fleet by using spring anchors, which bore a fresh broadside late in the battle.
13–14 September	Battle of Baltimore. A British fleet was unable to bombard Fort McHenry into submission with Congreve rockets and mortar shells. The British fleet was unable to approach the fort due to this fixed fortification's effective counter battery fire.
October	Robert Fulton launched the first steam-powered warship, the USS *Demologos*.
1815	
June	The *Demologos*, renamed the USS *Fulton* following the inventor's death, was commissioned. At 156 feet in length, the *Fulton* carried twenty-four thirty-two-pounder carronades. The *Fulton* was a ship-rigged catamaran with her paddlewheel protected between her twin hulls. The steamer's fifty-eight-inch wooden bulwarks led many to believe the *Fulton* was shot-proof. The *Fulton* was only effective for harbor defense.

CHAPTER 3

SHOT TO SHELL

T HE AGE OF SAIL WAS quickly coming to its end during the Napoleonic Wars. Little had changed during this two-hundred-year span of time. Ships and artillery remained virtually the same, while tactics only made significant changes during the era's final drama. The Industrial Age introduced new ordnance and motive power technologies, which caused a major revolution in ship design concepts, construction and composition. While seamen would feel relatively at home in ships of either the seventeenth or eighteenth centuries, sailors from Sir Edward Hawke's *Royal George* would have been overwhelmed by the new vessels and artillery of the mid-nineteenth century.

The Greek War of Independence witnessed the last battle fought wholly under sail and the first steam-powered warship to serve in battle. Even though the USS *Fulton* was the first steam-powered warship, the *Fulton* was primarily a harbor defense vessel and never served in combat. The first purpose-built steam-powered warship to actually participate in combat was the *Karteria*. Built in Great Britain for the Greek Navy, the *Karteria* served with distinction under the command of former Royal Navy officer Frank Hastings during the Greek War of Independence. As this conflict introduced steam power to naval warfare, the war truly marked the end of the Age of Sail. An Allied English, French and Russian fleet fighting for Greek independence defeated the Turks on October 20, 1827, at Navarino Bay in the last battle fought wholly under sail. Navies of the world recognized the advantages of steam over sail-power. Accordingly, the transition to steam was rapid and quickened even more for military purposes by the invention of the screw propeller. Side-paddle wheels took up the space that would have otherwise had mounted guns. Likewise, the paddle wheels themselves and their engines mounted on deck were very vulnerable to artillery fire. The screw propeller, conceived and created by several inventors, including John Ericsson, Francis Pettit-Smith and Joseph Ressel, enabled engine systems to be installed below the waterline, making screw-propelled warships virtually shot-proof. Furthermore, the British Admiralty tested which propulsion system had greater power. Two equally powered (two hundred horsepower engines) and weighted steam sloops, the 880-ton propeller-driven HMS *Rattler* and the 800-ton paddle-driven HMS *Alecto*, were chained together for a "tug of war." The *Rattler* pulled the *Alecto* stern first with a speed of 2.8 knots. By the late 1840s most warships were fitted with screw systems.

The Napoleonic Wars prompted the development of new types of artillery. Heavier guns with greater impact or projectiles with more destructive power were sought to gain battlefield superiority. Rockets, explosive shells and columbiads were all introduced; however, naval warfare still stayed the same. Wooden sailing warships had ruled the waves for centuries, and admirals seemed satisfied to fight sea battles in the traditional manner. Notwithstanding the new Nelsonian concepts of penetration and envelopment of an enemy's line, technology limited combat to cannonballs

Engraved for the Univerſal Magazine.

Sᵗ EDWARD HAWKE.
Printed for J. Hinton at yᵉ King's Arms, Newgate Street.

"Sir Edward Hawke," J. Hinton (publisher), engraving, ca. 1803. *Courtesy of The Mariners' Museum.*

bouncing off the sides of huge wooden ships of the line. New tactics of annihilation required equally destructive weaponry. Accordingly, old techniques of warfare ended when Brigadier General Henri-Joseph Paixhans published two books, *Nouvelle Force Maritime et Artillerie* in 1822 and *Experiences faites sur une arme nouvelle* in 1825, in which he advocated a system of naval gunnery based on standardization of caliber and the use of shellguns. While he admitted that his concepts were not new, his thoughts unified a series of ideas that proved to be extremely revolutionary. In 1824, Paixhans tested an eighty-pounder shellgun against an old eighty-gun of the line, *Le Pacificateur*, at Brest. The battleship was virtually demolished by only sixteen shells. Besides demonstrating the tremendous destructive power of explosive shells, Paixhans argued that modern warships should be steam-powered, iron-plated and armed with like-caliber shellguns.

Shells were far superior to solid shot in terms of naval combat. Whereas solid shot strove to penetrate (and often did not) the wooden sides of warships, shells were designed to explode in a ship's side, tearing an irregular hole that could sink a vessel. Sparks from the explosion could ignite fires on the damaged ship. Furthermore, the resulting splinters and shell fragments had nasty anti-personnel properties that could decimate a crew. Initially, the lower velocity required to propel shells against a target meant that shell guns could be lighter. This allowed more powerful guns to be mounted in a ship's battery, thereby increasing the weight of a warship's broadside.

Other ordnance improvements followed Paixhans's work. Harvard professor Daniel Treadwell introduced cast-iron smoothbore guns that were strengthened with wrought-iron cylinders (bands). Other gun designers worked on solving the problem of the weakness in cast iron.

"Bombardment of Fort McHenry, Baltimore, Maryland, September 13, 1814," Paul Schnitzler, oil painting, ca. 1814. *Courtesy of The Mariners' Museum.*

"Testing Columbiad at Fortress Monroe," engraving. *Courtesy of John Moran Quarstein.*

The object was to increase projectile weight and velocity. The 1844 *Princeton* disaster clearly demonstrated the problem with large wrought-iron guns. The welding of bands and the inherent weakness of wrought iron due to long exposure to intense heat made gun designers look for other solutions. John Dahlgren developed a nine-inch cast-iron gun for the U.S. Navy in 1850. He designed the gun to give the greatest weight of metal at the breech. Consequently, the smooth exterior and curved lines of the Dahlgren guns prompted some observers to call them "soda bottle guns." Dahlgren would produce guns in various sizes from nine-inch to twenty-inch. The U.S. Army also developed new smoothbore guns. Major George Bomford's combination of cannon, howitzer and mortar, commonly known as the columbiad seacoast gun, was improved in the 1840s by Captain Thomas Rodman. Rodman invented a process of casting a gun hollow and then cooling the tube from the inside out with a constant stream of water. This strengthened the gun and enabled the production of huge columbiads ranging in size from ten to twenty inches. The twenty-inch version was produced nineteen feet in length and weighed 115,000 pounds. It was capable of hurling a 1,600-pound projectile over six miles.

Even though large smoothbore shellguns became very popular, designers still sought to produce a more accurate and reliable weapon. The answer was found, in part, through the development of rifled cannons. Sardinian army officer Major Giovanni Cavalli introduced the first effective rifled gun in 1845. Cavilli's gun featured a two-grooved, rifled barrel with a ribbed, cylindrical conical shell. An explosive shell could now be hurled at a target with greater velocity, accuracy and penetrating power than that of smoothbore guns. Other designers, such as William Armstrong, Sir Joseph Whitworth and Robert Parker Parrott, created a variety of somewhat reliable muzzle-loading rifled guns. Each of these designs featured cast-iron tubes that had been grooved and then reinforced with wrought-iron band shrunk over the breech.

All of these new theories, engine systems and weapons were put to the test during the Mexican and Crimean Wars. The U.S. Navy was able to prove the value of steamers during the 1846–48 Mexican War. Steamers were critical tools in quick resupply from a base nine hundred miles away to maintain a very effective close blockade of the Mexican coast. In operations at Veracruz and up the Tabasco River, steamers proved most valuable where tide and wind proved difficult for sailing craft. Side-wheel frigates like the USS *Mississippi* and some light-draft steamers like the *Scorpion, Scourge, Spitfire* and *Vixen* were key to successful coastal operations. Whether shelling shore batteries during troop landings or towing sailing vessels into position, the effectiveness of steam power during the Mexican War prompted the U.S. Navy to authorize the construction of four additional large steam warships in March 1847.

Although steam power proved itself during the Mexican War, the power of explosive shells would prompt great changes to warship construction during the Crimean War. The stunning Russian naval victory at Sinope on November 30, 1853, proved the superiority of the new shell guns. Admiral Pavel Stepanovich Nakhimov's squadron totally destroyed a Turkish fleet. Thereafter, the Allied navies refused to engage the Russian batteries defending Sevastopol, fearing the impact of Russian shells on their ships. A stalemate continued until the French reread Paixhans's book and began the construction of floating iron batteries. Designed by Pierre Armand Guieysse, the *Lave*-class featured formidable vessels mounting eighteen 68-pounder shell guns in a casemate covered by 4-inch iron plating. These armorclads had a length of 167.5 feet, a draft of eight feet and were propelled by a 225-horsepower engine. Three of these batteries, *Devastation, Lave* and *Tonnante*, were towed into the Black Sea and used in the Allied assault against the Russian batteries at Kinburn on October 17, 1855. Anchoring just 800 yards from the forts, the French ironclads passed their trial by fire. After four hours of heavy cannonading, the armored floating batteries had suffered minimal damage. Only two French sailors were killed when a Russian shell entered a gunport. In turn, the Russian forts were shelled into submission. Kinburn proved the value of armored vessels against fixed fortifications.

Although the *Lave*-class achieved great success at Kinburn, the floating batteries had two weaknesses: speed and seaworthiness. Accordingly, Chief Constructor of the Imperial French Navy Stanislas Charles Henri Laurent Dupuy de Lome used this Crimean War experience to develop a new ironclad design that combined speed, protection and firepower. The *Gloire*, launched on November 24, 1859, was a 253-foot wooden steam-powered frigate covered with 4½-inch iron-plate. She mounted thirty-six guns and was capable of 13.5 knots. The Royal Navy, not to be outdone by the French, introduced an ambitious armorclad production program. The British produced several iron-plated floating batteries during the Crimean War. Once the war was over, the Royal Navy was quick to improve upon the floating battery design, building four additional batteries (*Erebus*, *Terror*, *Thunderbolt* and *Aetna*). In response to the *Gloire*, the HMS *Warrior* and HMS *Black Prince* were two of ten ironclads under construction in British shipyards by early 1861.

All of the technological and tactical changes during the Crimean War were observed and recorded by a team of U.S. Army officers headed by Major Richard Delafield (Delafield's team included Major Alfred Mordecai and Captain George Brinton McClellan). These observers produced a study that was commonly referred to as the Delafield Report. This survey recommended modernizing the United States military establishment based on the Allied combat experiences. Suggested improvements focused on advanced armaments and comprehensive fortifications required for coastal defense as well as the need for ironclad vessels to protect American harbors and interests abroad. The Delafield Report, noting that Great Britain and France had used "their greatest exertions to devise the means of destroying the sea-coast casemated defenses of their enemy," advised that the U.S. Navy should construct steam-powered, armored vessels armed with the most advanced ordnance to compete with modern European navies.

The Delafield Report was published after the U.S. Navy had already initiated its modernization program with the *Merrimack*-class steam screw frigates. The U.S. Navy continued its reliance on steam-powered wooden warships; this continued with the construction of the *Hartford*-class of screw sloops and other steamships like the *Narragansett*-class. While the public questioned the U.S. Navy's reluctance to construct ironclads, the refusal to enter into an arms race with European powers was due to several factors. United States overseas interests did not appear threatened by any European nation in the 1850s, and the U.S. Navy was content to allow the Europeans to complete costly experiments with ironclads. After all, the U.S. Navy was already heavily invested in the Stevens's Battery. This revolutionary warship concept was initiated in 1842 and by 1860 was still incomplete.

By 1860, naval warfare had evolved more in the forty-five years since the end of the Napoleonic Wars than during any previous historical era. Technology now ruled the waves. Steam power, screw propellers, ironclads, explosive shells and rifled cannons changed ship-to-ship and ship-to-fortification tactical concepts. When the Civil War erupted, no one realized how these new technologies would come into play.

"American Auxiliary Paddle Steamship *Savannah* 1819," Frederick A. Craven, model, ca. 1934. *Courtesy of The Mariners' Museum.*

1819

An iron barge, *Vulcan*, was the first to offer regular passenger service.

22 May

The *Savannah* became the first steamship to travel across the Atlantic from Savannah, Georgia, to Liverpool. The crossing was made primarily under sail.

1822

Brigadier General Henri-Joseph Paixhans published *Nouvelle Force Maritime et Artillerie*, in which he advocated a system of naval gunnery based on standardization of caliber and the use of shellguns.

June

Aaron Mercy became the first oceangoing iron ship when she steamed from the Thames across the Channel to Paris, France. The *Aaron Mercy* remained in service until 1855.

1824

Paixhans tested an eighty-pounder shellgun against an old ship of the line, *Le Pacificateur*. The wooden warship was virtually demolished by only sixteen shells.

1825

Construction of a granite dry dock, which had the capacity for repairing any size ship of the line, was begun at Gosport Navy Yard, Portsmouth, Virginia.

Paixhans published his second book, *Experiences faites sur une arme nouvelle*, in which he advocated that navies do away with solid shot altogether in favor of explosive shells fired from a few large-caliber guns.

1826

May

The British-built *Karteria* (*Perseverance*) of the Greek navy was the first purpose-built steamer to engage in combat. While commanded by former Royal Navy officer Frank A. Hastings, the *Karteria* destroyed twenty-seven Turkish vessels, bombarded Turkish land fortifications and served as a transport. The *Karteria* was blown up in 1831 during the Greek Civil War.

"The Battle of Navarino," C. Lanlois (artist), W. Spooner (publisher), aquatint, ca. 1827. *Courtesy of The Mariners' Museum.*

1827

July — Britain, France and Russia openly agreed to secure autonomy for Greece by the Treaty of London.

20 October — Battle of Navarino Bay. The Turkish-Egyptian fleet commanded by Admiral Ibrahim Pasha was anchored in a horseshoe formation to allow his ships' broadsides to command the entrance to Navarino harbor. An Anglo-Franco-Russian fleet with eleven ships of the line and nine frigates under the command of Vice Admiral Sir Edward Codrington arrived to force mediation between the Greeks and Turks. When Codrington's fleet anchored near the Turkish ships, an unintentional battle erupted. The battle featured close combat. The Turkish fire ships missed their targets and caused damage to their own ships. The superior training of the European powers was decisive and the Turkish fleet was destroyed in one hour. This engagement was the last major battle fought solely by wooden sailing ships.

1836 — France's Petit Smith and John Ericsson, working independently, took out patents for screw propellers.

1837

April — Ericsson's screw propeller was fitted on the forty-foot launch *Francis B. Ogden*, which towed a barge containing several senior Royal Navy officials down the Thames at ten knots.

18 May — The second USS *Fulton* was launched. The *Fulton* was a 700-ton side-wheeler, 180 feet in length with a beam of 35 feet. Her two engines produced 625 horsepower and could make 12 knots. The *Fulton* carried eight long 42-pounders and one long 24-pounder. Her first commander was Captain Matthew Calbraith Perry. She was primarily an experimental vessel.

"U.S. Ship
Pennsylvania,"
James Fulton
Pringle (artist),
William James
(engraver),
aquatint, ca. 1839.
*Courtesy of The
Mariners' Museum.*

18 July   USS *Pennsylvania* launched at the Philadelphia Navy Yard. She was built from 1821 to 1837. The *Pennsylvania* was the largest sailing warship ever built for the U.S. Navy and was designed to mount 136 guns; however, she was only armed with 120 guns (16 eight-inch shell guns, 104 thirty-two-pounder carronades). Her only voyage sent the warship from the Philadelphia Navy Yard to Gosport Navy Yard, where she arrived on January 2, 1838. The *Pennsylvania* was in ordinary and then served as a receiving shop from 1842 until her destruction in 1861. The USS *Pennsylvania* was a link to post–War of 1812 naval philosophy. Events of that war made it clear that the U.S. Navy needed powerful ships of the line stationed in every major port to lift a blockade. Since the U.S. Navy did not have adequate funding to build and maintain such a fleet, naval leaders decided to construct (or partially construct) these ships of the line and either keep them partially completed in ship houses or placed in ordinary rotting along the quays of various navy yards.

1838
27 November   <u>Attack on Veracruz, Mexico</u>. A French squadron commanded by Admiral Baudin attacked Veracruz. The powerful island fortress of San Juan d'Ulua was silenced using explosive shells. This is the first time the French navy used Paixhans's concepts in combat.

1839   Laird Shipyard produced the first iron-hulled warship, *Nemesis*, for the Bengal Marine (East India Company). Propelled by side-wheels, the *Nemesis* mounted two thirty-two-pounders and four six-pounders. The *Nemesis* successfully fought in the First China War (1841–43).

Theodore Timby of Syracuse, New York, designed and patented a "cordon of revolving towers" for land and sea fortifications. His concept was presented

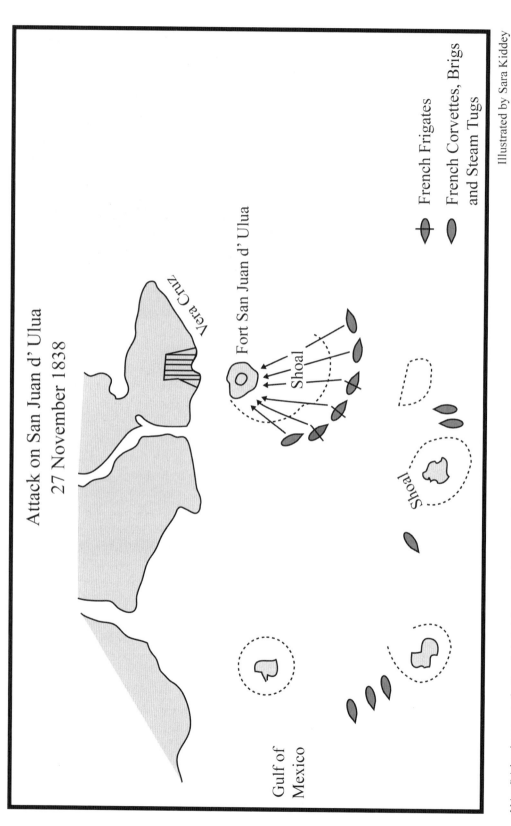

Attack on San Juan d' Ulua
27 November 1838

Vera Cruz

Fort San Juan d' Ulua

Shoal

Shoal

Gulf of
Mexico

French Frigates

French Corvettes, Brigs
and Steam Tugs

Illustrated by Sara Kiddey

Using Paixhans's concepts, the French shelled the supposedly impregnable Mexican fort into submission. The French shellguns outranged the old Mexican smoothbore artillery. Explosive shells proved to be extremely effective against fixed fortifications.

to President John Tyler; however, an Army-Navy Commission recommended against its development two years later.

1841

Swedish engineer John Ericsson arrived in the United States. He brought with him a 12-inch wrought-iron gun manufactured at the Mersey Iron Works near Liverpool named the "Orator." Renamed "Oregon," the gun had 3.5-inch wrought-iron bands shrunk on the breech, and its shot could penetrate 4.5 inches of wrought iron.

5 May

USS *Mississippi* was launched. The *Mississippi* and her sister ship USS *Missouri* marked the beginning of the real United States steam navy. The *Mississippi* was built at Philadelphia Navy Yard under the direct supervision of Captain Matthew Calbraith Perry. The *Mississippi* was armed with one nine-inch smoothbore, ten eight-inch smoothbores and one twelve-pounder. The *Mississippi*'s success prompted the construction of several of the side-wheel frigates and sloops for the U.S. Navy. The paddler design, however, had two major weaknesses: the paddle wheels were located on the sides of the ships, and the need to place much of the engine system on the main deck limited space for armaments. This limited firepower and vessel vulnerability made paddle propulsion an imperfect match for its military purpose. One shot could destroy either.

1842

The *Guadeloupe*, built by Laird in Great Britain for the Mexican navy, was launched as the first significant iron-hulled warship. This paddler was 175 feet in length and mounted two 68-pounder shellguns. Many naval observers considered it the strongest warship afloat.

April

U.S. Congress appropriated $250,000 to build the iron-hulled and iron-cased warship *Stevens Battery*. This appropriation was the first government sponsorship of iron warship construction. Robert L. Stevens of Hoboken, New Jersey, discovered that laminated iron plate 4.5 inches thick could withstand shot from a 64-pounder gun. Stevens's goal was to create a shot-proof warship faster than any other ship afloat and capable of mounting the most modern guns. The development of larger and more powerful wrought-iron guns prompted Stevens to increase the armor to 6.75 inches. Over $700,000 of federal and Stevens family money was spent on the project; yet it was incomplete by the outbreak of the Civil War.

7 May USS *Congress*, the last keel-up constructed U.S. Navy sailing warship, was commissioned. Rated as a forty-four-gun frigate, the *Congress* mounted ten eight-inch smoothbores and forty thirty-two-pounder guns.

24 May USS *Cumberland* launched.

1843 The *Great Britain* became the first propeller-driven vessel to cross the Atlantic Ocean.

Royal Navy ordered its first screw-driven vessel, the *Rattler*.

15 August USS *Missouri* destroyed by fire at Gibraltar.

9 September USS *Princeton* commissioned. The first steam screw warship constructed for the U.S. Navy, Captain Robert S. Stockton supervised the sloop's construction. John Ericsson designed two vibrating lever engines, three tubular iron boilers and six-bladed screw propeller (fourteen feet in diameter). The *Princeton* was the first screw-propeller warship in any navy, the first warship with machinery entirely below the waterline, the first to burn anthracite coal and the first to use fan blowers for her furnace fires.

5 December The first iron-hulled warship built in the United States, USS *Michigan*, was commissioned. This paddler-wheel steamer mounted only one eight-inch shellgun.

"Awful Explosion of Peace-Maker on Board the U.S. Frigate, *Princeton*," Currier & Ives, lithograph, ca. 1844. *Courtesy of The Mariners' Museum.*

1844

29 February

During a pleasure cruise on the Potomac River attended by over four hundred people, including President John Tyler, his department heads, congressmen and their families, the twelve-inch shellgun named the "Peacemaker" exploded, killing eight attendees, including Secretary of State Abel Upshur and Secretary of the Navy Thomas Gilmer. Robert Stockton and several others were severely injured. This event would cause the U.S. Congress to limit funds for ordnance and ship design development while simultaneously souring the relationship between the U.S. Navy and John Ericsson.

Robert Stockton's "Peacemaker" was a twelve-inch wrought-iron gun forged by Ward and Company of New York. It was bored and finished under the direction of John Ericsson at the Phoenix Foundry. The "Peacemaker" had the same bore and chamber as Ericsson's "Oregon" shellgun, but was greater in diameter to compensate for the "Oregon's" reinforcing bands. The process by which the "Peacemaker" was made appeared to be its undoing. The faulty welds and overexposure to intense heat in the manufacturing process caused Stockton's gun to explode. This event turned the U.S. Navy away from the production of large shellguns.

U.S. Navy Yard was established at Memphis, Tennessee.

1845

Major Giovanni Cavalli of the Sardinian Army introduced the first effective breech-loading rifled gun.

The last Treadwell-designed gun was manufactured. Wrought-iron guns were expensive to produce and were unreliable.

Lieutenant Thomas Jackson Rodman developed a process enabling the production of larger caliber shellguns. The Rodman Process entailed casting the gun tube around a hollow pipe the size of the bore, closed at the bottom.

A second pipe was inserted within a few inches of the base of the first pipe. When molten metal was poured into the mold, water was poured into the smaller pipe. It flowed out the bottom, through the larger pipe and ran out the top. Coals were heaped around the exterior of the casting to make sure that the gun cooled from the inside out.

April

The British Admiralty tested the power of screw-propeller-driven ships against paddle-wheel-powered ships. A tug of war was arranged between the screw-powered HMS *Rattler* (888 tons, 200 horsepower) and the paddler HMS *Alecto* (800 tons, 200 horsepower). On a totally calm day, the *Rattler* towed the *Alecto* stern just with a speed of 2.8 knots.

1846

Acting Naval Constructor John Luke Porter created plans for an iron-cased floating harbor defense battery.

1847

March

U.S. Congress authorized construction of four side-wheel frigates, *Susquehanna*, *Powhatan*, *Saranac* and *San Jacinto*. Naval leaders were highly impressed with the

	performance of the side-wheel frigate USS *Mississippi* during her operations off the Mexican coast in November 1846.
9 March	U.S. Navy conducted its first large-scale amphibious operation landing: sixty-five "surfboats," twelve thousand men, artillery, horses and supplies were landed at Veracruz, Mexico.
22 March	Commander Josiah Tattnall led the "Mosquito Flotilla" of small steamer- and schooner-rigged gunboats to attack Fort San Juan d'Ulua guarding the sea approaches to Veracruz.
1849	American Ben Chambers invented the first effective breechblock that prevented the escape of gases at the breech when firing a breech-loaded gun. The interrupted screw breechblock allowed the block to be inserted, then screwed and locked into place. The ability to seal gases emitted when powder was ignited gave the projective greater velocity.
1850 May	The Lancaster breech-loading, rifled cannon was introduced in Great Britain. John Adolph Bernard Dahlgren, director of the U.S. Navy Ordnance Department at the Washington Navy Yard, noted that the inferiority in overall number of ships might be offset by superior ordnance. He became the principle advocate for the U.S. Navy to mount shellguns in its ships. Dahlgren designed and produced the first nine-inch shellgun (made at Fort Pitt Foundry, Pittsburgh, Pennsylvania, in May 1850). The design developed into a curved shape with double vents. Dahlgren designed his guns to place the greatest weight of metal at the point of greatest strain, the breech. These guns, with their smooth exteriors, curved lines and weight of metal at the breech, resembled soda water bottles. The nine-inch shellgun was the most common broadside, carriage-mounted gun in the U.S. Navy during the Civil War. Dahlgren would eventually produce eight-, eleven-, fifteen- and twenty-inch versions.
1852 17 April	Gosport Navy Yard was the scene of experiments that tested the capacity of iron vessels in resisting the force of shells and cannonballs. The tests "proved that iron is not so invulnerable as many as heretofore supposed, and unsuited to such purposes."
1853 30 November	Battle of Sinope. A Turkish squadron, including seven frigates, three corvettes and three steamships, commanded by Vice Admiral Osman Pasha, anchored in the Sinope roadstead. Admiral Pavel Stepanovich Nakhimov brought his squadron (six ships of the line, two frigates and a brig) from Sevastopol and attacked the Turkish fleet at anchor. Many of the Russian ships were armed with sixty-eight-pounder shellguns. After two hours the Turkish fleet was destroyed: one frigate exploded and three burned. Only one small steamer escaped. The Turks lost 2,980 dead to the Russian losses of 37. This engagement proved the effectiveness of explosive shells upon wooden warships.

"Destruction of Turkish Squadron at Sinope," Read and Company, engraving, 1854. *Courtesy of The Mariners' Museum.*

1854	John Ericsson sent plans for a turreted, iron-cased ship to Napoleon III, Emperor of France.
8 March	Commodore Matthew Calbraith Perry returned to Japan.
28 March	France and Great Britain declared war on Russia, beginning the Crimean War.
17 October	French and British ships attacked Russian forts defending Sevastopol. The Allies were repulsed and several ships significantly damaged. France and Great Britain recognized that wooden ships couldn't engage land batteries mounting shellguns.
1855	Captain Cowper Coles of the Royal Navy developed a gun turret concept for shipboard use. The Coles turret turned on a circumferential rollerpath set within the ship. The armored (4.5 inches) portion came up through the main deck to form an iron-protected glacis. Therefore, the gun positions and turret operation systems were protected. Crewmembers entered the turret from a hollow cylinder within the ship.
15 June	USS *Merrimack* launched at Charleston Navy Yard, Boston Harbor.
July	Sir William G. Armstrong introduced the most successful breech-loading rifled gun. The Armstrong gun featured a steel tube with several spiral grooves of rifling. The tube was then covered by built-up rings of wrought iron welded together. The breech unscrewed for loading. The projectile either featured three rows of brass studs or was sheathed in lead to fit the grooves in the barrel. The extensive banding enabled the Armstrong gun to withstand greater pressure than most other contemporary rifled guns. The Armstrong guns were noted for long range and accuracy.
28 July	USS *Constellation* rebuilt as the last U.S. Navy sailing ship construction project.
17 October	Bombardment of Kinburn. Lessons learned at Sinope and during naval attacks against Sevastopol prompted the British and the French to begin the

construction of iron-cased floating batteries. These armorclads were designed specifically to confront the Russian land batteries. The French were able to send three of their armored floating batteries into the Black Sea before the British. The *Lave*-classes were virtually rectangular vessels 170 feet in length with a 47.5-foot beam. With a draft of 8.7 feet and protected by four inches of iron over 17 inches, the batteries mounted sixteen 50-pounder guns and two 12-pounders. However, underpowered with a 225-horsepower engine, the batteries could only make four knots.

The *Devastation*, *Lave* and *Tonnante* participated in the attack upon Fort Kinburn, guarding the entrance to Nikolaou Harbor at the mouth of the Dnieper and Bug Rivers. While supported by ten ships of the line and eighty other vessels, the new French batteries became the first steam-powered armored warships to be used in a fleet action.

The French ironclad batteries closed within nine hundred yards, and in two and a half hours the Russian fortification was destroyed. While repeatedly struck by Russian shot (*Tonnante*—sixty-six hits, *Devastation*—sixty-seven hits), the batteries proved to be shot-proof. The only casualties, two killed and twenty-four wounded, were caused by two hot shots entering the gunports of the *Tonnante*. When the Russian forts surrendered, the action proved the effectiveness of iron-cased vessels and rendered wooden warships obsolete.

Hot shot was developed in the late eighteenth century as a technique of enhancing the impact of shot upon wooden warships. Fixed fortifications had specialized furnaces constructed that would heat solid shot "red hot." The shot would be hoisted up to a gun emplacement in a bucket, placed by means of tongs in the muzzle of a cannon, slightly elevated and allowed to roll against the well-soaked wad that rested against a dry wad protecting the powder from moisture. Another soaked wad kept the shot in place. The shot would be quickly fired and then would lodge in the opponent's wooden ship, often causing the vessel to burn.

1856

The Royal Navy constructed three floating armored batteries, *Erebus*, *Glatton* and *Aetna*.

Sir Henry Bessemer announced that he had developed a process (known as the Bessemer process) by which air was blown through molten pig iron to decarbonize it, sufficient heat being generated by the reactions to keep the charge hot and liquid. The result was extremely malleable, mild steel.

20 February

The steam screw frigate USS *Merrimack*, called a "magnificent specimen of naval architecture," was commissioned at Charleston Navy Yard.

1857

4 May

USS *Roanoke* (one of five *Merrimack*-class frigates) was commissioned at Gosport Navy Yard.

21 May

USS *Minnesota* (one of five *Merrimack*-class frigates) was commissioned at Washington Navy Yard.

"La Gloire," Roche, engraving, ca. 1859. *Courtesy of The Mariners' Museum.*

1858

13 March — USS *Colorado* (one of five *Merrimack*-class vessels) was launched at Gosport Navy Yard.

1859

March — Captain Cowper Coles patented the idea of turrets aboard ships. His concept of centerline turrets gave the guns a wide arc of fire.

November — French navy launched the *Gloire* as an armored frigate. The *Gloire* was protected by a 4.5-inch belt of iron supported by 17 inches of wood. The ironclad mounted fourteen 8.8-inch and 6.4-inch rifled, breech-loading guns.

1860

16 February — USS *Merrimack* arrived at the Gosport Navy Yard and was immediately placed in ordinary for an overhaul and repair of her engines.

6 November — Republican candidate Abraham Lincoln elected the sixteenth president of the United States.

December — HMS *Warrior* launched. The *Warrior* was an all-iron vessel protected by a 4.5-inch armor belt. The ironclad mounted ten 110-pounder and four 70-pounder Armstrong breech-loading rifled guns as well as twenty-six 68-pounder muzzle-loading smoothbores. Capable of obtaining a combined (steam and sail) speed of 17.5 knots, the *Warrior* could escape what she could not destroy. The *Warrior*'s superior speed, armor and armament gave the ironclad the ability to destroy any other ship in the world.

20 December — South Carolina seceded from the Union.

26 December — Major Robert Anderson and 127 men abandoned Fort Moultrie on Sullivan's Island and transferred the garrison to Fort Sumter, an island in Charleston Harbor.

CHAPTER 4

WOOD TO IRON

T HE AMERICAN CIVIL WAR IS often considered the first modern, industrial war. Many factors, such as westward expansion and slavery, prompted the disagreement between the North and the South to evolve into combat. The war can be generally viewed as a conflict between agrarian and industrial societies over slave and free labor. Both North and South endeavored to mobilize all of their resources to wage total war. This experience revolutionized warfare, and it also changed forever America's political, social and economic fabric.

As the first total war, the two sections often relied on new technologies in their quest to achieve victory. Few other aspects of the Civil War witnessed such a reliance on new techniques and tools as the war along the rivers, coasts and oceans. The South was obviously caught at a disadvantage as an agrarian society faced with waging technological warfare. This situation became very apparent when Confederate leaders realized that their all-important commercial connection with Europe was threatened by the Union blockade. Immediately the Confederacy sought new or otherwise experimental equipment necessary to counter the Federal advantages. The Union would react by using its industrial strength to counter and then overwhelm Confederate efforts.

All of the recent technological changes in ordnance, motive power and ship design were observed and accepted by several American politicians, naval leaders, scientists and engineers. When the Confederate States of America was organized, the new nation was fortunate to follow the forward thinking of Stephen Russell Mallory, the prewar chairman of the U.S. Senate's Naval Affairs Committee. He was named the Confederate secretary of the Navy. Mallory immediately realized that the Confederacy could never match the North's superior shipbuilding capabilities unless a new "class of vessels hitherto unknown to naval service" was introduced to tip the balance in favor of the South. The secretary of the Navy knew that iron-cased warships armed with the most powerful rifled guns could destroy the North's wooden navy. Mallory considered

> the possession of an iron-armored ship as a matter of the first necessity. Such a vessel at this time could traverse the entire coast of the United States, prevent all blockades, and encounter, with a fair prospect of success, their entire Navy…unequality of numbers may be compensated by invulnerability; and thus not only does economy but naval success dictate the wisdom and expediency of fighting iron against wood

The question that then begged an answer: how could the agrarian South create such a warship?

The initial answer was found in the ashes of Gosport Navy Yard. Burned and abandoned by the Federals on April 20, 1861, the Confederacy found amidst the yard's ashes a way to jumpstart its ironclad navy. The steam screw frigate USS *Merrimack* was raised and placed into the undamaged

Stephen Russell Mallory, photograph, ca. 1870. *Courtesy of The Mariners' Museum.*

granite dry dock. Meanwhile, Mallory assembled a brilliant team, including scientist John Mercer Brooke, naval constructor John Luke Porter and engineer William Price Williamson. After careful consideration they agreed upon Brooke's concept of a sloped casemate and believed that an ironclad could be quickly configured by using the old engines and hull of the *Merrimack*. The transformation of the frigate *Merrimack* into the ironclad ram CSS *Virginia* was an amazing test of Confederate ingenuity and resources. The Confederacy was able to adapt whatever materials were available to create the blueprint for its ironclad fleet. The casemate design appeared to be best suited for the South. Mallory quickly approved the construction of five ironclads, hoping that once completed they would be able to adequately defend Southern harbors. The Confederates needed to build ironclads quickly at home or purchase armored vessels overseas before the North could counter with iron ships of its own.

News of the Confederate efforts to convert the *Merrimack* into an ironclad began to leak northward throughout the summer of 1861. Union Secretary of the Navy Gideon Welles already recognized that the U.S. Navy was outdated and needed an effective shipbuilding program to enforce the blockade of Southern ports. Welles quickly realized that the Union had to construct armorclad vessels capable of countering any ironclad the South might produce or purchase. The secretary of the Navy advised Congress that "much attention has been given within the last few years to the subject of floating batteries, or steamers." Based on Welles's recommendation,

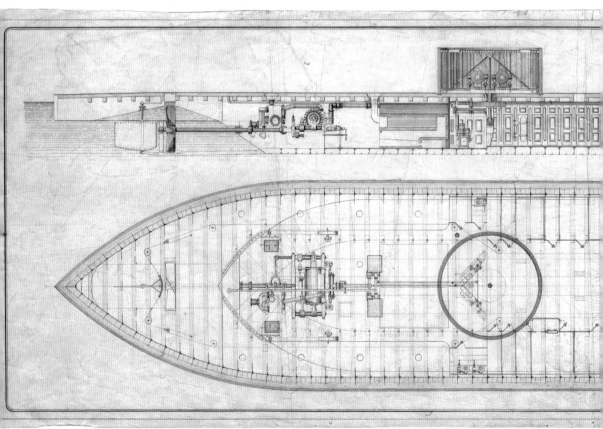

"U.S. Ironclad Steamer *Monitor*," John Ericsson, plans, 1862. *Courtesy of The Mariners' Museum.*

Congress appropriated $1.5 million for the construction of armored warships and authorized the appointment of an Ironclad Board to review designs. The board consisted of Flag Officer Joseph Smith, Flag Officer Hiram Paulding and Captain Charles Henry Davis, and they considered sixteen designs. Two were quickly selected: the European floating battery *New Ironsides* and the iron clapboard frigate *Galena*. Questions about the *Galena* brought the vessel's backer, Cornelius Bushnell, in contact with the brilliant Swedish-American engineer John Ericsson. When Ericsson shared with Bushnell a model of his tower battery, Bushnell promoted the acceptance of the Ericsson Battery by the Ironclad Board. Ericsson's ironclad was a completely new concept in naval design. His genius could be found everywhere in the project. The *Monitor*, as the warship would eventually be named, was an engineering marvel, containing numerous patents created by Ericsson. The ironclad's most impressive feature was its steam-powered, rotating, circular turret designed to contain two large shellguns. The turret was protected by eight inches of curved iron plates and the gunports were equipped with shutters. It was completely shot-proof, as it was virtually awash with the sea. Only the turret and pilothouse protruded from the deck. All of the ship's machinery, magazine and quarters were positioned below the waterline. Everything about the ironclad was so technologically advanced and it looked so different that when first seen by Lieutenant James Henry Rochelle he exclaimed, "Such a craft as the eyes of a Seamen never looked upon before."

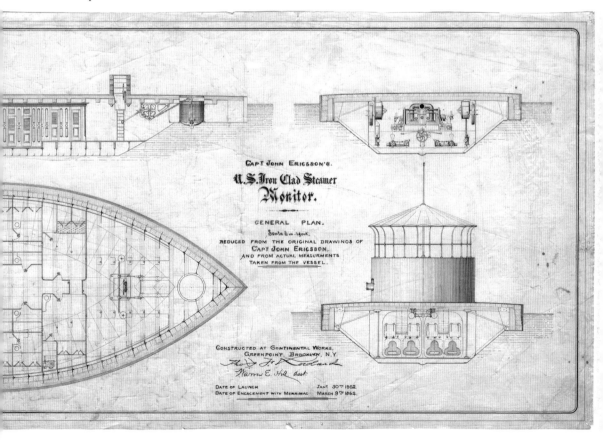

As workmen at Gosport Navy Yard and Continental Iron Works in Brooklyn labored on their ironclads, other technological and design changes began to emerge. The Confederates recognized that, due to British and French neutrality, it would take considerable time and effort to purchase ironclads from Europe and redouble their efforts to produce ironclads throughout the South. Along the Mississippi River four casemate-style ironclads were laid down. The construction of iron warships was also begun in Mobile, Savannah, Charleston and Wilmington.

In the meantime, the U.S. Army assumed a far more aggressive approach to the control of western rivers. On August 7, 1861, Quartermaster General Montgomery Meigs awarded a contract to build seven ironclads to James B. Eads. The *City*-class ironclads, designed by Naval Constructor Samuel M. Pook, were called "Pook's Turtles" because these ships featured an armored casemate. Vessels like the USS *Cairo* were armed with fourteen guns, had a draft of six feet and a speed of nine knots. Several other casemate-style ironclads were built in late 1861 and gave the Federals an overwhelming naval superiority on the Mississippi River when campaigning began in February 1862.

Ordnance improvements initiated before the war would also be introduced to naval warfare in 1862. The Parrott gun, developed by West Point graduate Robert Parker Parrott, was produced in 100- and 150-pounder versions for the U.S. Navy. These rifled guns, distinguished by their single reinforcing band on the breech, gave the Union a valuable alternative to heavy shellguns and mortars. A rifle's flat trajectory, velocity range and accuracy made it a useful naval weapon. Parrott rifles would prove very effective against fixed masonry fortifications. The conically shaped solid shot bored into a fort's brick sides and could reduce these coastal defenses. Likewise, the Confederates, recognizing Mallory's admonition to produce rifled guns, utilized the services of the brilliant John Mercer Brooke. An Annapolis graduate and assistant to Matthew Fontaine Maury, Brooke developed an outstanding rifle gun in the summer of 1861. The Brooke gun was a rifled cast-iron weapon with a wrought-iron reinforcing band at the breech. Its heavy, tapered tube was strengthened with a single-, double- or triple-band. These guns featured a hookslant rifling and were produced in several calibers. Brooke created an armor-piercing bolt that was capable of penetrating 8 inches of iron, backed by 18 inches of wood at 260 yards. These bolts would eventually prove rather effective against Union ironclads. In addition to these ordnance improvements, the Confederacy experimented with torpedoes. Guided by research conducted by Matthew Fontaine Maury, the Confederates created explosive devices that could be used on spars or as floating defensive tools. These torpedoes (mines) would not have an impact until later in the war.

Union and Confederate navies quickly reacted to the war's outbreak and used much of 1861 seeking ways to achieve victory along the Southern coast. Naval leaders all recognized that the key was either maintaining or breaking the blockade. They realized that only with new warships and weapons would they prevail over their enemy.

The smoke had barely cleared from Gosport Navy Yard when the Confederates initiated their own efforts to transform warfare. The Southern ironclad building program was hampered by the agrarian economy, whereas the North was well suited to modernize its fleet and quick to take action. By the end of 1861 several ironclads were either in the water or nearing completion. While the CSS *Manassas* was the first ironclad ship to be deployed, it was a poorly conceived warship. The *Manassas*'s tactical victory at the Head of the Passes was due in part to the perceived power of the ram rather than based on what actual damage the ironclad had inflicted on the Federal wooden warships. Ram fever was born! Nevertheless, the Federals countered elsewhere with powerful steamers with superior armaments. DuPont's tactics at Port Royal Sound gave the Federals a grand victory. The sound was transformed into a repair base and coaling station, which enhanced the effectiveness of the Union blockade. It became very clear that the North's shipbuilding and industrial advantages could only be overcome if the Confederacy could find the means to defend Southern ports. The new technological and tactical concepts considered in 1861 would change naval warfare forever in 1862.

1861

5 January	Fort Morgan, at the entrance to Mobile Bay, seized by Alabama militia.
9 January	The *Star of the West*, commanded by Captain John McGowan, United States Revenue Marine (USRM), attempted to resupply the Union garrison of Fort Sumter. The *Star of the West* was forced to abandon this effort due to Confederate artillery fire. This cannonade was the first Confederate shot fired at a vessel flying the United States flag during the war.
10 January	Forts Jackson and St. Phillip, guarding the Mississippi route to New Orleans, were captured by Louisiana militia.
12 January	Fort Barrancas and the Pensacola Navy Yard seized by Alabama and Florida militia troops. Union troops occupied Fort Pickens on Santa Rosa Island.
14 January	South Carolina declared any attempt to resupply Fort Sumter an act of war.
19 January	Commonwealth of Virginia proposed a national peace conference.
20 January	Ship Island, Mississippi seized by Confederate militia.
26 January	Louisiana passed an ordinance of secession.
2 February	Congressman William P. Chilton of Alabama introduced a resolution "that the Committee on Naval Affairs be instructed into the propriety of constructing by this government of two iron-plated frigates and such iron-plated gunboats as may be necessary to protect the Commerce and provide the safety of the Confederacy."
9 February	Jefferson Finis Davis elected president of the Confederate States of America.
11 February	Commander John Dahlgren, chief of Naval Ordnance, urged Congress to approve the building of more steam-powered gun-sloops and an "iron-cased" ironclad.

John Adolph Bernard Dahlgren was born in Philadelphia, Pennsylvania, on November 13, 1809. He was the son of a Swedish diplomat. Initially rejected a midshipman's commission in the U.S. Navy, he served in the merchant marines to gain experience.

He received an acting midshipman's appointment in 1842. Dahlgren was detailed to the Washington Navy Yard in 1847. He established and directed the U.S. Navy's ordnance department. During this assignment he developed a bronze boast howitzer, the smoothbore shellgun known as the Dahlgren gun and a rifled gun for naval service.

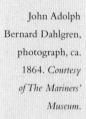

John Adolph
Bernard Dahlgren,
photograph, ca.
1864. *Courtesy
of The Mariners'
Museum.*

14 February	Confederate Congress authorizes "the Committee on Naval Affairs to procure…all such persons versed in naval affairs as they may deem it advisable to consult with."
18 February	In his inaugural address President Jefferson Davis suggested "that for the protection of our harbors and commerce on the high seas a Navy adapted to those objects will be required."
20 February	Confederate Department of the Navy was established.
21 February	Stephen Russell Mallory of Florida appointed secretary of the navy for the Confederacy. He was perhaps one of Jefferson Davis's better cabinet appointments and one of only two men who served in the same cabinet post throughout the war. Mallory was born in 1812 in Trinidad. He moved to Key West when he was a young boy and became inspector of customs at nineteen. He became an attorney in 1839, fought as a volunteer in the Seminole War, served as a judge and rose to political prominence. Mallory was elected senator from Florida in 1851 and became chairman of the Senate Committee on Naval Affairs in 1854. While serving as committee chairman, Mallory worked to modernize the U.S. Navy. He secured appropriations to construct steam screw frigates and sloops of war. Mallory's efforts to champion the construction of an iron-cased battery, designed by Robert L. Stevens, proved unsuccessful, but brought him in contact with European efforts to construct ironclads. His tenure as chairman of the Committee on Naval Affairs prepared him to create the Confederate navy from virtually nothing.

27 February	U.S. Congress authorized construction of seven steam sloops of war. Secretary of the Navy Gideon Welles noted that "steam, as well as heavy ordnance, has become an indispensable element of the most efficient naval power."
4 March	President Abraham Lincoln inaugurated.
7 March	Gideon Welles of Hartford, Connecticut, took office as the Union secretary of Navy. Born in 1802, Welles studied at Norwich Academy. Upon graduation be turned to journalism and politics. Welles helped to organize the Democratic Party in Connecticut and his connections with Andrew Jackson resulted in his appointment as postmaster of Hartford. During the Polk administration, Welles was named head of the Naval Bureau of Provisions and Clothing. His increasing dislike of slavery prompted him to join the Republican Party in 1854.
15 March	Confederate Congress authorized the construction or purchase of ten gunboats for coastal defense.
23 March	USS *Cumberland* arrived in Hampton Roads.
31 March	Welles ordered 250 men from the Brooklyn Navy Yard to reinforce the Gosport Navy Yard.
6 April	Lieutenant John L. Worden departed Washington, D.C., en route to Pensacola, Florida, with orders for the USS *Sabine* to reinforce Fort Pickens on Santa Rosa Island.
10 April	USS *Pawnee*, captained by Commander Stephen C. Rowan, departed Hampton Roads for relief of Fort Sumter. Secretary of the Navy Gideon Welles ordered Flag Officer Charles Stewart McCauley, commandant of the Gosport Navy Yard, to place the USS *Merrimack* in condition to steam to a Northern yard "or, in case of danger from unlawful attempts to take possession of her, that she may be placed beyond their reach." Welles instructs McCauley to guard public property within Gosport Navy Yard and to "exercise your judgment in discharging the responsibilities that resolves on you." The secretary also cautioned the commandant that "there should be no steps taken to give needless alarm, but it may be best to order most of the shipping to sea or other stations."
	Charles Stewart McCauley was born on February 3, 1793, in Philadelphia, Pennsylvania, and was appointed a midshipman in 1808. McCauley served on Lake Ontario during the War of 1812. In 1834 he was given command of his first ship. McCauley was promoted to captain in 1839 and during the Mexican War commanded the Washington Navy Yard. He was commander of the Pacific Squadron, 1850–53, and in 1855 was detailed as commander of the Home Squadron. Flag Officer C.S. McCauley was assigned to Gosport Navy Yard in 1860. He was a poor choice for this critical command as McCauley was over-aged, unwell and unfit for duty due to his reliance on drink.
11 April	Commander James Alden ordered to report to Flag Officer McCauley to take command of the USS *Merrimack*.
	McCauley telegraphed Welles that it would take a month to revitalize the *Merrimack*'s dismantled engines.

"Fort Sumter," John Ross Key, oil painting. *Courtesy of The Mariners' Museum.*

12 April	Welles considered McCauley "feeble and incompetent for the crisis" and detailed the U.S. Navy's chief engineer, Benjamin Franklin Isherwood, to Gosport to prepare the *Merrimack* for sea. Isherwood was appointed first assistant engineer in the newly established U.S. Navy Corps of Engineers in 1844. In 1848 he was appointed to chief engineer.
	General P.G.T. Beauregard ordered the bombardment of Fort Sumter.
3:20 a.m.	Major Robert Anderson declined last opportunity to surrender Fort Sumter.
4:30 a.m.	First Confederate shell burst over the fort. Bombardment of the fort began.
7:30 a.m.	Captain Abner Doubleday fired the first answering round.
	Even though shelling throughout April 12 had little effect on Sumter's wall, Confederate hot shot had ignited several fires within the fort.
1:00 p.m.	Federal relief expedition appeared outside Charleston harbor. Miscommunications and bad weather prevented most of the relief force from arriving. No effort was made to resupply Fort Sumter.
5:00 p.m.	Due to limited ammunition, only six of Fort Sumter's cannon replied to the Confederate bombardment.
13 April	Lieutenant John L. Worden was seized near Montgomery, Alabama, following his mission to Fort Pickens. He was the U.S. Navy's first prisoner of war. John Lorimer Worden was born in Westchester County, New York, on March 12, 1818. He joined the U.S. Navy in 1834 and spent much of his career at the Naval Observatory.
12:00 p.m.	Fires raged throughout Fort Sumter.
1:48 p.m.	Flagstaff of Fort Sumter shot away.
2:30 p.m.	Former Senator Louis T. Wigfall rowed out to Fort Sumter and negotiated surrender of the fort.
14 April	Commander James Alden and Chief Engineer B.F. Isherwood arrived at Gosport Navy Yard. Isherwood immediately began work on the *Merrimack's* engine system.
	Fort Sumter occupied by Confederate troops.

"Gosport Navy Yard," engraving, 1861. *Courtesy of John Moran Quarstein.*

15 April   Lincoln called for 75,000 volunteers from states "loyal to the Union."

16 April   Flag Officer Garrett J. Pendergrast, commander of the USS *Cumberland*, was ordered to keep his ship in Gosport Navy Yard "and, in case of invasion, insurrection, or violence of any kind, to suppress it, repelling assault by force."

Secretary Welles ordered McCauley to remove all public property from Gosport. Besides the *Merrimack*, the *Dolphin*, *Germantown* and *Plymouth* were the only warships in relatively good condition to warrant removal.

17 April   Virginia seceded from the Union.

Benjamin F. Isherwood completed emergency repairs to the *Merrimack* and reported to McCauley that the frigate would be ready to leave port the next day.

The citizens of Norfolk and Portsmouth organized a "Vigilant Committee." Several ships were sunk off Sewell's Point as obstructions blocking Union access to Gosport Navy Yard.

18 April   Chief Engineer B.F. Isherwood reported the *Merrimack* ready for sea; however, McCauley, as commandant of Gosport Navy Yard, refused to release the frigate from the yard.

John Letcher, governor of the Commonwealth of Virginia, ordered Major General William Booth Taliaferro of the Virginia Militia to assume command of troops assembling in the Norfolk area and to occupy the Gosport Navy Yard.

Governor Letcher named Catesby ap Roger Jones and Robert Pegram as captains in the Virginia State Navy. Pegram was instructed by the governor to "assume command of the naval station, with authority to organize naval defenses, enroll and enlist seamen and marines, and temporarily appoint warrant officers, and to do and perform whatever may be necessary to preserve and protect the property of the commonwealth and of the citizens of Virginia."

Flag Officer Hiram Paulding was detailed to take command of Gosport Navy Yard. Welles ordered that on "no account should the arms and munitions be permitted to fall into the hands of insurrectionists…should it finally become necessary, you will, in order to prevent that result, destroy the property." Paulding left the Washington Navy Yard with one hundred marines onboard the eight-gun steamer USS *Pawnee*.

19 April   The Baltimore Riot began. The Sixth Massachusetts Regiment suffered four men killed and thirty-nine men wounded. Approximately twelve civilians were killed.

Maryland threatened to leave the Union.

President Abraham Lincoln proclaimed a blockade of the Southern coastline.

General Taliaferro advised yard commandant C.S. McCauley that he planned to assume possession of Gosport Navy Yard on behalf of the "sovereign state of the Commonwealth of Virginia."

Fort Norfolk, containing over three hundred thousand pounds of gunpowder, was occupied by the Virginia Militia.

Flag Officer C.S. McCauley refused to allow Lieutenant Thomas O. Shelfridge of the USS *Cumberland* to take the brig *Dolphin* to Craney Island and stop the sinking of any more ships in the channel.

20 April

12:00 p.m.   Flag Officer C.S. McCauley dismissed workmen from Gosport Navy Yard.

1:00 p.m.   Gosport's loyal workmen, marines and sailors began to scuttle ships and destroy property that could not be removed.

8:00 p.m.   Flag Officer Paulding arrived at Gosport Navy Yard with 100 marines and 350 men of the Third Massachusetts Volunteers. The *Pawnee* was stocked with combustibles including 40 barrels of gunpowder, 11 tanks of turpentine, 12 barrels of cotton waste and 181 flares.

The yard was partially destroyed as a result of this action. The USS *Pennsylvania*, *Germantown*, *Raritan*, *Columbia*, *Dolphin*, *Delaware*, *Columbus*, *Plymouth* and *Merrimack* were either burned or sunk. United States Frigate (USF) *United States* was abandoned as a "venerable relic."

As the ships burned in the harbor, buildings throughout the yard were set on fire. The two huge ship houses were quickly engulfed by flames. Ship House A contained the partially completed seventy-four-gun *New York*, which was consumed by fire as she sat on the stocks. Since everything would not burn, sailors and marines rushed through the yard laying powder trails to destroy the valuable machinery and facilities. When efforts to break off the trunnions of the over one thousand cannons in the yard with sledgehammers proved futile, the guns were spiked with wrought-iron nails. Two officers, Commander John Rodgers and Captain Horatio Gouverneur Wright, were assigned the task of mining the granite dry docks. Their work was purportedly foiled by a petty officer who did not wish the explosion to damage nearby homes of his prewar friends.

"Burning of Gosport Navy Yard," engraving. Courtesy of John Moran Quarstein.

21 April
4:30 a.m. Paulding's command left the burning Gosport Navy Yard on board the USS *Yankee*, USS *Pawnee* and USS *Cumberland*.

Confederates occupied Gosport Navy Yard. The yard immediately became a tremendous asset. Over 1,085 cannons were captured and these weapons would be used throughout 1861 to defend the Southern coastline. The yard's granite dry dock and workshops helped create the initial Confederate navy. The Federals provided the Confederacy with military property worth $4,810,056.68. Overnight, the Confederacy gained the infrastructure to construct the vessels to challenge the Federal blockade. The Richmond press gloated over the abundance of equipment and supplies, stating, "We have enough to build a navy of iron-plated ships."

22 April Flag Officer Franklin Buchanan, commandant of the Washington Navy Yard, resigned his U.S. Navy commission. Captain Samuel Francis DuPont relieved Buchanan. A Maryland native and grandson of a signer of the Declaration of Independence, Buchanan was born September 17, 1800. He was appointed midshipman in the U.S. Navy in January 1815. Franklin Buchanan was the first superintendent of the U.S. Naval Academy at Annapolis and during the Mexican War's siege of Veracruz, he commanded the sloop of war *Germantown*. He was commander of Matthew C. Perry's flagship, the USS *Susquehanna*, when Perry opened Japan to American trade. Buchanan was promoted captain in 1855. Able, courageous and experienced, Franklin Buchanan was perhaps the most aggressive senior officer to join the

Confederate Navy. His strategic flair, discipline and heroic qualities made him respected and admired by all those around him. "A typical product of the old-time quarter deck, as indomitably courageous as Nelson, and as arbitrary," Lieutenant J.R. Eggleston described Buchanan.

Flag Officer French Forrest, CSN, assumed command of Gosport Navy Yard. A fifty-year naval veteran known as a "blusterer of the real old-tar school," Forrest had gained considerable fame during the Mexican War while commanding the *Cumberland* and *Raritan*. Noted for his immaculate dress, stern countenance and flowing white hair, Forrest was one of the most senior officers to join the Confederate navy.

23 April　Flag Officer Hiram Paulding, aboard the USS *Pawnee*, arrived in Washington, D.C., and reported the loss of Gosport Navy Yard.

Major General Robert E. Lee assigned Colonel Andrew Talcott, Virginia State Engineers, to "proceed up the James River to the vicinity of Burwell's Bay, and select the most suitable point, which in your judgment, should be fortified in order to prevent the ascent of the river by the enemy."

24 April　USS *Cumberland* captured two Confederate blockade-runners, the tug *Young America* and schooner *George M. Smith*, in Hampton Roads.

26 April　Stephen Mallory advised Confederate President Jefferson Davis to "adopt a class of vessels hitherto unknown to naval services. The perfection of a warship would doubtless be a combination of the greatest known ocean speed with the greatest known floating battery and power of resistance."

27 April　President Lincoln extended the blockade to include the coasts of Virginia and North Carolina.

29 April　Major General R.E. Lee commissioned the Confederate States Receiving Ship (CSRS) *Confederate States* (formerly USF *United States*) as the first ship in the Virginia State Navy.

Mound City, Illinois shipyard owner James Eads suggested to Gideon Welles to build iron warships to control the Mississippi River. This concept was passed on to the U.S. Army as Welles felt the need to concentrate on finding ships to enforce the blockade.

Lieutenant Catesby ap Roger Jones assigned to command water batteries on Jamestown Island. Jones entered the U.S. Navy as a midshipman on June 18, 1836. He served under his uncle, a hero of the War of 1812, Commodore Thomas Jones. Promoted to master on September 14, 1848, and lieutenant on May 12, 1849, Jones was then assigned to the Washington Navy Yard. During the 1850s, Jones worked on artillery experiments with Captain John Dahlgren, chief of the U.S. Navy Ordnance Bureau. Jones served on the maiden voyage of the USS *Merrimack* to test the frigate's cannons.

2 May   Brevet Lieutenant General Winfield Scott wrote President Lincoln suggesting what should be done to defeat the Confederacy. Scott further elaborated on his plan on May 3. This concept was the celebrated Anaconda Plan. In essence, Scott's plan intended to strangle the South into submission. Scott believed this could be achieved by enforcing a blockade, splitting the Confederacy along the line of the Mississippi River, creating land operations and featuring amphibious operations.

3 May   The gunboat USS *Yankee*, commanded by Lieutenant Thomas O. Selfridge, entered the York River chasing a schooner and was forced to retreat due to Confederate cannon fire from Gloucester Point. The pre-Revolutionary War earthworks on Gloucester Point were defended by a section of the Richmond howitzers commanded by Lieutenant J. Thompson Brown. This action was the first shot fired in defense of the Commonwealth of Virginia during the war.

4 May   USS *Cumberland* captured the *Mary and Virginia* carrying coal and schooner *Theresa C.* containing cotton off Fort Monroe. Captain Lawrence Rosseau at New Orleans was ordered to determine the availability of wrought-iron plates "of any given thickness from two and one-half to five inches." Rosseau later reported that none could be rolled of that thickness.

6 May   Confederate Congress passed an act recognizing state of war with the United States and authorized the issuing of Letters of Marque to private vessels.

9 May   Secretary of the Navy Stephen Mallory ordered Commander James D. Bulloch, CSN, to Great Britain to purchase ships, guns and ammunition.

The iron-hulled merchant vessel *Fingal* (CSS *Atlanta*) was launched at Thomson Shipyard, Glasgow, Great Britain.

10 May   Mallory advised the Confederate Congress's Committee on Naval Affairs that "I regard the possession of an iron-armored ship as a matter of the first necessity. Such a vessel at this time could traverse the entire coast of the United States, prevent all blockades, and encounter, with a fair prospect of success, their entire Navy…But inequality of numbers may be compensated by invulnerability; and thus not only does economy but naval success dictate the wisdom and expediency of fighting with iron against wood."

13 May	Queen Victoria proclaimed Great Britain's neutrality.
14 May	Mallory instructed Captain Lawrence Rousseau and Captain Duncan Ingraham to identify sources of iron-plate in the South.
	USS *Minnesota* captured schooners *Mary Willis*, *Delaware Farmer* and *Emily Ann* in Hampton Roads.
16 May	Commander John Rodgers purchased the steamboats *Tyler*, *Lexington* and *Conestoga*. These vessels were converted into gunboats commonly referred to as "timberclads."
17 May	USS *Minnesota* captured the bark *Star* in Hampton Roads.
18 May	Contract issued to raise the scuttled USS *Merrimack* from the Elizabeth River.
19 May	The gunboats USS *Monticello* and USS *Thomas Freeborn* shelled Confederate batteries at Sewell's Point and were forced to retire by Confederate counter-battery fire. Flag Officer French Forrest used 196 of the over 1,000 cannons found at Gosport Navy Yard to defend the entrance to the Elizabeth River.
21 May	John A. Stevenson of New Orleans presented a plan to Secretary of the Navy Stephen R. Mallory to break the blockade. Stevenson proposed acquiring powerful tugboats and to alter things "as to make them comparatively safe against the heaviest guns afloat, and by preparing their bow in a peculiar manner…render them capable of sinking by collision the heaviest vessels ever built." Stevenson also noted that we "have no time, place, or means to build an effective navy. Our ports are, or soon will be, all blockaded. On land we do not fear Lincoln, but what shall we do to cripple him at sea?"
22 May	Major General Benjamin Franklin Butler assumed command of the Union Department of Virginia headquartered at Fort Monroe.
23 May	Following the brief occupation of Hampton, Virginia, by the 1st Vermont Regiment, three slaves owned by Colonel Charles King Mallory of the 115th Virginia Militia escaped to Fort Monroe.
24 May	General Butler declared the three runaway slaves "contraband of war."
	The Union base Camp Hamilton was established in Elizabeth County, Virginia near Fort Monroe. The fortified camp was named in honor of General-in-Chief Winfield Scott's military secretary Colonel Schulyer Hamilton.
25 May	USS *Minnesota* captured bark *Winfred* near Hampton Roads.
27 May	Union troops occupied Newport News Point and constructed the fortified position called Camp Butler. Federal control of this point closed the riverine link between Norfolk and Richmond.
30 May	*Merrimack* was raised and moved into Gosport's Dry Dock #1. Contracts were issued to raise the *Germantown* and *Plymouth* from the Elizabeth River.
3 June	Mallory instructed Lieutenant John Mercer Brooke to develop an ironclad design for construction in the South.
5 June	USRM *Harriet Lane* engaged Confederate Batteries at Pig Point at the mouth of the Nansemond River.
10 June	Union forces from Fort Monroe, Camp Hamilton and Camp Butler commanded by Brigadier General Ebenezer Pierce were defeated by Confederate troops

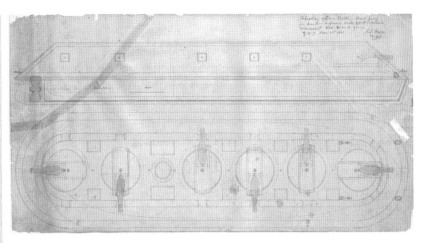

"Floating Steam Battery Bomb Proof for Harbor Defense," John Luke Porter, plan, 1861. *Courtesy of The Mariners' Museum.*

commanded by Colonel John Bankhead Magruder at Big Bethel Church, Virginia. This was the first land battle of the war.

15 June Rifled Sawyer gun on Fort Calhoun (Rip Raps Battery) shelled Confederate batteries at Sewell's Point.

CSRS *Confederate States* was organized as a school ship and armed with nineteen guns (thirty-two-pounders and nine-inch columbiads) to also serve as a blockship.

18 June CSS *Teaser*, commanded by Lieutenant Robert Randolph Carter, CSN, was assigned to help defend the James River at Jamestown Island. This former steam tug was armed with a thirty-two-pounder banded rifle and detailed to observe Union naval operations at the mouth of the James River.

23–24 June Report on Confederate homefront ironclad design completed by Lieutenant John Mercer Brooke, Naval Constructor John Luke Porter and Chief Engineer William Price Williamson. The panel recommended that the *Merrimack* be transformed into an ironclad.

24 June Tennessee State Legislature requested that the Confederate government appropriate $250,000 to enhance defense of the Western rivers.

25 June Gideon Welles learned that the Confederates were building an iron-cased ram in New Orleans and a powerful floating battery in Mobile Bay, Alabama.

26 June USS *Minnesota* captured bark *Sally Magee* off Hampton Roads.

27 June Blockade Strategy Board held its first meeting and recommended that Confederate ports should be closed by stationing ships off each major Confederate port. Board membership included Captain Samuel Francis DuPont, USN; Commander Charles Henry Davis, USN; Brigadier General John Gross Barnard, USA; and U.S. Coast Survey Superintendent Alexander Bache.

28 June Lieutenant John Mercer Brooke began to study and experiment with projectiles and rifled guns.

Side-wheel steamer *St. Nicholas* was captured by Captain George Hollins, CSN, on the Potomac River.

Captain DuPont of the Blockade Strategy Board recommended that two ports, one in South Carolina and one in either Georgia or Florida, be occupied for use as coal depots for the blockading fleet. DuPont believed the blockade could not be effective without these coaling stations.

29 June Steamer *St. Nicholas*, commanded by Captain George Hollins, CSN, captured schooners *Margaret* and *Mary Pierce* and the brig *Monticello*.

1 July USS *Minnesota* captured schooner *Sally Mears* in Hampton Roads.

7 July Two floating torpedoes were picked up in the Potomac River by USS *Resolute*.

10 July USS *Minnesota* captured the Confederate brig *Amy Warwick* in Hampton Roads.

11 July Secretary of the Navy Stephen R. Mallory ordered Flag Officer French Forrest to begin the transformation of the *Merrimack* into an ironclad.

18 July Secretary of the Navy Stephen R. Mallory reported:

> *The frigate Merrimack has been raised and docked at the expense of $6,000, and the necessary repairs to hull and machinery to place her in her former condition was estimated by experts at $450,000. The vessel would then be in the river, and by the blockade of the enemy's fleets and batteries rendered comparatively useless. It has therefore been determined to shield her completely with 3-inch iron, placed at such angles as to render her ball-proof, to complete her at the earliest moment, to arm her with the heaviest ordnance, and to send her at once against the enemy's fleet. It is believed that thus prepared she will be able to contend successfully against the heaviest of the enemy's ships and to drive them from Hampton Roads and the ports of Virginia. The cost of this work is estimated by the constructor and engineer in charge at $172,523, and as time is of the first consequence in this enterprise I have not hesitated to commence the work and to ask Congress for the necessary appropriation.*

21 July Union army commanded by Brigadier General Irvin McDowell defeated by Confederate forces commanded by Generals Joseph E. Johnston and P.G.T. Beauregard at the First Battle of Manassas (Bull Run).

24 July Tredegar Iron Works received contract to produce iron plate for the *Merrimack* conversion project.

30 July Secretary of the Navy S.R. Mallory conferred about the creation of a western armored fleet.

31 July Aeronaut John LaMountain made his first successful balloon flight from Fort Monroe observing Confederate defenses throughout the Hampton Roads area.

3 August U.S. Congress appropriated $1.5 million for ironclad ship construction.

Secretary of the Navy Gideon Welles was authorized to "appoint a board of three skillful officers to investigate the plans and specifications that may be submitted for the construction or completing of iron or steel-clad steamships or steam batteries." Flag Officer Joseph Smith, Flag Officer Hiram Paulding and Commander Charles Henry Davis named to Ironclad Board.

From a Photograph by Brady.

Gideon Welles

"Secretary of the Navy Gideon Welles," engraving, ca. 1880. *Courtesy of the Virginia War Museum.*

John LaMountain made first balloon ascent from a warship, USS *Fanny*, in Hampton Roads to observe Confederate batteries in Sewell's Point.

7 August James B. Eads received contract from U.S. Army to build seven shallow-draft ironclads based on the design provided by Naval Constructor Samuel Pook. Known as "Pook's Turtles," this class of river ironclad was more commonly referred to as the *City*-class. The USS *St. Louis* was one of the "Pook's Turtles." This flat-bottomed, light-draft stern-wheeler was 175 feet in length with a 51 foot 2 inch beam. The *St. Louis* was armed with four forty-two-pounders and seven thirty-two-pounders.

Confederate troops commanded by Brigadier General John Bankhead Magruder burned Hampton, Virginia, to preclude its use by Union forces.

John LaMountain made another successful balloon flight from Fort Monroe, Virginia.

Advertisements were placed in Northern newspapers soliciting seagoing ironclad designs.

9 August Confederate privateer *York* captured schooner *George G. Baker* off Cape Hatteras, North Carolina. The USS *Union* recaptured the *George G. Baker* and forced the *York* to be scuttled by her own crew.

10 August John LaMountain made a second aerial reconnaissance from the deck of the USS *Adriatic*. The balloon soared over two thousand feet in the air, which enabled a thorough inspection of Confederate-held Norfolk. LaMountain advised Major General B.F. Butler that he could create a balloon that could "shell, burn, or destroy Norfolk."

12 August Timberclads *Tyler*, *Lexington* and *Conestoga* were positioned at the confluence of the Ohio and Mississippi Rivers. Mallory ordered Lieutenant John Mercer Brooke to conduct iron-plating tests.

15 August CSS *Manassas* was launched as a privately funded privateer. The *Manassas* was 143 feet in length, displaced 387 tons and was protected by one inch of iron plate backed by wood. The ironclad privateer was armed with one sixty-four-pounder muzzle loading smoothbore and a cast-iron ram.

Deadline for advising Ironclad Board that a design would be submitted.

16 August President Abraham Lincoln proclaimed that the inhabitants of the Confederate States were in a state of insurrection and outlawed all trade with them.

17 August Major General John Ellis Wool assumed command of the Union Department of Virginia at Fort Monroe.

23 August Confederate Congress appropriated $800,000 for the construction of four ironclads on the Mississippi River—two at New Orleans and two at Memphis.

26 August A squadron commanded by Flag Officer Silas Horton Stringham left Hampton Roads with nine hundred troops led by Major General Benjamin Franklin Butler en route to Hatteras Inlet, North Carolina. Since Hatteras Inlet was the main channel into Pamlico Sound, it was an entrance for blockade runners to bring supplies to Virginia via the Great Dismal Swamp and Albemarle-Chesapeake Canals as well as an outlet for Confederate privateers preying upon Union commerce. The Hatteras operation was the first Union effort to attack the Southern coastline.

28 August	Flag Officer Stringham began bombardment of Fort Clark and Fort Hatteras guarding the entrance to Hatteras Inlet, North Carolina.
10:00 a.m.	Union fleets, mounting over 147 heavy cannon, began the bombardment of both Confederate forts. The Confederate counter-battery fire was ineffective.
11:45 a.m.	Major General B.F. Butler began the landing of his 880-man-strong command.
6:00 p.m.	Fort Clark was abandoned.
29 August	Flag Officer Samuel Barron, CSN, surrendered Hatteras Inlet. It was the first major Union naval victory of the war.
30 August	CSS *Harmony*, a seventy-eight-ton side-wheel tug built in Philadelphia, attacked the forty-four-gun sailing frigate USS *Savannah* off Newport News Point. The *Harmony* was armed with two thirty-two-pounders. These antiquated smoothbore shellguns were modernized at Gosport by Commander A.B. Fairfax. Fairfax, head of the Gosport Navy Yard's Ordnance Department, rifled these guns with seven bands and grooves and then banded the breech. The *Harmony*'s attack upon the *Savannah* was considered a naval "repetition of the combat between David and Goliath"; however, the test of these rifled guns proved successful. The *Savannah* suffered significant damage from the *Harmony*'s shells.
31 August	CSS *Teaser* shelled Camp Butler on Newport News Point.
1 September	President Abraham Lincoln learned of the Union capture of Hatteras Inlet, North Carolina.
2 September	Lieutenant John Mercer Brooke and Lieutenant Catesby ap Roger Jones conducted iron-plating shot-proof tests and experiments at Jamestown Island.
5 September	Franklin Buchanan was commissioned captain in the Confederate States Navy.
8 September	Cornelius S. Bushnell accidentally met Cornelius Delameter of Delameter Iron Works on the steps of the Williard Hotel in Washington, D.C. Delameter advised Bushnell to meet with Swedish-American inventor John Ericsson to find answers to questions about the *Galena*'s stability.
9 September	C.S. Bushnell gave plans of *Galena* to John Ericsson.
10 September	C.S. Bushnell met with John Ericsson and reviewed *Monitor* plans.
	USS *Pawnee* captured blockade runner *Susan Jane* in Hatteras Inlet. Blockade runners were unaware that the Federals had occupied this strategic entrance to the North Carolina Sounds.
11 September	C.S. Bushnell met with John A. Griswold and John F. Winslow to solicit support of Secretary of State William Seward and Secretary of the Navy Gideon Welles for the *Monitor* design.
12 September	CSS *Manassas* (converted from the tugboat *Enoch Train*) commissioned into the Confederate navy. President Abraham Lincoln and Cornelius Bushnell met to discuss the *Monitor* concept.
13 September	CSS *Patrick Henry* shelled Newport News Point. The *Patrick Henry* was previously the bay steamer *Yorktown*. This fast side-wheeler was appropriated

C.S. Bushnell, photograph, ca. 1860. *Courtesy of The Mariners' Museum.*

by the Confederate navy and armed with ten heavy guns, including two thirty-two-pounder rifles and a ten-inch shellgun. The *Patrick Henry* featured a one-inch iron shield to protect her engines and was the most powerful Confederate warship in Virginia waters until the emergence of the CSS *Virginia*.

President Abraham Lincoln and Cornelius Bushnell met with the Ironclad Board. The three officers (Smith, Paulding and Davis) "all were surprised at the novelty" of Ericsson's design. When the meeting concluded, Lincoln looked at the model and remarked, "All I have to say is what the girl said when she stuck her foot into the stocking. It strikes me there's something in it."

C.S. Bushnell met with John Ericsson in New York and persuaded him to go to Washington, D.C., to discuss his ironclad plans.

14 September C.S. Bushnell and John Ericsson met with the Ironclad Board. Despite an initial rejection, Ericsson persuaded the board otherwise. At 3:00 p.m., the *Monitor* (Ericsson Battery) concept was accepted.

16 September The Ironclad Board submitted a report that noted, "For river and harbor service we consider ironclad vessels of light draught, or floating batteries thus shielded, as very important." The Ironclad Board reviewed the plans and proposals for seventeen ships, of which three were recommended for construction: *Galena*, *Monitor* and *New Ironsides*.

17 September Troops landing from the USS *Pawnee* captured Ocracoke Inlet, North Carolina.

18 September E.C. Murray received a contract to build CSS *Louisiana* and Tift Brothers received a contract to build the CSS *Mississippi*. Both ironclads were built in New Orleans.

Secretary of the Navy Gideon Welles appointed Flag Officer Louis Malesherbes Goldsborough as commander of the North Atlantic Blockading Squadron. Born in Washington, D.C., on February 18, 1805, Goldsborough was commissioned a lieutenant in 1825. He commanded a steamboat expedition during the Seminole War and captained the ship of the line USS *Ohio* during the Mexican War. Prior to the Civil War, Goldsborough was superintendent of the U.S. Naval Academy.

22 September John Ericsson received letter of confirmation that his "ironclad gunboat" design was accepted by the Ironclad Board.

23 September Flag Officer L.M. Goldsborough assumed command of the North Atlantic Blockading Squadron.

27 September James Eads began construction of the *City*-class ironclad *St. Louis*. Within a week six other ironclads were laid down, including *Pittsburg*, *Carondelet*, *Louisville*, *Mound City*, *Cairo* and *Cincinnati*.

Cornelius Bushnell, John A. Griswold, John Winslow and John Ericsson formed a partnership to build *Monitor*. John Ericsson completed all blueprints for the ironclad's construction.

1 October The Confederate North Carolina Squadron (Mosquito Fleet) commanded by Flag Officer William Lynch, including CSS *Curlew*, CSS *Raleigh* and CSS

Junaluska, captured the gunboat USS *Fanny* (soon to be rechristened CSS *Fanny*) in Pamlico Sound, North Carolina.

4 October Government contract issued to John Ericsson and partners for the construction of "Ericsson's Battery" signed.

Chief Engineer Alban C. Stimers was named the U.S. Navy's superintendent for the Ericsson's Battery project.

Construction of CSS *Mississippi* started in New Orleans.

7 October Contract for the construction of the ship house at Greenpoint Ship Yard, Long Island, New York, issued to Allan Deckerman.

8 October H. Abbott and Son of Baltimore, Maryland, were contracted to produce all of the one-inch iron plate for the Ericsson's Battery project.

9 October CSS *Ivy*, a side-wheeler armed with one eight-inch shellgun, one thirty-two-pounder rifle and two twenty-four-pounder howitzers, shelled Union blockades at the Head of the Passes, Louisiana. The Federals were surprised by the range of the Confederacy's gunboat's rifle.

10 October USS *Daylight* destroyed a Confederate battery near Lynnhaven Roads, Virginia.

11 October CSS *Manassas*, commanded by Flag Officer George Nichols Hollins and supported by the gunboats *Ivy* and *James L. Day*, attacked the Union fleet, including the USS *Richmond*, *Vincennes*, *Water Witch*, *Nightingale* and *Preble*, near the Head of the Passes, Mississippi River. The *Manassas* rammed and damaged the USS *Richmond* and the *Vincennes* was injured by shellfire. Lieutenant Frederick Hill of *Richmond* recalled the attack:

> *I had been soundly sleeping, when I was rudely awakened by a tremendous shock, followed by the sound of the rattle we used as a signal to night quarters. Jumping into my trousers, with my coat in one hand and my sword in the other, I, with the other wardroom officers, rushed on deck…Emerging from the hatchway, I saw on the port side amid ships a smokestack just above our hammock nettings from which belched streams of black smoke…the ram…cleared herself from us and dropped slowly a stern in the darkness.*

The *Manassas* had been seriously damaged from her attack on the USS *Richmond*. Her ram was broken off, one engine was out of operation and the smokestack had collapsed over a ventilator, causing noxious fumes to spread through the ironclad. The *Manassas* ran onto the riverbank. The Union squadron fled the scene as three fire rafts came down the river. The *Richmond* and *Vincennes* ran aground, attempting to escape. In the panic, the *Vincennes* was temporarily abandoned. Both Union warships floated by daylight. The Confederates' attack forced the Union ships out of the Head of the Passes, but did not end the Federal blockade of the mouth of the Mississippi River.

12 October Lieutenant Catesby ap Roger Jones reported to the Secretary of the Navy Stephen Russell Mallory about iron-plating tests on Jamestown Island. The

Catesby ap Roger
Jones, photograph,
ca. 1870. *Courtesy
of The Mariners'
Museum.*

report noted that the sloped sides of the *Merrimack*'s casemate would greatly enhance the shot-proof qualities of the shield; however, it must be clad with four inches of iron, preferably with two layers of two-inch plate. These findings forced Tredegar Iron Works to rework its machinery to produce two-inch iron plate.

13 October — Flag Officer L.M. Goldsborough advised Secretary of the Navy Gideon Welles: "Nothing, I think, but very close work can possibly be of service in accomplishing the destruction of the *Merrimack*."

Goldsborough ordered the steam tugs *Dragon* and *Zouave* to remain in constant company with the sail-powered USS *Congress* and *Cumberland* "so as to tow them into an advantageous position in case of an attack from the *Merrimack* or any other quarter."

USS *St. Louis* launched from Eads's shipyards.

14 October — Citizens of Chincoteague Island, Virginia, took an oath of allegiance in the presence of Lieutenant A. Murry of the USS *Louisiana* and proclaimed their "abhorrence of the secession heresy."

15 October — USS *New Era* was launched as a timberclad. Construction was then immediately begun transforming the vessel into the ironclad USS *Essex*.

Construction of CSS *Louisiana* started in New Orleans.

Construction of CSS *Arkansas* commenced in Memphis, Tennessee.

THE CONFEDERATE IRON-CLAD "LOUISIANA" ON THE WAY TO FORT ST. PHILIP.

19 October	Worthington Pumps purchased for the *Monitor*.
22 October	USS *Carondelet* launched.
23 October	Construction of the *Monitor*'s rudder was begun.
25 October	*Monitor*'s keel laid at Continental Iron Works, Greenpoint, Brooklyn, New York.
	Thomas Rowland of Continental Iron Works signed a contract with John Ericsson to construct the single-turreted ironclad at .075 cents per pound.
29 October	Flag Officer Samuel Francis DuPont's expedition to Port Royal Sound, South Carolina, departed Hampton Roads. Consisting of seventy-seven vessels, it was the largest U.S. Navy fleet ever assembled to that date.
31 October	Construction of the CSS *Eastport* was begun at Cerro Gordo, Tennessee.
1 November	Major General George Brinton McClellan named general in chief of the U.S. Army.
5 November	Confederate squadron of small gunboats commanded by Flag Officer Josiah Tattnall defending Port Royal Sound dispersed by USS *Ottawa*, *Pembina*, *Seneca* and *Pawnee*.
7 November	Flag Officer S.F. DuPont's squadron captured Port Royal Sound.
9:00 a.m.	DuPont's flotilla steamed into Port Royal Sound and his large ships began a steady, circling movement between the Forts Beauregard and Walker, guarding the sound's entrance. While forty-one guns were mounted in these forts, none could match the heavier calibers of DuPont's guns. The constantly moving steam-powered ships were difficult targets for the poorly trained Confederate gunners. The well-trained Union crews were able to repeatedly hit the fixed targets provided by the forts. Smaller Union gunboats were also in position on Fort Walker's flank, out of range of effective Confederate counter-battery fire, and were able to enfilade the fort, dismounting guns one by one.
2:00 p.m.	The dispirited Confederates, running out of ammunition, abandoned Fort Walker.
3:30 p.m.	Fort Beauregard was abandoned by the Confederates. Flag Officer Tattnall was able to rescue some of the Confederate troops with his gunboats and ferried them to Hilton Head, South Carolina.

The Union capture of Port Royal Sound provided the South Atlantic Blockading Squadron with an important coaling and repair station, thereby enabling the squadron to maintain a close blockade of Savannah and Charleston. The engagement also proved that fixed coastal fortifications were unable to block steam-powered, well-armed warships from entering harbors.

Construction of the USS *Benton* was initiated at Mound City, Illinois.

8 November	Alabama legislature appropriated $150,000 to construct the ironclad CSS *Baltic* at Selma, Alabama. The *Baltic*, originally a cotton carrier, was a poorly conceived project. The ironclad was plated with four inches of iron and armed with four guns.
11 November	Thaddeus Sobieski Constantine Lowe made his first balloon observations of Confederate forces outside of Washington, D.C., from the balloon boat *G.W. Parke Custis*.
	Thomas Rowland of Continental Iron Works advised John Ericsson that he had 175 men at work on the ironclad project.
	Lieutenant Catesby ap Roger Jones detailed the executive officer of the *Merrimack*.
12 November	The *Fingal* ran the blockade into Savannah as the first successful Confederate government blockade-runner. The *Fingal* brought with her perhaps the largest single shipment of war material into the Confederacy, including thirteen thousand Enfield rifles and four hundred barrels of gunpowder.
15 November	Chief Engineer Alban Stimers authorized the first payment of $50,000 for work on the Ericsson Battery project.
16 November	Secretary of the Navy Stephen Russell Mallory advertised for plans and bids to build four seagoing ironclads capable of carrying four heavy guns each.
	Iron deck beams were installed in Ericsson's Battery.
18 November	Chief Surgeon Algernon S. Garnett detailed to serve as surgeon of the *Merrimack*.
22 November	Union gunboats shelled Confederate defenses at the mouth of the Warwick River.
25 November	Confederate Secretary of the Navy approved the first armorplate shipment to Gosport Navy Yard for use in cladding the *Merrimack*.
	Lieutenant John Taylor Wood detailed to the *Merrimack* and assigned the task of recruiting crewmembers. A prewar instructor at the U.S. Naval Academy in Annapolis, Maryland, Wood was the grandson of U.S. President Zachary Taylor and the nephew by marriage of Confederate President Jefferson Davis. These family connections would serve him well with his task.
26 November	Flag Officer Josiah Tattnall engaged the Union fleet with four gunboats in Cockspur Roads below Savannah, Georgia, in an effort to lure the Federal ships under the guns of Fort Pulaski.
29 November	Lieutenant John Lorimer Worden reported to Washington, D.C., following his seven-month imprisonment in a Confederate POW Camp.
30 November	Lieutenant Charles Carroll Simms was assigned to the *Merrimack*.
2 December	CSS *Patrick Henry*, commanded by Commander John Randolph Tucker, was damaged during a two-hour duel with Union gunboats near Newport News Point.

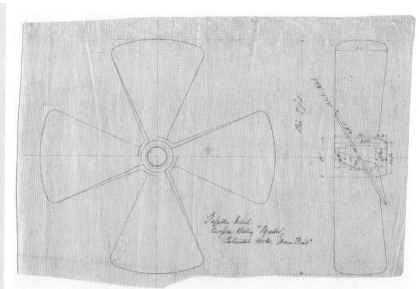

3 December	Officers John Randolph Eggleston, Henry Hungerford Marmaduke, Marshall P. Jordan and Eugenius Alexander Jack detailed to the *Merrimack*.
4 December	Ericsson Battery investors received second payment of $37,500.
5 December	Wooden bulwark installed on the Ericsson Battery.
7 December	Captain Reuben T. Thom's Company C, Confederate States Marine Corps
20 December	arrived at Gosport Navy Yard to guard the *Merrimack*.
26 December	Flag Officer Franklin Buchanan visited Gosport Navy Yard to review *Merrimack*'s conversion.
	Flag Officer Josiah Tattnall with the CSS *Savannah, Resolute, Sampson, Ida* and *Barton* attacked the Union blockading ships at the month of the Savannah River. The Federal fleet was forced out to sea.
29 December	CSS *Patrick Henry* engaged four Union gunboats off Pig Point after Federal vessels had shelled Confederate batteries.
	CSS *Sea Bird*, commanded by Flag Officer William Lynch, evaded Union cannon fire and captured a large schooner laden with water for Fort Monroe.
31 December	Ericsson Battery had its boilers installed and hull painted. Chief Engineer Alban Stimers tested the ironclad's engines and propellers.

CHAPTER 5

THE POWER OF IRON OVER WOOD

T HE RUSH TO ORGANIZE AND equip Federal and Confederate navies in 1861 would have great dividends for both sides in 1862. February 1862 would witness the first major naval actions in the Western theater. Major General Ulysses S. Grant relied upon the ironclad fleet commanded by Flag Officer Andrew Hull Foote. Foote's ironclads overwhelmed Fort Henry on the Cumberland River, yet the ironclads were repulsed during an attack against Fort Donelson on the Tennessee River. Foote was wounded during the engagement, and the Pook Turtles were found not to be shot-proof. Since the Confederates still did not have any operational ironclads in the Mississippi region, the *City*-class armorclads gave the Federals a tremendous advantage.

Overall, the Confederates were just not ready to defend their port cities against the Federal onslaught in early 1862. The Union navy appeared able to move along the Southern coastline at will. Flag Officer L.M. Goldsborough and Brigadier General Ambrose E. Burnside collaborated in the capture of Roanoke Island. The resulting loss of the North Carolina Sounds as well as Fernandina, Florida, considerably weakened the Confederacy. The success of these Union amphibious operations caused Union Major General George B. McClellan to plan a strike against the Confederate capital at Richmond by way of the Virginia Peninsula. McClellan believed that his 121,500-man army could operate using the James and York Rivers. The Confederates did not appear to have sufficient resources available to contend with such a huge movement until the CSS *Virginia* emerged from the Elizabeth River on March 8, 1862.

The CSS *Virginia*'s destruction of the USS *Cumberland* and USS *Congress* off Newport News Point on March 8, 1862, proved the power of iron over wood. These wooden warships were simply outmatched by the new technologies of rifled guns, iron plating and steam power. Steam power also enabled the reintroduction of the ram as a highly effective tactical tool. The *Virginia*, despite all of its flaws, appeared to be the most powerful naval vessel in American waters. Northern leaders viewed the *Congress–Cumberland* disaster as the greatest calamity since the Union defeat at Bull Run on July 21, 1861, and feared that the Confederate ironclad might soon attack Washington, D.C., or New York City. A virtual miracle occurred when the USS *Monitor* entered an eerie Hampton Roads awash in the glow of the burning Congress. The next day, March 9, 1862, revolutionized naval warfare. The *Monitor* and *Virginia* fought for over four hours and this first duel between ironclad ships ended in a draw. The March 9 events reinforced the power of armor cladding and heavy guns as well as introduced the new technologies of a rotating turret and ship operations below the waterline.

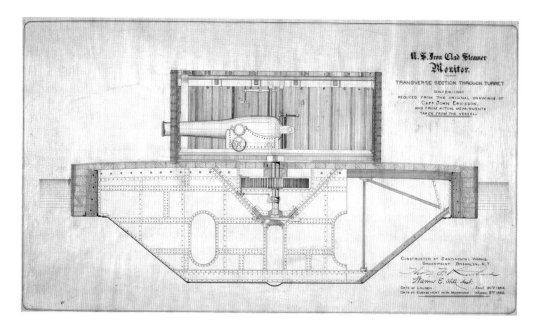

"U.S. Ironclad Steamer *Monitor*," John Ericsson, plan, 1861. *Courtesy of The Mariners' Museum.*

The *Monitor* and *Virginia* influenced ship construction for the next fifty years. North and South concentrated on building more of their ironclad designs. Once ironclads were introduced as the key to naval success, the South's agrarian society was unable to match Northern industrial strength. The two ironclads under construction at New Orleans typified the problems faced by the Confederate ironclad design. When Flag Officer David Glasgow Farragut attacked the masonry coastal forts, Fort St. Phillip and Fort Jackson, defending the riverine approach to New Orleans, the CSS *Louisiana* engines were not operational and it could only serve as a floating battery. The CSS *Mississippi* was still under construction. The privately converted CSS *Manassas* was an ill-conceived warship and was the only functional ironclad defending New Orleans. All three ironclads would be destroyed: the *Manassas* ran aground near Fort Jackson and was burned, while the *Louisiana* and *Mississippi* were scuttled by their own crews to prevent their capture. New Orleans fell, in part, due to the Confederacy's weak transportation and manufacturing infrastructure, which did not allow the time to complete ironclad construction projects.

Meanwhile, on April 10, 1862, Captain Quincy Adams Gilmore began his bombardment of Fort Pulaski on Cockspur Island defending the approaches to Savannah, Georgia. The next day the garrison surrendered. Gilmore's heavy ordnance, including several thirty-pounder rifled Parrott guns, mounted on Big Tybee Island blew a hole in the fort's walls. Fort Macon, guarding Beaufort, North Carolina, surrendered on April 25, 1862, following a massive bombardment by siege mortars and rifled guns. Fixed masonry fortifications proved vulnerable to conical solid shot from rifled guns. These projectiles bored into the brick face of forts and made forty years of coastal defense construction along the Southern coastline virtually worthless.

Following the March 8–9, 1862 engagement, the CSS *Virginia* and the USS *Monitor* maintained a stalemate in Hampton Roads. The *Virginia*'s mere existence paralyzed the Union fleet operations in support of Union General George B. McClellan's Peninsula Campaign. Flag Officer L.M.

Goldsborough declared the James River closed to Union shipping. He also feared that the Confederate ironclad might strike Union transports in the York River and lower Chesapeake Bay. Only the *Monitor*, Goldsborough hoped, could hold the Confederate ironclad in check. This tactical situation caused McClellan to besiege the Confederate Warwick-Yorktown Line for almost four weeks. President Abraham Lincoln traveled to Fort Monroe to find a way to break this stalemate. The president helped to orchestrate the capture of Norfolk on May 10, 1862. The makeshift *Virginia's* twenty-two-foot draft made the ironclad unable to steam up the James River to Richmond. She was scuttled by her own crew early on the morning of May 11, 1862. The riverine door to Richmond was now left undefended. The *Monitor*, accompanied by the ironclads USS *Galena* and USRMS *Naugatuck* (*Stevens Battery*) as well as two wooden gunboats, USS *Aroostook* and USS *Port Royal*, steamed up the James River in an effort to capture the Confederate capital. Forts on the lower James, like Huger and Jamestown Island batteries, were unable to block the Union advance. The Federal flotilla was finally halted by Confederate batteries atop Drewry's Bluff. The *Galena's* clapboard plating proved unable to stop plunging solid shot and the Union ironclad was severely crippled. The *Monitor* could not sufficiently elevate her eleven-inch Dahlgrens to shell the Confederate batteries. The one-hundred-pounder Parrott on the *Naugatuck* burst. These problems forced the Federals to fall back downriver. The acclaimed *Monitor* proved not be the "super ship"; however, the Union navy had already ordered more monitors. The Confederates simultaneously realized that they must build better and more ironclads if the South had any hope of winning the war.

Even though the Confederate navy had initiated the construction of four ironclads on the Mississippi River in 1862, only one unfinished vessel survived the Union onslaught. The CSS *Arkansas* was towed from Memphis up the Yazoo River to Greenwood, Mississippi. Lieutenant Isaac Newton Brown took charge of the vessel and somehow was able to complete her construction. Brown managed to scrape together wood, iron and guns to ready the *Arkansas*. Unlike all other Confederate ironclads, sides of the *Arkansas's* casemate were perpendicular, although the ends were slanted. The ersatz Confederate ironclad was plated with railroad T-iron. Iron supplies were so limited that the stern section of the casemate and the pilothouse were not plated. Armed with ten guns and manned with a crew of two hundred men, the *Arkansas* steamed down the Yazoo River in mid-July.

Awaiting the Confederate ironclad were the combined squadrons, including Farragut's steam sloops of war, Porter's mortar schooners, Charles Davis's ironclads and Charles Ellet's rams. The whole of the Western navy was anchored above Vicksburg. The entire force had been assembled by July 1; however, the fleet could not take action because of the lack of infantry support. Farragut, nevertheless, was anxious to go back down the Mississippi, as he knew the river was falling and he did not want his large vessels stranded. The Federals had heard about the Confederate ironclad up the Yazoo; yet, no Union commander seriously believed that the Southerners could construct an ironclad under such primitive conditions. A force was sent into the Yazoo on July 15 to investigate. As the *Carondelet*, *Tyler* and *Queen of the West* entered the Yazoo they encountered the CSS *Arkansas*. In the engagement that followed, the *City*-class ironclad *Carondelet* was seriously damaged by cannon fire from the *Arkansas* and left disabled. The *Arkansas* chased the two wooden gunboats into the Mississippi where the Confederates found the entire Union fleet at anchor. The Confederate ironclad, now commanded by

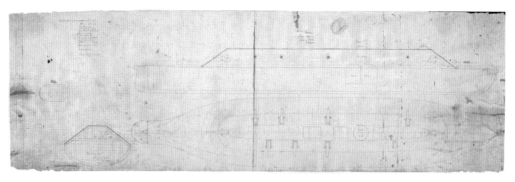

"CSS *Merrimac*," John Luke Porter, plan, 1861. *Courtesy of The Mariners' Museum.*

Lieutenant Henry Stevens because Brown had been wounded, steamed slowly through the entire Union fleet. The *Arkansas* was struck several times by Union shot and shell; however, she inflicted injury upon several Union vessels. The USS *Lancaster* was seriously damaged as the *Arkansas* escaped downriver to Vicksburg. Farragut was embarrassed and angered by the *Arkansas*'s foray and sent his ships after the *Arkansas*. The *Hartford* and other wooden steamers could not spot the *Arkansas* when they passed Vicksburg that evening. The next day Farragut ordered Davis to send a force to Vicksburg to destroy the Confederate ironclad as it lay along the wharf at Vicksburg. The USS *Essex* steamed alongside the *Arkansas* and poured shot into the Confederate ironclad. One shell entered a gun port and decimated half of the *Arkansas*'s available crew. The *Essex*, damaged herself from the Confederate batteries, moved downriver as the rams *Sumter* and *Queen of the West* attempted to cripple the *Arkansas*. Somehow the Confederate ironclad survived this fierce attack. Nevertheless, when the *Arkansas* moved downriver to support the Confederate army's attack upon Baton Rouge, the *Arkansas*'s engines broke down and she was scuttled on August 6, 1862.

The events of 1862 had taught Union and Confederate naval leaders that ironclads were the key to victory. The two-day engagement in Hampton Roads is still considered the greatest naval engagement of the Civil War. The *Virginia*'s victory on March 8 proved the superiority of armored steam-powered warships over wooden sailing vessels. The USS *Monitor*'s arrival that evening saved the Union wooden naval fleet in Hampton Roads and reinforced that only an ironclad could stop another ironclad. The *Monitor* was the true progenitor of the modern warship. Ericsson's concept combined a series of new technologies, including low profile and revolving turret, which made the world's navies take notice. The *London Times* noted that "there is not now a ship in the English navy apart from these two [HMS *Warrior* and HMS *Ironsides*] that it would not be madness to trust an engagement with that little *Monitor*."

The ironclad boom following the Battle of Hampton Roads caused an intense appreciation for Ericsson's design in the North. Less than three weeks after the battle, Ericsson and his partners received a contract to build "six boats on the plan of the *Monitor* for $400,000 each." Contracts were also issued to other builders to produce the improved, larger *Passaic*-class of monitors. The monitor design was continually modified by other shipbuilders. James Eads and Alban Stimers both created variations of low freeboard, turreted, armored warships. Even the USS *Roanoke*, originally a sister ship of the USS *Merrimack*, was converted into an ironclad. The hull was plated and three turrets were installed on the deck. The *Roanoke* was not a success.

The *Monitor* may have been the ship of the future, but there were numerous flaws in the design. Monitors were basically floating batteries, having to be towed from port to port. The ships were so unseaworthy, as seen in the USS *Monitor*'s sinking on the morning of December 31, 1862, that they could not serve their primary function as blockading ships. The monitor design was far better suited for harbor defense and service along the inland waterways. These ironclads had insufficient armaments (two guns per turret), inadequate gun elevation and a slow volume of fire. The *Monitor* was not a factor during the Drewry's Bluff engagement due to these problems.

As the Federals focused on the monitor designs, the Confederate 1862 experience prompted major changes in the South's ironclad production program. While the CSS *Virginia* was a makeshift prototype and had won a great victory on March 8, Confederate leaders recognized the ironclad's limitations. Even though the Confederates endeavored to build several other huge ironclads, such as the *Louisiana* and *Arkansas*, in 1862, these were designed as offensive weapons to challenge the blockade. The Confederates just did not have the industrial and technological resources to build this type of warship and turned to European sources for oceangoing ironclads. Secretary of the Navy Stephen R. Mallory recognized that it was far more important to defend the Confederate harbors, as these outlets were critical to maintaining the overseas trade connection. The experience at New Orleans, Port Royal Sound and Roanoke Island taught Mallory that the South could not rely on traditional coastal forts to guard its harbors. Harbor defense ironclads and other new weapons like torpedoes were required to maintain an in-depth system to protect Southern ports against Federal naval attack.

The 1862 experience prompted Naval Constructor John Luke Porter to modify the Confederate ironclad design into a smaller, lighter draft vessel more appropriate for riverine service and harbor defense. The first of these new style ironclads was the CSS *Richmond*. This flat-bottomed, shallow-draft ironclad design would be recreated in several lengths throughout the South. Nevertheless, the improved design could not resolve several inherent problems: poor propulsion systems, construction delays, limited industries producing iron and machinery, an overtaxed transportation network and a lack of sufficiently skilled workers. Most of the ironclads laid down in 1862 would not be ready for service until 1864 as a result of Confederate shipbuilding challenges.

Neither of the two warships that started the ironclad revolution survived 1862. The *Virginia*, her bad engines and deep draft that limited her range, was scuttled by her crew on the morning of May 11, 1862. It was, as crewmember Richard Curtis reflected, "a sad finish for such a bright beginning." The *Virginia* "had never been the effective fighting machine that the hopes of her friends and fears of her enemies had made her" and her destruction was a tremendous blow to the Confederacy. The *Monitor* continued to support Union operations in eastern Virginia throughout the Peninsula Campaign. The Union ironclad became a symbol of the Northern industrial superiority and her success in Hampton Roads prompted the U.S. Navy to send the unseaworthy ironclad south to Beaufort, North Carolina. Declared not "a seagoing vessel" by her executive officer Samuel Dana Greene, the *Monitor* floundered in a gale off Cape Hatteras early in the morning of December 31, 1862. The two ironclads were no more, but their legacy would dominate naval warfare for decades to come.

1862

2 January   Flag Officer L.M. Goldsborough ordered USS *Louisiana, Lockwood, I.N. Seymour, Shawseen* and *Whitehall* to depart Hampton Roads to Hatteras Inlet, North Carolina. The *Whitehall* returned to its Newport News station due to engine trouble. Goldsborough assembled a squadron to support an operation against Roanoke Island, North Carolina. Flag Officer L.M. Goldsborough urged Brigadier General Ambrose E. Burnside to embark his expedition to Hatteras Inlet, North Carolina. Congressman John Winslow (an investor in the *Monitor* project) informed John Ericsson that if the *Monitor* were successful he would obtain a guarantee that twenty ironclads would be constructed.

6 January   Flag Officer A.H. Foote requested more sailors to crew his ironclad flotilla. Major General Henry Halleck approved that soldiers could be transferred to serve aboard the *City*-class ironclads then being readied for active duty.

Ericsson and partners received $37,500 payment from the U.S. Navy.

7 January   Lieutenant L.S. Phelps reported to Flag Officer A.H. Foote about Confederate fortifications along the Cumberland and Tennessee Rivers. The fort guarding Dover, Tennessee, known as Fort Donelson, was considered formidable. Flag Officer Foote moved down the Mississippi River to Columbus with the tinclads *Tyler* and *Lexington* and one of the two ironclads then available to him, the USS *Essex*. En route Foote encountered one submarine battery (torpedo).

Major General George B. McClellan ordered Brigadier Ambrose E. Burnside to join Flag Officer L.M. Goldsborough at Fort Monroe and then proceed to Hatteras Inlet, North Carolina. Burnside was to capture Roanoke Island. Once successful, Burnside was detailed to operate against Fort Macon, New Bern and Beaufort.

9 January   Flag Officer David Glasgow Farragut appointed to command the Western Gulf Blockading Squadron.

David Glasgow Farragut was born at Campbell's Station, Tennessee, on July 5, 1801. He was adopted by Commander David D. Porter following the death of his mother. Farragut was commissioned a midshipman on December 17, 1810, and assigned to the USS *Essex*. While standing alongside the Norfolk quay in early 1811, the young and diminutive Farragut was splashed with a watering pot by some seaman "to make him grow." Farragut quickly snagged one of the fellows with a boat hook and drove off the others with a dirk. When Porter learned of this "engagement," he noted that Farragut was "three pounds of uniform and seventy pounds of fight." A prize master at twelve, Farragut was promoted to lieutenant in 1822, to commander in 1944 and to captain in 1855. He married a Norfolk girl in 1843 and resided there until Virginia's Secession. He was forced to move to New York because of his Union sympathies; however, his Southern connections made him suspect. His stepbrother David Dixon Porter, interviewed Farragut and assured Assistant Secretary of the Navy Gustavus Fox that Farragut was indeed loyal to the Union.

"John L. Worden," engraving, ca. 1862.

Courtesy of The Mariners' Museum.

10 January	Commander William Smith, captain of the USS *Congress*, reported, "I have not yet devised any plan to defend us against the *Merrimack* unless it be with hard knocks." Flag Officer L.M. Goldsborough ordered the armed tugs *Zouave* and *Dragon* to remain constantly in company with the USS *Congress* and the USS *Cumberland* so as to tow them to an advantageous position in case of attack from the *Merrimack*.
	Flag Officer L.M. Goldsborough ordered USS *Henry Brinker* to Hatteras Inlet, North Carolina.
11 January	Gosport Navy Yard's blacksmiths and finishers signed a public testament volunteering "to do any work that will expedite the completion of the *Merrimack*, free of charge, and continue on until eight o'clock every night."
	Union ironclads *Essex* and *St. Louis* engaged Confederate gunboats in the Mississippi River near Lucas Bend, Missouri.
	Flag Officer L.M. Goldsborough ordered USS *Delaware*, *Philadelphia*, *Hunchback*, *Morse*, *Southfield*, *Commodore Barney* and *Commodore Perry* to Hatteras Inlet, North Carolina.
12 January	The one-hundred-day construction timetable for Ericsson's Battery expired.
	Union amphibious operation to Roanoke Island, North Carolina, departed Fort Monroe under command of Flag Officer L.M. Goldsborough and Brigadier General Ambrose E. Burnside.

13 January	Lieutenant John Lorimer Worden detailed as commander of Ericsson's Battery.
	Flag Officer L.M. Goldsborough's squadron arrived off Hatteras Inlet.
14 January	USS *Carondelet* commissioned. A *City*-class river ironclad, the *Carondelet*, displayed 512 tons and was 175 feet in length with a six-foot draft. Powered by a center wheel, this casemate ironclad was armored with 2.5-inch iron plate. The *Carondelet* was armed with four eight-inch smoothbores, one forty-two-pounder rifle, six thirty-two-pounder rifles, one fifty-pounder rifle, one thirty-pounder rifle and one twelve-pounder rifle.
15 January	Major General Mansfield Lovell, CSA, and Lieutenant Thomas B. Huger, CSN, took over fourteen steamers at New Orleans. Each ship was fitted with one heavy cannon and a heavy iron ram. The cannon was "to be used in case the stern of any of the [Union] gunboats should be exposed to fire, for they are entirely unprotected behind, and if attempting to escape by flight would be vulnerable by shot from a pursuing vessel."
16 January	Lieutenant John L. Worden arrived in New York and assumed command of the U.S. steamer built by Captain Ericsson. Even though Worden recognized the ironclad as an experiment, he was "induced to believe that she may prove a success. At all events, I am quite willing to be an agent in testing her capabilities."
	James Eads launched four *City*-class ironclads: USS *Cincinnati*, *Louisville*, *Mound City* and *Pittsburg*.

John Ericsson, photograph. *Courtesy of The Mariners' Museum.*

20 January "Ericsson Battery" was officially named the USS *Monitor*. Assistant Secretary of the Navy Gustavus Vasa Fox asked Ericsson for a suggestion, to which the inventor replied:

> *In accordance with your request, I now submit for your approbation a name for the floating battery at Greenpoint. The impregnable and aggressive name of this structure will admonish the leaders of the Southern rebellion that the batteries on the banks of their rivers will no longer present barriers to the entrance of Union forces. The ironclad intruder will thus prove a severe monitor to those leaders. But there are other leaders who will also be startled and admonished by the booming of the guns from the impregnable iron turret. "Downing Street" will hardly view with indifference this last Yankee notion, this monitor. To the Lords of the Admiralty the new craft will be a monitor…On these and many similar grounds I propose to name the new battery* Monitor.

21 January Flag Officer William Lynch observed the Union fleet off Hatteras Inlet and noted the importance of Roanoke Island: "Here is the great thoroughfare from Albemarle Sound and its tributaries, and if the enemy obtain lodgments or succeed in passing here he will cut off a very rich country from Norfolk market."

23 January Roanoke Island expedition crossed the Hatteras Inlet bar and entered Pamlico Sound.

24 January Union lighthouse ship went aground at Cape Henry, Virginia, and was captured by the Confederates.

25 January Flag Officer French Forrest wrote Major General Benjamin Huger: "I have just learned that one of the enemy's vessels has been driven ashore with several hundred gallons of oil on board…We are without oil for the *Merrimack* and the importance of supplying this deficiency is too obvious for me to urge anything more in its support."

City-class river ironclad USS *Cairo* commissioned.

26 January Flag Officer Josiah Tattnall completed a resupply of Fort Pulaski while engaging a Union squadron in Wassau Sound.

27 January Workmen finished iron plating the *Merrimack*.

28 January Lieutenant Samuel Dana Greene detailed to the *Monitor* as executive officer.

Captain John Marston, commander of the USS *Roanoke* and senior officer in Hampton Roads whilst Flag Officer L.M. Goldsborough was in North Carolina waters, responded to Secretary of the Navy Gideon Welles's suggestion that the USS *Congress* be transferred to Boston, stating, "as long as the *Merrimack* is held as a rod over us, I would by no means recommend that she should leave this place."

30 January John Ericsson informed that the *Monitor*'s two eleven-inch Dahlgren guns would be transferred from the USS *Dacotah*.

10:00 a.m.	USS *Monitor* launched at Greenpoint, Continental Iron Works. Assistant Secretary of the Navy G.V. Fox telegraphed Ericsson, "I congratulate you and trust that she will be a success. Ready her for sea, as the *Merrimack* is nearly ready at Norfolk and we wish to send her there."
4:30 p.m.	All of the *Monitor's* turret armor was placed aboard the ironclad.
31 January	*City*-class river ironclad *St. Louis* commissioned.
2 February	Flag Officer David Glasgow Farragut departed Hampton Roads aboard the USS *Hartford* en route to assuming command of the Western Gulf Coast Blockading Squadron.
6 February	Flag Officer A.N. Foote captured Fort Henry on the Cumberland River. Foote's command included ironclads USS *Essex, Carondelet, Cincinnati* and *St. Louis.*
	CSS *Louisiana* launched at Jefferson City, Louisiana. The *Louisiana's* construction was delayed by labor problems, shortages of material and an inoperative motive system.
7 February	Lubricating oil for the *Merrimack* arrived at Gosport Navy Yard from Richmond.
	Flag Officer L.M. Goldsborough's squadron bombarded defenses of Roanoke Island, North Carolina. Fort Bartow was heavily damaged by naval gunfire. Brigadier General Ambrose Burnside's troops were landed on Roanoke Island.
8 February	
9:00 a.m.	Union Fleet continued bombardment of Roanoke Island
4:00 p.m.	Obstructions cleared that enabled Union fleet to pass into Albemarle Sound.
5:00 p.m.	Fort Bartow surrendered.

CSS *Curlew* disabled by Union gunfire ran aground and destroyed. Lynch's squadron retreated up the Pasquotank River.

The Confederates were shocked by the loss of Roanoke Island, as Brigadier General Henry A. Wise wrote:

> *Such is the importance and value, in a military point of view, of Roanoke Island, that it ought to have been defended by all the means in the power of the Government. It was key to all the rear defenses of Norfolk. It unlocked two sounds, eight rivers, four canals, and two railroads...It guarded more than four-fifths of all Norfolk's supplies of corn, pork, and forage, and it cut the command of General Huger off from all of its most efficient transportation. It endangers the subsistence of his whole army, threatens the navy yard at Gosport, and to cut off Norfolk from Richmond and both from railroad communication with the South. It lodges the enemy in a safe harbor from the storms of Hatteras, gives them a rendezvous, and a large, rich range of supplies, and the command of the seaboard from Oregon Inlet to Cape Henry.*

Flag Officer Franklin Buchanan ordered Commander John Randolph Tucker to keep the CSS *Patrick Henry* and CSS *Jamestown*, positioned off

Mulberry Island Point, in constant readiness to cooperate with the *Merrimack* when that ship was ready for service.

10 February Flag Officer William Lynch's Mosquito Squadron retreated up the Pasquotank River to Elizabeth City, North Carolina, after Roanoke Island surrendered. A Union naval expedition, led by Commander Stephen Clegg Rowan, steamed up the Pasquotank and engaged the Confederate naval force. The CSS *Ellis* was captured, the CSS *Seabird* was sunk; the CSS *Black Warrior, Fanny* and *Forrest* were scuttled. Several Confederate vessels attempted an escape to Norfolk, Virginia, via the Great Dismal Swamp Canal at the South Mills Lock. The CSS *Raleigh* and *Beaufort* entered the canal; however, the CSS *Appomattox* was too large and was scuttled as an obstruction.

Flag Officer Franklin Buchanan advised Secretary of the Navy Stephen R. Mallory that the *Merrimack* had not yet received her crew "not withstanding all my efforts to procure them from the Navy."

11 February Food and other supplies were stored in the *Merrimack*.

13 February *Merrimack* floated in dry dock for the first time. Lieutenant Catesby ap Roger Jones, who had shown "a want of faith in her ability to float," noted immediately that there were serious problems with the still incomplete warship.

14 February USS *Galena* launched at the Maxson Ship Yard in Mystic, Connecticut. The *Galena* was designed by Samuel Pook and was one of three experimental ironclads. Their model featured 3½-inch clapboard iron plating in a tumblehome design to help deflect shot. The *Galena* was armed with two 100-pounder rifles and four 9-inch Dahlgrens.

Flag Officer A.N. Foote's squadron was repulsed at Fort Donelson, Tennessee. The ironclads *Louisville, St. Louis* and *Carondelet* were severely damaged by plunging fire from Confederate shore batteries. Foote's flagship, USS *St. Louis*, was struck fifty-nine times by shot and lost steering control. Foote was seriously wounded during the engagement.

15 February Lieutenant John Pine Bankhead of the USS *Pembina* discovered a battery of "tin can" torpedoes in the Savannah River. Bankhead removed one of the "infernal machines" for examination, but deemed it more prudent to endeavor to sink the remaining ones than to attempt to remove them. The Confederates deployed a variety of "torpedoes" (mines to protect waterways and harbors). Bankhead encountered electric mines (submarine batteries), which had been invented by Mathew Fontaine Maury.

Flag Officer Josiah Tattnell's gunboat squadron attacked Union batteries on Venus Point on the Savannah River.

16 February Brigadier General U.S. Grant forced Confederates to "unconditionally surrender" Fort Donelson, Tennessee.

17 February *Merrimack* was launched, commissioned and rechristened as the CSS *Virginia*. "There were no invitations to governors and other distinguished men, no sponsor nor maid of honor, no bother of wine, no brass band, no blowing of steam whistles, no great crowds to witness this memorable event," remembered William Cline.

"CSS *Virginia* in Dry Dock," ca. 1862. *Courtesy of John Moran Quarstein.*

Gosport Navy Yard Commandant French Forrest ordered Executive Officer Catesby ap Roger Jones "to receive on board the *Virginia* immediately after dinner today, all the officers and men attached to the vessel with baggage, hammocks, etc., and have the ship put into order throughout. She will remain where she is to coal and receive her powder."

19 February   *Monitor* experienced steering problems during her trial run in New York Harbor. Chief Engineer Alban Stimers reported that the steering required significant repairs and that *Monitor* made only six knots.

20 February   Lieutenant John L. Worden received orders from Secretary of the Navy Gideon Welles to "Proceed with the USS *Monitor*, under your command, to Hampton Roads, Virginia."

Major General John Ellis Wood, commander of the Union Department of Virginia at Fort Monroe, Virginia, reported to Secretary of War Edwin Stanton: "We want a larger naval force than we have at present."

21 February   Captain John Marston of the USS *Roanoke* reported to Gideon Welles "by a dispatch from General Wool, I learn that the *Merrimack* will positively attack Newport News within five days, acting in conjunction with the *Jamestown* and *Yorktown* from the James River, and the attack will be at night."

23 February   When he heard that the *Merrimack* had finally been launched, Captain Gershom Jacques Henry Van Brunt, commander of the USS *Minnesota*, advised the Navy Department that "the sooner she gives us the opportunity to test her strength the better."

24 February   USS *Benton* was commissioned. The *Benton* was converted from a catamaran snag boat known as Submarine No. 7. She was 202 feet in length with a 9-foot draft and powered by a stern paddlewheel. Nicknamed the "Old Warhorse,"

"Franklin Buchanan," engraving. *Courtesy of The Mariners' Museum.*

the *Benton* was armed with two 9-inch Dahlgrens, seven 42-pounder rifles and seven 32-pounder rifles.

USS *Essex* was commissioned.

Flag Officer Franklin Buchanan named commander of the Confederate James River Defenses with the CSS *Virginia* as his flagship. This command also included CSS *Patrick Henry*, *Jamestown*, *Teaser*, *Raleigh* and *Beaufort*. Secretary of the Navy Mallory advised Buchanan:

> *The* Virginia *is a novelty in naval construction, is untried, and her powers unknown; and hence the department will not give specific orders as to her attack upon the enemy. Her powers as a ram we regarded as very formidable, and it is hoped you will be able to test them. Like a bayonet change of infantry, this mode of attack, while the most destructive, will commend itself to you in the present scarcity of ammunition. It is one also that may be rendered destructive at night against the enemy at anchor. Even without guns the ship would, it is believed, be formidable as a ram. Could you pass Old Point and make a dashing cruise in the Potomac as far as Washington, its effect upon the public mind would be important to our cause. The condition of our country, and the painful reverses we have just suffered, demand our utmost exertions; and unconvinced as I am that the opportunity and the means for striking a decisive blow for our navy are now, and for the first time, presented, I congratulate you upon it, and know that your judgment and gallantry will meet all just expectations. Action, prompt, and successful just now, would be serious importance to our cause.*

25 February	USS *Monitor* commissioned in New York as a fourth-rate ship. Captain John A.B. Dahlgren called the vessel "a mere speck, like a hat on the surface." Commander D.D. Porter, who had been assigned the task of assessing the ironclad's combat capabilities, declared the *Monitor* "a perfect success, and capable of defeating anything that then floated."

Lieutenant John L. Worden mustered the handpicked volunteer crew of sixteen officers and forty-nine men on board the *Monitor*. The men were primarily recruited from the receiving ship *North Carolina*.

The *Virginia* started loading coal and ammunition.

Flag Officer French Forrest reported that the lack of gunpowder would delay the CSS *Virginia*'s sortie. Lieutenant Catesby ap Roger Jones advised Lieutenant John Mercer Brooke that the *Virginia* was "not sufficiently protected below the water. We are least protected where we most need it. The constructor should have put on six inches [of iron] where we now have one." Naval Constructor J.L. Porter had miscalculated the ironclad's displacement, which caused the Confederate ironclad to ride too high in the water. |
| **26 February** | CSS *Germantown* moved to the entrance of the Elizabeth River to serve as a blockship. This powerless floating battery was armed with seven cannons and fitted with a sand-filled bulkhead seven feet thick. The CSRS *Confederate States* would eventually join the *Germantown* as another floating battery to guard the entrance created in the double-tow of obstructions near the mouth of the Elizabeth River. The *Confederate States* was armed with nineteen cannons. The *Confederate States* was formerly the frigate *United States*. This venerable relic, originally launched May 10, 1797, formerly mounted forty-four guns. She had been in ordinary at Gosport Navy Yard since 1849.

USS *Monitor*'s departure from New York Harbor was delayed by lack of ammunition for her guns. |
| **27 February** | Flag Officer French Forrest reported the lack of gunpowder delayed any attack of the *Virginia* against the Union blockaders.

USS *Monitor* developed a steering malfunction due to an unbalanced rudder. The problem was corrected by Ericsson and Alban Stimers by installing a series of pulleys between the title and the steering wheel drum. |
| **28 February** | Flag Officer Franklin Buchanan arrived at Gosport Navy Yard to assume his command and he found the *Virginia* still not ready for combat: |

> *She is by no means ready for service. She requires eighteen thousand two hundred pounds of powder, howitzers are not fitted and mounted on the upper deck to repel boats and boarders and none of the port shutters are fitted on the ship. Much of the powder has now arrived, and other matters shall not detain us…the shutters for two bow and quarter ports, I will have temporarily placed there to keep out shot and shells. The last of our powder and shells will be received on board on Wednesday… I feel confident that the acts of the* Virginia *will give proof of the desire of her officers and crew to meet the views of the Department as far as practical.*

1 March	Mechanics continued work repairing the *Monitor*'s steering apparatus.
2 March	Flag Officer Franklin Buchanan advised Major General John Bankhead Magruder,

> *It is my intention to be off Newport News early on Friday morning next unless some accident occurs to the* Virginia *to prevent it, this I do not anticipate. You may therefore look out for me at the time named. My plan is to destroy the frigates first, if possible, and then turn my attention to the battery on the shore. I sincerely hope that acting together we may be successful in destroying many of the enemy.*

3 March	Major General John Bankhead Magruder advised General R.E. Lee that the Army of the Peninsula would not be able to cooperate with Buchanan's attack on Newport News Point. Magruder believed "that no one ship can produce such an impression upon the troops at the Newport News as to cause them to evacuate." The Army of Peninsula commander advocated that the *Virginia* be deployed as a floating battery guarding the James River.
4 March	USS *Monitor* successfully completed her sea trials. Master's mate George Frederickson reported in the *Monitor*'s log about the trials:

> *First of firing blank cartridges, second a stand of grape, third with canister with a full charge of powder 2:15 with 30 pounds steam making 50 revolutions turned with helm hard a starboard turned in four minutes and fifteen seconds within a compass of three times her length and proceeded towards the yard against strong ebb tide vessel going at the maximum speed of G one quarter knots an hour. Greatest number of revolutions attained was 64.*

The *Monitor* lost two crewmembers. George Frederickson noted in the *Monitor*'s log, "Norman McPherson and John Atkins deserted taking the ship's cutter and left for ports unknown so ends this day."

5 March	As the *Monitor* prepared to leave New York Harbor another steering malfunction delayed departure.
6 March	Last gunpowder shipment arrived for the CSS *Virginia*.

Captain Thomas Kevill and thirty-one members of the United Artillery (Company E, Forty-first Virginia Volunteer Infantry) mustered on board the CSS *Virginia*. The men of the United Artillery filled the ironclad's roster. Kevill assumed command of one of the *Virginia*'s nine-inch Dahlgrens.

Secretary of the Navy S.R. Mallory wrote Flag Officer Franklin Buchanan,

> *I submit for your consideration the attack of New York by the* Virginia. *Once in the bay, she could shell and burn the city and the shipping. Such an event would eclipse all the glories of the combats of the sea…peace would inevitably follow. Bankers would withdraw their capital from the city. The*

"Seth Low," James Bard, oil painting. *Courtesy of The Mariners' Museum.*

Brooklyn Navy Yard and its magazines and all the lower part o the city would be destroyed, and such an event, by a single ship, would do more to achieve our immediate independence than would the result of many campaigns.

USS *Monitor* was ready to leave New York for Hampton Roads.

11:00 a.m. *Monitor* taken undertow by the USS *Seth Low.*

4:00 p.m. *Monitor* and *Seth Low* join gunboats USS *Currituck* and *Sachen.* This flotilla rounded Sandy Hook en route to Hampton Roads just as Secretary of the Navy Gideon Welles changed the *Monitor*'s orders and directed the ironclad to steam to Washington, D.C. Since the *Monitor* was out of communication range when the message arrived, the orders were transmitted from New York to Hampton Roads, where they awaited the *Monitor*'s arrival.

7 March General Joseph Eggleston Johnston completed the withdrawal of his 40,000-strong Confederate army from Manassas to Fredericksburg on the Rappahannock River.

CSS *Virginia* was ready for sea trials. A heavy gale kept the unseaworthy ironclad at Gosport Navy Yard.

Major General John Bankhead Magruder advised Buchanan that the Army of the Peninsula would not cooperate with the *Virginia*'s planned attack on Newport News.

USS *Monitor* was struck by a heavy gale along the New Jersey coast. Acting Assistant Paymaster William Keeler noted that in the morning "the top of every wave that breaks against our side rolls unobstructed over the deck dashing and foaming at a terrible rate. The wind continued to increase after dinner with a heavier sea pouring across our deck with an almost resistless force, every now and then breaking against our smoke pipes…sending a torrent of water down on our fires." Executive Officer Samuel Dana Greene stated later in the day "that there was imminent danger that the ship would founder." When Greene hailed and ordered the *Seth Low* to tow the *Monitor* toward calmer waters, the ironclad was saved. George Geer remembered the trip, recalling, "I was not a bit sea sick and stood the trip well. Our only difficulty was that the water washed into us and kept us all soaking wet and did not give us any chance to sleep."

Franklin Buchanan met with the commanders of his escort-armed tugs, Lieutenant Joseph W. Alexander of the CSS *Raleigh* and Lieutenant William Harwar Parker of the CSS *Beaufort*. Flag Officer Buchanan detailed his plans to attack Newport News Point and reminded them that if the battle turned against them, he would hoist a new signal "Sink Before Surrender."

Lieutenant John Dabney Minor observed Union fleet dispositions late in the afternoon: "I reconnoitered the enemy off Newport News and Old Point and was glad to be able to report that they were not in such force as I had been led to suppose."

8 March

3:00 a.m.   *Monitor* struck by the final force of the heavy gale that threatened the ironclad the day before. Waves were once again crashing over the *Monitor*'s deck. Executive Officer Greene "began to think that the *Monitor* would never see daylight" as the wheel rope jumped off the steering wheel and the ironclad began to sheer, stressing its towline with the *Seth Low*.

6:00 a.m.   USS *Monitor* was able to ride out the heavy seas and continued her course toward Hampton Roads.

8:00 a.m.   Major General George Brinton McClellan met with President Abraham Lincoln and reviewed the operational strategy of the Army of the Potomac. Because of the Confederate retreat to the Rappahannock River, McClellan believed that his Urbana Plan was no longer viable and advised the president that the Army of the Potomac should be moved to Fort Monroe.

10:00 a.m.   The *Virginia*'s casemate was coated with a thick layer of "ships grease" to help deflect shot.

10:30 a.m.   McClellan held a "council of war" with his corps commanders. The generals all agreed that the Army of the Potomac should move against the Confederate capital by way of the Chesapeake Bay.

10:45 a.m.   Flag Officer Franklin Buchanan inspected his ironclad's engines and its ability to withstand his proposed tactics with the *Virginia*'s Chief Engineer H. Ashton Ramsay. When Ramsay advised Buchanan that all of the machinery was securely braced and the ten-mile trip downriver would be sufficient to test the engine's reliability, Buchanan declared, "I am going to ram the *Cumberland*. I am told she has the new rifled guns, the only ones in their whole fleet we have cause to fear. The moment we are out in the Roads, I'm going to make right for her and ram her."

11:00 a.m.   Buchanan hoisted his flag officer's red pennant over the *Virginia* and ordered the crew to cast off. Workmen dashed off the ship without completing many minor details.

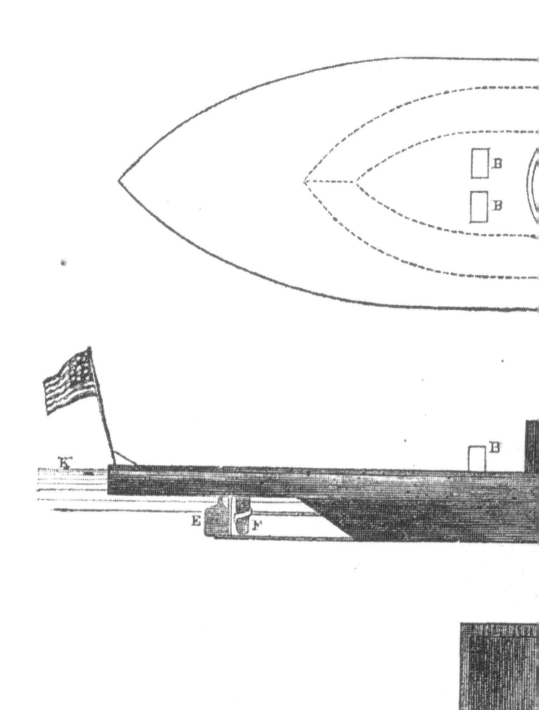

A, Revolving Turret.—B. B. Smoke-pipe.—C, Pilot-house.—D. Anchor We[...] K. K. Water-line.—L. Da[...]

"View of the USS *Monitor*," engraving, ca. 1862. *Courtesy of John Moran Quarstein.*

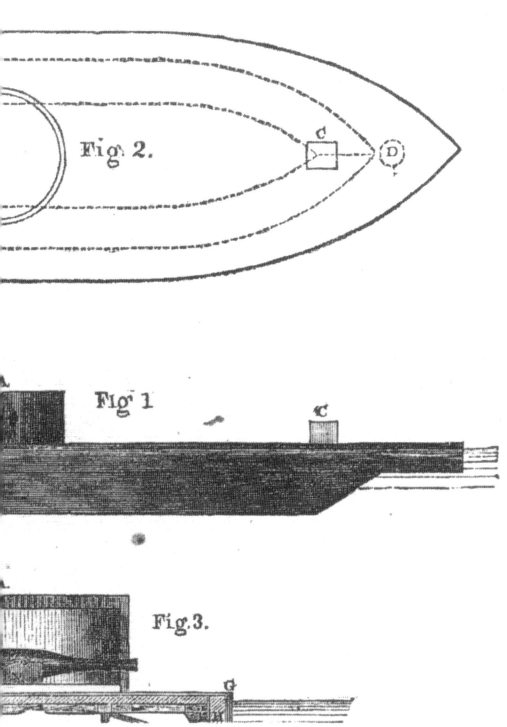

Fig. 2.

Fig. 1

Fig. 3.

Rudder.—F, Propeller.—G, Iron Armor.—H, Braces for Deck Beams.— Gun.—M, Gun-carriage.

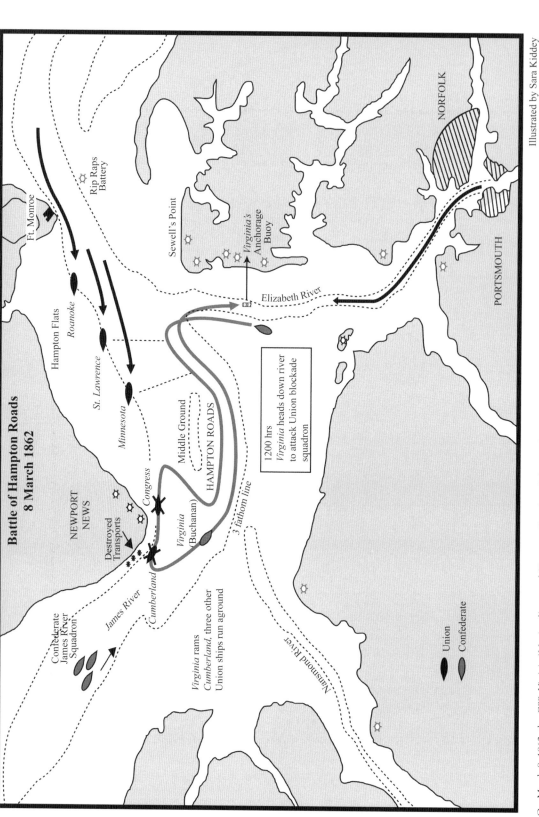

**Battle of Hampton Roads
8 March 1862**

Ft. Monroe

Rip Raps Battery

Hampton Flats

Roanoke

NEWPORT NEWS

St. Lawrence

Minnesota

Destroyed Transports

Congress

Middle Ground

HAMPTON ROADS

Sewell's Point

Virginia's Anchorage Buoy

Elizabeth River

NORFOLK

1200 hrs
Virginia heads down river
to attack Union blockade
squadron

PORTSMOUTH

Cumberland

Virginia (Buchanan)

3 fathom line

James River

Confederate James River Squadron

Virginia rams
Cumberland, three other
Union ships run aground

Nansimond River

Union

Confederate

Illustrated by Sara Kiddey

On March 8, 1862, the CSS *Virginia* (*Merrimack*) entered Hampton Roads and destroyed two Union wooden warships off Newport News Point. The *Virginia's* range was limited by her twenty-two-foot draft. As the USS *Cumberland* and USS *Congress* were destroyed, Union frigates *Minnesota*, *Roanoke* and *St. Lawrence* ran aground. *Minnesota* and *St. Lawrence* were damaged by shellfire as the *Virginia* returned to her anchorage off Sewell's Point.

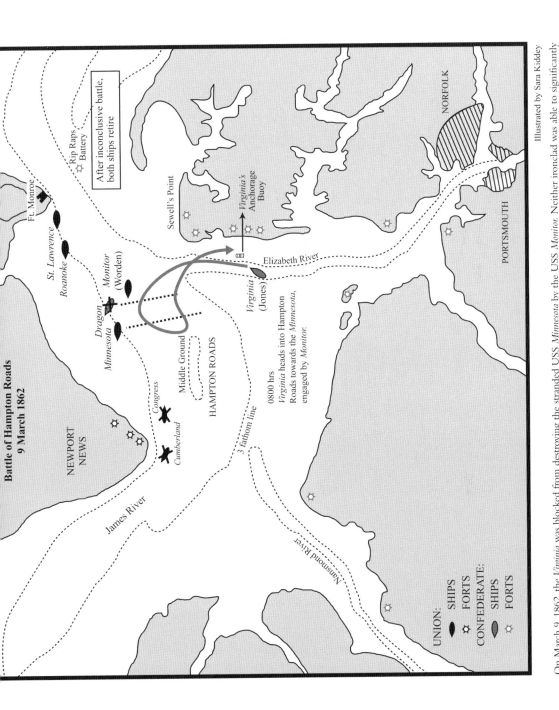

Battle of Hampton Roads
9 March 1862

NEWPORT NEWS

Ft. Monroe

St. Lawrence

Roanoke

Monitor (Worden)

Dragon

Minnesota

Congress

Cumberland

Middle Ground

HAMPTON ROADS

3 fathom line

James River

Nansemond River

Rip Raps Battery

After inconclusive battle, both ships retire

Sewell's Point

Virginia's Anchorage Buoy

Elizabeth River

Virginia (Jones)

0800 hrs
Virginia heads into Hampton Roads towards the Minnesota, engaged by Monitor.

NORFOLK

PORTSMOUTH

UNION:
SHIPS
FORTS
CONFEDERATE:
SHIPS
FORTS

Illustrated by Sara Kiddey

On March 9, 1862, the *Virginia* was blocked from destroying the stranded USS *Minnesota* by the USS *Monitor*. Neither ironclad was able to significantly damage its opponent.

THE "MERRIMAC" PASSING THE CONFEDERATE BATTERY ON CRANEY ISLAND, ON HER WAY TO ATTACK THE FEDERAL FLEET.

11:30 a.m. The banks of the Elizabeth River thronged with thousands of cheering citizens. Surgeon Dinwiddie Phillips commented that "Most of them, perhaps, attracted by our naval appearance, and descriptions of witnessing our movements through the water. Few, if any, entertained an exalted idea of our efficiency, and many predicted a total failure." Lieutenant William Parker of the CSS *Beaufort* remembered, "No voice broke the silence of the scene; all hearts were too full for utterance, for all realized that the fact that there was to be tried the great experiment of the ram and ironclad in naval warfare."

12:30 p.m. The *Virginia*'s trial run down the Elizabeth River proved that the ironclad was as unmanageable as a "water-logged" log. The warship was slow (five knots) and ran so close to the river bottom (twenty-two-foot draft) that a towline from the CSS *Beaufort* was needed to help the huge ironclad round a bend in the river. Major William Norris believed the *Virginia* "was in every respect ill-proportioned and top-heavy; and what with her immense length and wretched engines, she was a little more manageable than a timber-raft."

1:00 p.m. As the *Virginia* passed Craney Island, Flag Officer Franklin Buchanan informed the crew, "Sailors in a few minutes you will have the long awaited opportunity to show your devotion to your country and our cause...The Confederacy expects every man to do his duty, beat to quarters."

Buchanan then pointed to the Union fleet in Hampton Roads and exclaimed, "Those ships must be taken...Go to your guns!" Midshipman Hardin Littlepage recalled that Buchanan "also told us that the Confederates had complained that they were not taken near enough to the enemy and assured us that there should be no such complaint this time, for he intended to head directly for the *Cumberland*."

1:30 p.m. The CSS *Virginia* dropped its towline from the *Beaufort* and entered Hampton Roads at high tide. The *Virginia* appeared "like the roof of a very big barn belching forth smoke as from a chimney on fire."

2:20 p.m. The *Virginia* and her consorts, CSS *Raleigh* and CSS *Beaufort*, exchanged fire with Union forces at Newport News Point. The *Beaufort* fired the first Confederate shot of the day. The first shot from the CSS *Virginia*'s forward seven-inch Brooke rifle struck the *Cumberland*'s starboard rail, injuring several Marines.

2:55 p.m. The *Virginia* and the fifty-two-gun sailing frigate *Congress* traded salvos. Shot from the *Congress* bounced off the Confederate ironclad like "pebble stones." Lieutenant John Randolph Eggleston remembered the scene: "The view from my station was restricted to the gun port, some three by four feet. For a time only the distant shores were visible, till suddenly the port became the picture of a great ship. It was the *Congress* only about a hundred yards distant. But for an instant she was visible, for suddenly there leaped from her sides the flash of thirty-five guns, and as many shot and shell were hurled from it high into the air." As by a miracle, no projectile entered into the wide-open ports. The Confederate ironclad replied and unleashed her broadside of four guns against the *Congress*.

Hot shot and shell ignited two fires on the hapless frigate and the *Congress* appeared critically damaged.

3:00 p.m. USS *Monitor*, towed by the USS *Seth Low*, passed Cape Henry and entered the Chesapeake Bay.

The CSS *Virginia* did not stop to complete the destruction of the *Congress*, but continued on toward the *Cumberland* "like some devilish and superhuman monster, or the horrid creature of a nightmare." The *Cumberland* kept up her fire against the oncoming ironclad, but her shot "struck and glanced off, having no more effect than peas from a pop-gun."

3:05 p.m. CSS *Virginia* steamed over the anti-torpedo obstructions surrounding the *Cumberland* and rammed the sloop of war in its starboard quarter. The *Cumberland* was mortally wounded; the ramming was only made worse by a simultaneous shot from the *Virginia*'s bow rifle, which killed ten men. The Union warship immediately began to sink with the *Virginia*'s ram trapped within the *Cumberland*'s hull.

3:06 p.m. As the weight of the *Cumberland* rested upon the ram, the *Virginia*'s engines refused to reverse and the Confederate ironclad began to settle. The poorly mounted ram broke off and freed the *Virginia*. Ashton Ramsay noted, "Like a wasp we could sting but once leaving the sting in the wound."

3:08 p.m. The *Virginia* floated fifty yards apart from the *Cumberland* as the two ships continued to bombard each other. Acting Master's Mate Charles O'Neil remembered that the "shot and shell from the *Merrimack* crashed through the wooden sides of the *Cumberland* as if they had been made of paper carrying huge splinters with them and dealing death and destruction." The *Cumberland* turned into a slaughterhouse and the sloop's death toll was 121. The *Virginia* also received significant damage from her encounter with the *Cumberland*. The ironclad's smokestack was riddled; the damaged funnel caused the gundeck to fill with smoke and the *Virginia*'s speed was lessened. Three broadsides from the *Cumberland* shot away the starboard anchor, starboard cutter, guard howitzers, stanchions and iron railings. The

"*Virginia* Attacking *Cumberland*," Alexander Charles Stuart, oil painting. *Courtesy of The Mariners' Museum.*

"Gun Deck of *Cumberland*," J.O. Davidson, engraving, ca. 1880. *Courtesy of John Moran Quarstein.*

Cumberland's gunners aimed at the *Virginia*'s gunports, hoping to send solid shot inside the casemate. Lieutenant Catesby ap Roger Jones reported, "Our aft nine-inch gun was loaded and ready for firing, when its muzzle was struck by a shell which broke it off and fired the gun. Another gun also had its muzzle shot off; it was broken so short that at each subsequent discharge its port was set on fire."

3:10 p.m.   USS *Minnesota* ran aground off Salter's Creek.

3:35 p.m.   Lieutenant George Upham Morris ordered his men to abandon ship. Morris commanded the remaining gun crews to "give them a broadside boys, as she goes." The *Cumberland* sank in fifty feet of water. "She went down bravely, with her colors flying," Catesby ap Roger Jones remembered.

3:40 p.m.   CSS *Virginia*, due to her deep draft and poor steering, was forced to steam up the James River to turn around. While this maneuver was executed, the Lieutenant John Taylor Wood struck the *Congress* with several shells from the seven-inch stern Brooke rifle. The *Virginia* also destroyed two Union transports and captured one other, which was anchored along a wharf.

4:00 p.m.   USS *Monitor* neared Cape Henry lighthouse. Louis Stodder recorded in the *Monitor*'s logbook that he "heard heavy firing in the distance."

USS *Roanoke* ran aground on the Middle Ground Shoal.

4:05 p.m.   CSS *Virginia* steamed within two hundred yards of the stranded *Congress*. The *Congress*'s stern was quickly demolished and the main deck was "literally reeking with slaughter." The USS *Zouave* was struck by several shells from the ironclad, which destroyed the tug's figurehead and pilothouse. When a shell hit the *Zouave*'s rudderpost, the disabled vessel broke off action and fled the scene.

4:20 p.m.   Lieutenant Joseph B. Smith, acting commander of the *Congress*, was struck by a shell fragment, which tore off his head and a portion of his shoulder. The ship's command evolved onto the shoulders of Lieutenant Austin Pendergrast.

4:40 p.m.   USS *Congress* surrendered.

5:00 p.m.   CSS *Raleigh* and *Beaufort* steamed alongside the *Congress*. The Union frigate was boarded to remove the wounded and to complete the ship's destruction when rifle and cannon fire from Camp Butler, commanded by Brigadier General Joseph King Fenno Mansfield, forced the Confederate gunboats to back away from the *Congress*. USS *Roanoke* floated off the Middle Ground Shoal and moved away from the action to the protection of Fort Monroe.

5:05 p.m.   Flag Officer Franklin Buchanan ordered Lieutenant Robert Dabney Minor to take the *Virginia*'s remaining cutter over to the *Congress* to complete the frigate's destruction. A volley of musketry hit the boat and Robert Minor was seriously wounded. The CSS *Teaser*, commanded by Lieutenant William Webb, picked up the survivors in a bold dash.

5:20 p.m.   Buchanan, standing atop the *Virginia* and enraged by the Union actions under a flag of truce, shot at the Federal soldiers on the shore. He was severely wounded in the thigh. Buchanan was carried below and ordered Catesby Jones to "plug hot shot into her and don't leave her until she is afire." Jones assumed command of the *Virginia.*

5:30 p.m. USS *St. Lawrence* ran aground on the Hampton Flats.

5:45 p.m. *Congress* was destroyed by hot shot and shell. The *Virginia* then left the Federal frigate burning "stem to stern."

6:00 p.m. Jones steered the Confederate ironclad back into Hampton Roads to destroy the grounded Union frigates. Shells from the *Virginia* damaged the USS *Minnesota* and the USS *St. Lawrence.* The *St. Lawrence* had a shell lodged in her main mast and over a dozen shells struck the *Minnesota.*

7:00 p.m. General Wool reported the destruction of the *Congress* and *Cumberland* to Washington, D.C., via telegraph. Wool's chief of staff, Colonel Le Grand B. Cannon, noted that the land-based armament at Fort Monroe was "as useless as musket-balls against the ironclad." General George McClellan immediately replied and authorized Wool to abandon Camp Butler on Newport News Point. McClellan telegraphed, "The performances of the *Merrimac* places a new aspect upon everything, and may very probably change my whole plan of campaign, just on the eve of execution." The Union general telegraphed Major General John Dix in Baltimore, "See that Fort Carroll is placed in a condition for defense as rapidly as possible in case the *Merrimac* should run by Fort Monroe."

8:00 p.m. Darkness and receding tide compelled Jones to steam the *Virginia* to her mooring at Sewell's Point. As the *Congress* spars and ropes "glittered against the dark sky in dazzling lines of fire," Jones vowed to destroy the Federal fleet the next day.

St. Lawrence floated and was towed toward Fort Monroe.

9:00 p.m. The USS *Monitor* entered Hampton Roads. Worden met Captain John Marston of the USS *Roanoke* and acting commander of Union naval forces in Hampton Roads. Marston rescinded the orders he had received from Secretary of the Navy Gideon Welles to immediately send the *Monitor* to Washington, D.C. He recognized that the best way to stop any Confederate ironclad assault against Washington was to defend the wooden frigates in Hampton Roads. Marston ordered Worden to station the *Monitor* near the *Minnesota* and to protect that warship from the *Virginia.*

10:00 p.m. Lieutenant John L. Worden wrote his wife, "The *Merrimac* has caused sad work amongst our vessels. She can't hurt us."

Crew of the CSS *Virginia* received their supper.

Catesby ap Roger Jones inspected the CSS *Virginia* for battle damage. The smokestack was riddled, a leak in the bow was discovered, two nine-inch Dahlgren barrels were partially shot off, several iron plates were cracked and much of the super-structure equipment—flag staffs, cutters, railings, etc.— were lost. The crew did not know that the ram was missing. Jones believed that the *Virginia* could fight again the next day.

"Sinking of the *Congress*," J.O. Davidson, engraving, ca. 1880. *Courtesy of John Moran Quarstein.*

11:00 p.m.   USS *Monitor* anchored next to the *Minnesota*. As the *Congress* continued to send an eerie glow across Hampton Roads, one of the *Virginia*'s crew "chanced to be looking in the direction of the *Congress* when there passed a strange-looking craft, brought out in bold relief by the brilliant light of the burning ship, which at once he proclaimed to be the *Ericsson*."

11:05 p.m.   Worden and Greene went on board the *Minnesota* and met with Captain G.J.H. Van Brunt. Van Brunt doubted that the ironclad could aid the *Minnesota*. Paymaster Keeler recalled, "the idea of assistance or protection being offered to the huge thing by the little pygmy at her side seemed absolutely ridiculous."

When Confederate Secretary of the Navy S.R. Mallory learned of the CSS *Virginia*'s destruction of the *Congress* and *Cumberland* he noted:

> *It will be remembered that the* **Virginia** *was a novelty in naval architecture, wholly unlike any ship that ever floated; that her heaviest guns were equal novelties in ordnance; that her motive power and obedience to her helm were untried, and her officers and crew strangers, comparatively, to the ship and to each other; and yet, under all these disadvantages, the dashing courage and consummate professional ability of Flag Officer Buchanan and his associates achieved the most remarkable victory which naval annals record.*

9 March
12:00 a.m.   The USS *Congress* exploded. "Certainly a grander sight was never seen, but it went right to the marrow of our bones." William Keeler recalled:

> *The night we arrived I was on deck and witnessed the explosion of the burning* Congress, *a scene of the most terrible magnificence. She was wrapped in one sheet of flame, when suddenly a volcano seemed to open instantaneously, almost beneath our feet and a vast column of flame and fire shot forth till it seemed to pierce the skies. Pieces of burning timbers, exploding shells, huge fragments of the wreck, grenades and rockets filled the air and fell sparkling and hissing in all directions. It did not flash up and*

vanish in an instant, but seemed to remain for a moment or two, an immense column of fire, one end on the earth the other in the heavens. It soon vanished and a dense thick cloud of smoke hid every thing from view. We were about two miles from the wreck and the dull heavy explosion seemed almost to lift us out of the water.

2:00 a.m. Captain Van Brunt attempted to float the USS *Minnesota* at high tide, but the frigate remained stuck in the mud.

5:30 a.m. William Cline reported that the crew of the CSS *Virginia* "began the day with two jiggers of whiskey and a hearty breakfast."

6:00 a.m. *Virginia* slipped her mooring at Sewell's Point but could not steam into Hampton Roads due to heavy fog.

7:00 a.m. President Lincoln met with Captain John Dahlgren and lamented the news of the Confederate ironclad's stunning victory. A cabinet meeting was held later in the morning. Gideon Welles observed the "frantic" Secretary of War Edwin Stanton. Stanton believed that "the *Merrimac*…would destroy every city on the coast under contribution, could take Fortress Monroe; McClellan's mistaken purpose to advance must be abandoned."

8:00 a.m. CSS *Virginia* entered Hampton Roads and moved toward the *Minnesota*.

8:30 a.m. Lieutenant Hunter Davidson fired the first shot of the day from the forward seven-inch Brooke gun at the *Minnesota*. The range was one thousand yards. Another shot quickly followed, "exploding on the inside of the ship, causing considerable destruction and setting the ship on fire." It appeared that the *Virginia* would make short work of the *Minnesota*. USS *Monitor* then moved from alongside of the *Minnesota* and blocked the *Virginia*'s approach to the stranded frigate. Lieutenant James Henry Rochelle of the CSS *Patrick Henry* noted, "Such a craft as the eyes of seamen never looked upon before—an immense shingle floating in the water, with a gigantic cheesebox rising from its center."

"Monitor-Merrimack," engraving, ca. 1862. Courtesy of John Moran Quarstein.

"*Monitor*—CSS *Virginia*," Alexander Charles Stuart, oil painting. Courtesy of The Mariners' Museum.

8:35 a.m. *Monitor* and *Virginia* began circling each other, in concentric circles, testing their opponents' armor. The battle was primarily fought at a range of less than one hundred yards. Often the ships almost touched each other as each ironclad endeavored to gain an advantage.

10:05 a.m. *Monitor* broke off action and steamed into a shoal to reload ammunition in the turret. Worden hoped that by firing his heavy shot, 168-pound spherical projectiles using 15 pounds of powder from his eleven-inch Dahlgrens, such pounding would loosen or break the *Virginia*'s iron plates.

10:10 a.m. Lieutenant Catesby Jones realized that the *Virginia* had the wrong ammunition with which to fight another ironclad. This was a tremendous disadvantage. The *Virginia* had only explosive shells, hot shot and canister to use against wooden ships. Chief Engineer Ashton Ramsay wrote, "If we had known we were to meet her [the *Monitor*], we would have at least been supplied with solid shot for our rifled guns." Therefore, while the *Monitor* replenished its ammunition, the *Virginia* steamed toward the *Minnesota*.

10:15 a.m. *Virginia* began shelling the *Minnesota*, but due to leaking from the loss of her ram, she ran aground.

10:30 a.m. *Monitor* began bombarding the *Virginia* with shot testing "every chink in our armor."

11:15 a.m. Chief Engineer Ashton Ramsay of the *Virginia* coaxed enough power out of the old engines to free the ironclad from the shoal. Lieutenant Jones decided to ram the *Monitor* and maneuvered the *Virginia* into position.

11:45 a.m. *Monitor* eluded ramming and was only hit with a glancing blow. This action caused no damage to the *Monitor*; however, the *Virginia* developed a new leak at her bow. The *Monitor* also fired both of her eleven-inch Dahlgrens at the *Virginia* when she was rammed. The shot struck just above the stern pivot gun port, which forced the *Virginia*'s iron shield in three inches.

"Monitor vs. Virginia," Thomas Skinner, painting. *Courtesy of The Mariners' Museum.*

11:50 a.m. When the *Monitor* avoided the *Virginia*'s attempt to ram her, the Union ironclad moved away from the action. The *Virginia* steamed toward the *Minnesota*. The *Minnesota* and the tug *Dragon* were shelled. Several shells struck the *Minnesota* and ignited a fire. One shell struck the *Dragon*. The *Dragon*'s boiler burst and the tug, which had been alongside the *Minnesota* to tow that vessel to safety, sunk.

12:10 p.m. *Monitor* attempted to ram the *Virginia*. Lieutenant Worden decided to strike the larger ironclad's vulnerable propeller and rudder. A steering malfunction caused the *Monitor* to miss the fantail of the *Virginia*, as the *Monitor* passed the stern of the *Virginia*; a shell from the seven-inch Brooke rifle commanded by Lieutenant John Taylor Wood struck the *Monitor*'s pilothouse. Worden was wounded and the *Monitor* broke off action.

12:25 p.m. Catesby Jones believed that the *"Monitor* has given up the fight and ran into shoal water." As Jones considered how to strike at the *Minnesota*, Worden was taken to his cabin. Lieutenant Greene conferred with the seriously wounded Worden. Worden advised, "Gentlemen, I leave it with you, do what you think best. I cannot see, but do not mind me. Save the *Minnesota* if you can."

12:30 p.m. The *Virginia* could not get closer than one mile to the *Minnesota*. The pilots warned Lieutenant Jones that the tide was falling fast. Jones concurred with the ironclad's officers and decided to return to the Elizabeth River.

12:40 p.m. Lieutenant Samuel Dana Greene assumed command of the *Monitor*. The *Monitor* was brought back into action. Greene mistook the *Virginia*'s course toward Sewell's Point as a sign of defeat and proclaimed, "We had evidently finished the *Merrimac*." The *Monitor* did not pursue the *Virginia* and steamed to a defensive position near the *Minnesota*.

1:30 p.m. Assistant Secretary of the Navy G.V. Fox, who observed the entire engagement, was received on board the USS *Monitor*. Fox told the *Monitor*'s officers, "Well,

gentlemen, you don't look as though you just went through one of the greatest naval conflicts on record." Major General George McClellan telegraphed Fox and asked, "Can I rely on the *Monitor* to keep the *Merrimack* in check, so that I can make Fort Monroe a base of operations?" Fox replied, "The *Monitor* is more than a match for the *Merrimack*, but she might be disabled in the next encounter…The *Monitor* may, and I think will, destroy the *Merrimack* in the next fight; but this is hope not certainty."

2:00 p.m.　Lieutenant J.L. Worden was taken to Fort Monroe for medical attention.

3:30 p.m.　CSS *Virginia* returned to Gosport Navy Yard.

Civilians and soldiers crowded the riverbank as the *Virginia* passed, "cheering, waving of handkerchiefs, flags, hats, and caps; people hallooing themselves hoarse, hundreds of small boats lining our course up river, and approaching as near as they dared the battle-scarred monster that had passed through such a fiery ordeal."

5:00 p.m.　Chief Engineer Alban Stimers telegraphed John Ericsson: "You have saved this place to the nation by furnishing us with the means to whip an ironclad frigate that was, until our arrival, having it all her way with our most powerful vessels."

Captain John A.B. Dahlgren noted when he learned about the *Monitor–Virginia* engagement, "Now comes the reign of iron—and cased sloops are to take the place of wooden ships."

10 March　Lieutenant Thomas O. Selfridge was named commander of the USS *Monitor*.

Lieutenant John Mercer Brooke began producing wrought-iron steel-tipped armored piercing "bolts" for 6.4- and 7-inch Brooke rifles.

CSS *Virginia* was placed in dry dock at Gosport Navy Yard for repairs.

USS *Whitehall* was accidentally destroyed by fire off Fort Monroe.

Confederate Secretary of State Judah Benjamin sent propaganda messages to European nations stating that "success of our iron-clad steamer *Virginia* (late the *Merrimac*) in destroying three first class frigates in her first battle, evinces our ability to break for ourselves the much-vaunted blockade, and ere the lapse of ninety days we hope to drive from our waters the whole blockading fleet."

8:00 a.m. USS *Monitor* steamed through the Union fleet in a "victory procession." Lieutenant Greene described the scene: "Cheer after cheer went up from the frigates and small craft for the glorious little *Monitor* and happy, indeed, we did all feel. I was the captain of the vessel that had saved Newport News, Hampton Roads, Fortress Monroe, (as General Wool himself said) and perhaps your Northern ports."

11:00 a.m. President Abraham Lincoln visited the wounded Lieutenant Worden at the Washington, D.C., home of Lieutenant Henry W. Wise. Lincoln told Worden, "You have done me more honor, sir, than I can ever do to you."

11 March Lieutenant Robert Dabney Minor advised Lieutenant John Mercer Brooke that he deserved "the gratitude and thanks of the Confederacy for the plan of the now celebrated *Virginia*."

Assistant Engineer Charles Schroeder was detailed to the CSS *Virginia*.

12 March Lieutenant William N. Jeffers was named commander of the USS *Monitor*.

Chief engineer of the Army of the Potomac, Brigadier General John Gross Barnard, informed the Assistant Secretary of the Navy G.V. Fox that "the possibility of the *Merrimac* appearing again paralyzes the movements of this army." Fox replied that the *Monitor* should be able to defeat the Confederate ironclad; however, "great dependence upon her" was not wise.

Flag Officer L.M. Goldsborough advised Major General G.B. McClellan that the James River was closed to Union operations and that the U.S. Navy could not attack the Confederate water batteries at Yorktown and Gloucester Point guarding the entrance to the York River.

13 March The Rip Raps Battery (Fort Calhoun) was renamed in honor of Major General John Ellis Wool for Wool's calming presence on March 8, 1862.

14 March Brigadier General Ambrose E. Burnside captured New Bern, North Carolina.

16 March Flag Officer A.H. Foote's squadron began the bombardment of Island No. 10.

17 March Major General George B. McClellan initiated the transfer of the Army of the Potomac to Fort Monroe. Eventually, 389 vessels delivered 121,500 men, 14,592 animals, 1,244 vehicles, 44 artillery batteries "and the enormous quantity of equipage…required for an army of such magnitude."

Chief Engineer Alban Stimers completed repairs to the *Monitor*'s pilothouse. Stimers placed a shell of solid oak covered with three inches of wrought iron, laid in three layers, around the structure. The pilothouse's sides were reconfigured from perpendicular to a slope of thirty degrees to deflect shot.

CSS *Nashville* escaped through the blockade from Beaufort, North Carolina.

Captain Augustus Hermann Drewry's Southside Artillery was assigned to Drewry's Bluff.

18 March Brigadier General Samuel Peter Heintzelman's III Corps arrived at Fort Monroe.

20 March   President Jefferson Davis responded to questions about the riverine defense of Richmond. He noted that the

> position at Drewry's Bluff, seven or eight miles below Richmond...was chosen to obstruct the river against such vessels as the Monitor. The work was being rapidly completed. Either Fort Powhatan or Kennon's Marsh, I found to be proper positions, will be fortified and obstructed as at Drewry's Bluff, to prevent the ascent of the river by ironclad vessels. Blocking the channel where sufficiently narrow by strong lines of obstructions, filling it with submersive batteries and flanking the obstructions by well-protected batteries of the heaviest guns, seems to offer the best and speediest chances of protection with the means at our disposal.

21 March   Flag Officer Josiah Tattnall was named commander of the CSS *Virginia*.

24 March   Captain Sidney Smith Lee, formerly executive officer of Gosport Navy Yard, was ordered to replace Flag Officer French Forrest as commandant of Gosport. Forrest was reassigned as head of the Office of Orders and Details, C.S. Navy Department, Richmond.

25 March   Major General Henry W. Halleck telegraphed Flag Officer A.N. Foote: "It is stated by men just arrived from New Orleans that the rebels are constructing one or more ironclad rivers boards to send against your flotilla. Moreover, it is said that they are to be cased in railroad iron like the *Merrimack*. If this is so I think a single boat might destroy your entire flotilla, pass our batteries and sweep the Western rivers."

27 March   Secretary of War Edwin Stanton instructed Charles Ellet Jr., "You will please proceed immediately to Pittsburgh, Cincinnati, and New Albany and take measures to provide steam rams for defense against ironclad vessels on the Western waters."

28 March   Secretary of War Edwin Stanton telegraphed Charles Ellet, "The rebels have a ram at Memphis. Lose no time." Stanton advised General Halleck about the Ellet ram concept: "They are the most powerful steamboats, with upper cabins removed, and bows filled in with heavy timber. It was not proposed to wait for putting on iron. This was the mode in which the *Merrimack* will be met. Can you not have something of the kind speedily prepared at St. Louis also?"

29 March   Flag Officer Josiah Tattnall arrived at Gosport Navy Yard and assumed command of the *Virginia* while she was still in dry dock. Tattnall had joined the U.S. Navy in 1812 and fought his first engagement during the Battle of Craney Island on June 22, 1813. He served with distinction in the Algerian War and Mexican War as well as in China as commander of the East India Squadron. Josiah Tattnall was known as the "beau ideal of a naval officer." Many fellow officers believed that Tattnall "possessed all the traits which are found in heroic characters." Almost six feet tall with long arms and a protruding lower lip, Tattnall was feared in his younger days as a cutlass expert. Tattnall reluctantly

resigned his U.S. Navy commission when Georgia left the Union and served as commander of the Savannah Squadron until assigned to the CSS *Virginia*. Mallory instructed Tattnall, "Do not hesitate or wait for orders, but strike when, how, and where your judgment may dictate."

2 April Major General George B. McClellan and staff arrived in Hampton Roads aboard the *Commodore*. McClellan advised Lincoln that "effective naval cooperation will shorten this operation by weeks."

4 April CSS *Virginia* had left dry dock after the completion of significant repairs and improvements, including additional iron plating below the waterline and the installation of a twelve-foot-long steel-tipped ram. The ram was designed by Lieutenant John Mercer Brooke to strike beneath the *Monitor*'s armor belt and penetrate the Union ironclad's half-inch iron hull.

Union Army of the Potomac began its march up the Peninsula toward the Confederate capital at Richmond. Minor skirmishes occurred at Big Bethel, Langhorne's (Causey) Mill and Young's Mill. Union forces occupied Confederate First Peninsula Defensive Line.

5 April McClellan's march up the peninsula halted at Lee's Mill. Major General John Bankhead Magruder's thirteen-thousand-man army defended a line of comprehensive fortifications (Second Peninsula Defensive Line) that reached twelve miles across the peninsula from Yorktown on the York River to Mulberry Island Point on the James River. Chief Engineer of the Army of the Potomac Brigadier General John Gross Barnard declared the Warwick–Yorktown line "one of the most extensive known to modern times."

"The assuming and maintaining of the line by Magruder was one of the boldest exploits ever performed by a military commander," wrote Confederate General Jubal A. Early. The CSS *Virginia* secured Magruder's James River flank. Flag Officer L.M. Goldsborough was so intimidated by the CSS *Virginia*'s presence that he declared the James River closed to Union shipping and refused to use naval forces to attack the Confederate Yorktown and Gloucester Point batteries defending the York River.

6 April Battle of Shiloh, Pittsburgh Landing, Tennessee.

McClellan decided to besiege the Confederate Warwick–Yorktown Line.

7 April Confederates surrendered Island No. 10 to Flag Officer A.H. Foote's squadron.

8 April General R.E. Lee, military advisor to President Jefferson Davis, asked Secretary of the Navy S.R. Mallory to order the *Virginia* to strike the Union transports in the York River.

10 April Union batteries on Tybee Island initiated bombardment of Fort Pulaski on Cockspur Island. Fort Pulaski was a key defensive work that guarded the riverine approaches to Savannah, Georgia. This brick moat-encircled fort was commanded by Colonel Charles Olmstead. General R.E. Lee believed that Pulaski was one of the most powerful forts in the South. However, the Federals, guided by engineer Captain Quincy Adams Gilmore, emplaced

heavy smoothbores, mortars and Parrott rifles. The Union cannons opened
fire at 8:15 a.m. In just five hours the rifled guns had breached the thick brick
walls of Pulaski. As darkness ended the cannonade, the hole had widened to
enable the Federals to shell the fort's interior.

11 April Union batteries continued bombardment. When Federal rifled projectiles
began to strike the fort's magazine, Pulaski surrendered. The loss of Pulaski
closed Savannah to blockade runners. More importantly, it proved the power
of heavy rifled guns to destroy masonry fortifications. The fall of Fort Pulaski
placed every Southern port protected by prewar coastal brick forts at risk.

The CSS *Virginia* was finally ready for her third foray into Hampton Roads.
The Confederate ironclad was supported by the James River Squadron: the
CSS *Patrick Henry, Jamestown, Teaser, Beaufort* and *Raleigh.*

6:00 a.m. *Virginia* left Gosport Navy Yard and steamed down the Elizabeth River to
Sewell's Point.

7:10 a.m. *Virginia* entered Hampton Roads. The Federal transports fled the harbor to the
protection of Fort Monroe. The USS *Monitor*, which had just been reinforced by
the iron-hulled USRMS *Naugatuck (Stevens Battery)* armed with a one-hundred-
pounder Parrott rifle, stayed in the channel between Fort Monroe and the Rip
Raps. The Union ironclad had strict orders not to engage the *Virginia* unless the
Confederate ironclad moved into the open waters of the Chesapeake Bay. Flag
Officer Tattnall refused to take his ironclad out of Hampton Roads and the
Monitor would not accept the *Virginia*'s challenge. *Monitor* crewmember William
Keeler observed the scene:

> *Each party steamed back and forth before their respective friends till
> dinnertime, each waiting for the other to knock the chip off his shoulder…She*

had no desire to come under fire of the Fortress and all the gunboats, to say nothing of rams, while engaged with us, neither did the Monitor with her two guns desire to trust herself to the tender mercies of the gunboats and Craney Island and Sewell's Point batteries while trying the iron hull of the monster. I had a fine view of her at a distance of about a mile through a good glass and I tell you she is a formidable looking thing. I had but little idea of her size and apparent strength until now.

3:00 p.m. With all of the Union fleet's attention placed on the moves of the CSS *Virginia*, the CSS *Jamestown*, commanded by Lieutenant Joseph Barney, captured two brigs and an Accomack schooner off Newport News Point and towed them to Norfolk.

4:00 p.m. CSS *Virginia*, flying the captured transport's flag upside down under her own colors as an act of disdain, fired several shells at the *Naugatuck* and returned to Gosport Navy Yard.

12 April General Joseph Eggleston Johnston was placed in command of all Confederate naval and military operations in Hampton Roads. Flag Officer Josiah Tattnall was greatly troubled by this change in command:

This would place me, with reference to the Army, in a position never held hither to by a officer of my rank in any naval service…If therefore, I am to be placed under the command of an army officer, and, being a seaman, am to hold my action and reputation subject to the judgment of a landsman, who can know nothing of the complicated nature of naval science, I earnestly solicit to be promptly relieved from my command.

Some younger man, whose backbone is more supple than fifty years of naval pride have made mine, can be found, I hope for the sake of harmony, to take my place and carry out the views of the Government.

Somehow, Secretary Mallory was able to convince Tattnall to retain his command.

15 April William Keeler reflected on the *Monitor*'s inactivity: "Lunch at twelve, of whiskey and crackers of which I don't partake, but am sorry to say <u>all</u> the rest do. Dinner at two which we draw out as long as possible, after which we loaf around deck (those who have cigars smoke them) and wish for the *Merrimac*."

16 April Elements of the Army of the Potomac attempted to break the Confederate Warwick–Yorktown line at Dam No. 1. The Vermont Brigade was repulsed by elements of Cobb's Legion, Fifteenth North Carolina and Second Louisiana.

18 April Confederate gunboats CSS *Teaser*, *Raleigh* and *Jamestown* were transferred from Norfolk up the James River to support the Confederate Warwick–Yorktown right riverine flank at Mulberry Island.

Confederate Congress endeavored to create a more effective defense of Southern harbors and passed an act authorizing contracts for the purchase of not more than six ironclads to be paid for in cotton.

Sewell's Point

The Union & Lincoln Guns

Jamestown capturing Schooners

"The Second Trip of the *Merrimac*," Theodore R. Davis, engraving, May 3, 1862. *Courtesy of John Moran Quarstein.*

On the Beach.

Schooners leaving

The Octorora & Naugatuck shelling the Merrimac.

Union mortar boats, led by Commander David Dixon Porter, began a five-day bombardment of Fort Jackson, one of two forts defending the Mississippi River approach to New Orleans.

19 April Captain Thomas Kevill and the United Artillery reassigned to the Sewell's Point battery.

Battle of South Mills, North Carolina. Confederates repulsed a Union attack near the North Carolina entrance to the Dismal Swamp Canal. The Federals' threat to Norfolk was halted.

CSS *Mississippi* was launched at Jefferson City, Louisiana.

Mortar schooner USS *Maria J. Carlton* was sunk by Confederate counter-fire while bombarding Fort Jackson, Louisiana.

CSS *Mississippi* was launched by Tift Brothers at Jefferson City, Louisiana.

20 April CSS *Patrick Henry* and *Beaufort* were assigned to the defense of Mulberry Island Point.

21 April USS *Galena* commissioned.

24 April The Tift brothers complained to the commander of the New Orleans defenses that the full mobilization of the militia was harming the effort to complete the

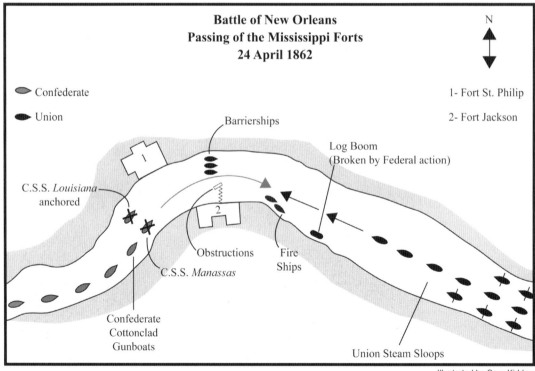

Battle of New Orleans
Passing of the Mississippi Forts
24 April 1862

N

Confederate

Union

1- Fort St. Philip

2- Fort Jackson

Barrierships

Log Boom
(Broken by Federal action)

C.S.S. *Louisiana* anchored

Obstructions

C.S.S. *Manassas*

Fire Ships

Confederate
Cottonclad
Gunboats

Union Steam Sloops

Illustrated by Sara Kiddey

Flag Officer David Glasgow Farragut steamed up the Mississippi River past obstructions, fire ships and two powerful masonry fortifications toward New Orleans. The Confederate ironclads were unable to block Farragut's path. The CSS *Louisiana*'s power path did not work and she was ineffective as a floating battery. The CSS *Manassas* was severely damaged as she attempted to ram Federal vessels and was destroyed on the riverbank. Farragut's steam sloops were protected by iron chains draped over her sides.

CSS *Mississippi*: "The officers of companies are taking from the shipyard our carpenters and laborers, and thus crippling our operations in trying to save the *Mississippi*." Lovell exempted the shipyard laborers from military duty.

Commander Charles Flusser's squadron, including the USS *Lockwood*, *Whitehead* and *Putnam*, blocked the mouth of the Albemarle and Chesapeake Canal by sinking obstructions in the lock.

Flag Officer David Farragut attacked and passed Confederate Forts Jackson and St. Philip. The action included a fierce engagement with Confederate naval forces. A fire raft set Farragut's grounded flag ship, USS *Hartford*, afire.

Percival Drayton and David Glasgow Farragut, photograph, ca. 1864. *Courtesy of The Mariners' Museum.*

Farragut's resolute leadership saved the ship. Meanwhile, the USS *Varuna* was rammed and sunk by two Confederate steamers. However, the Union fleet annihilated the Confederate squadron. The CSS *Manassas* was grounded and destroyed. The CSS *Warrior, Stonewall Jackson, General Lovell, Breckinridge* and *General Quitman* were destroyed. The CSS *Landis* and *W. Burton* surrendered, while the CSS *Absolute* and *Governor Moore* escaped. The ironclad *Louisiana*, which served as a floating battery, did little to block the Union advance.

The CSS *Mississippi* scuttled to prevent her capture by Farragut's fleet. The *Mississippi* was designed by the Tift Brothers and was 260 feet in length with a 12-foot-6-inch draft. Plated with 3.75 inches of iron, this ironclad was designed to mount twenty guns and was considered by the Confederates as "the strongest…most formidable war vessel that had ever been built." The three engines were unable to power the vessels' three screw propellers because of delays producing a shaft at Tredegar Iron Works in Richmond.

Construction of the CSS *Chicora* was initiated at Charleston, South Carolina. The *Chicora* was a *Richmond*-class ironclad designed by John L. Porter. The ironclad was plated with four inches of iron plate. She was 172 feet 6 inches in length with a 12-foot draft and was armed with two 9-inch Dahlgrens and four 6.4-inch Brooke rifles.

25 April Fort Macon, guarding the entrance to Bouge Sound, North Carolina, surrendered to Union forces commanded by Brigadier General John G. Parke. Parke had isolated the "old-style, strong, stone, casemated work, mounting 67 guns commanded by Colonel Moses J. White."

On March 23, he had decided to besiege the fort. Using eight-inch siege mortars and thirty-pounder Parrott guns, Parke initiated a bombardment at dawn on April 25. Union naval vessels, including USS *Daylight, State of Georgia, Chippewa* and *Gemsbok*, attempted to pass the fort. Fort Macon's sea face battery forced the Federal warships to retreat. Parke's artillery fire was effective and the Confederates capitulated in the late afternoon. The fall of Fort Macon reinforced the power of Parrott rifles against fixed masonry fortifications.

CSS *Arkansas* was launched at Memphis, Tennessee.

Acting assistant paymaster, William Keeler, of the USS *Monitor* noted that "there are three great evils in both our army and navy which if corrected would render them much more efficient—the first is whiskey, the second is whiskey, and the third is whiskey."

26 April The city of New Orleans capitulated to Flag Officer David Glasgow Farragut.

27 April USS *Galena*, captained by Commander John Rodgers, arrived in Hampton Roads.

28 April Forts Jackson and St. Philip surrendered. CSS *Louisiana, Defiance* and *McRae* scuttled to prevent capture.

1 May USS *Alligator* launched at Neafie Shipyard, Philadelphia. The *Alligator* was a submarine invented by the Frenchman Brutus de Villeroy. The submarine was forty-seven feet in length and was armed with two spar torpedoes. At first propelled by oars, a crank-operated screw propeller was installed later.

CSS *Richmond* was launched at Gosport Navy Yard. The *Richmond* was the first of J.L. Porter's *Richmond*-class ironclads.

Secretary of the Navy S.R. Mallory ordered all moveable equipment to be transferred from Gosport Navy Yard to yards being established at Richmond, Virginia, and Charlotte, North Carolina.

USS *Marblehead*, commanded by Lieutenant Somerville Nicholson, shelled Confederate batteries and wharves at Yorktown.

3 May General Joseph E. Johnston ordered the abandonment of the Confederate Warwick–Yorktown line. During the evening the Confederates covered their retreat with a massive bombardment of Union siege lines.

4 May Union naval forces captured the transport *Beauregard*, filled with coal for the CSS *Virginia*, off Ragged Island.

Union troops occupied Yorktown; however, as Federal soldiers crossed into the abandoned Confederate positions they encountered torpedoes. These "land-mines" were actually eight- and ten-inch columbiad shells fitted with a percussion cap ignition system, which exploded when stepped upon. Brigadier General Gabriel Rains invented these torpedoes, which were criticized as unethical weapons.

McClellan organized pursuit of the Confederate army, which resulted in skirmishes at Lee's Farm, Skiffes Creek Bridge and Whitaker's Mill.

Captain Thomas Jefferson Page, CSN, held the Confederate Gloucester Point batteries in action until 11:00 a.m. The boat crew from USS *Wachusett* raised the United States flag over the Gloucester Point batteries.

Confederates burned guard boat *General Scott* and sloop *Champion*, both loaded with Confederate Army supplies, to prevent capture. Union naval forces also captured two schooners at Gloucester Point.

5 May President Abraham Lincoln boarded the United States Revenue Mariner Ship (USRMS) *Miami* and left Washington, D.C., en route to Fort Monroe, Virginia.

The Battle of Williamsburg raged along a series of fourteen redoubts constructed in 1861 between College and Queen's Creeks known as the Williamsburg (Third Defensive) line. The battle began when Brigadier General Joe Hooker attacked Fort Magruder (Redoubt 6—the center of the Confederate line) but was repulsed. The Union line was driven back until Brigadier General Philip Kearny's division arrived to stabilize their position. Meanwhile, Brigadier General Winfield Scott Hancock's brigade occupied four redoubts on the Confederate left. Confederate efforts to dislodge the Federals failed. That night, successful in delaying the Union advance, the Confederates abandoned their remaining redoubts and continued their withdrawal to Richmond. The Confederate evacuation of the peninsula left Norfolk and Portsmouth isolated and open to Federal attack.

7:00 p.m. CSS *Jamestown* towed a brig containing heavy guns and ordnance intended for the CSS *Richmond* to Richmond. The CSS *Patrick Henry* towed the *Richmond* to the Rocketts Navy Yard at Richmond.

127

6 May President Abraham Lincoln, accompanied by Brigadier General Egbert L. Viele, Secretary of the Treasury Salmon P. Chase and Secretary of War Edwin M. Stanton, arrived during the evening at Fort Monroe's Engineer Wharf. The president had been invited to Fort Monroe by Major General John Ellis Wool in conjunction with Wool's desire to strike against Norfolk.

USS *Wachusett*, *Chucera* and *Sebago* escorted army transports up the York River to Eltham's Landing near West Point, Virginia.

7 May USS *Currituck* steamed up the Pamunkey River and captured the *American Coaster* and *Planter*.

Battle of Eltham's Landing. Brigadier General William Buell Franklin landed his division at Eltham's Landing to cut off the Confederate army retreat to Richmond. Major General G.W. Smith's Confederate command stopped Franklin's advance inland. Federal troops retreated under the protection of Union gunboats. This action ended Federal efforts to intercept the Confederate march to Richmond.

CSS *Virginia* emerged into Hampton Roads but could not induce the USS *Monitor* into combat. Acting Assistant Paymaster William Keeler noted that the *Virginia*

> *again made her appearance and another just after dinner while she was in status quo under Craney Island, apparently chewing the bitter end of reflection and ruminating sorrowfully upon the future. She remained there smoking, reflecting, and ruminating till nearly sunset, when she slowly crawled off nearly concealed in a huge murky cloud of her own emission, black and repulsive as the perjured hearts of her traitorous crew. The water hisses and boils with indignation as like some huge shiny repine she slowly emerges from her loathsome lair with the morning light, vainly seeking with glaring eyes some mode of escape through her meshes of the net, which she feels, is daily closing her in. Behind her she already hears the hounds of the hunter and before we the ever-watchful guards whom it is certain death to pass. We remain in the same position we have occupied since the fight—a sort of advance guard for the fleet.*

President Lincoln met with Major General John Ellis Wool and Flag Officer L.M. Goldsborough at Fort Monroe, Virginia, to plan how to capture Norfolk and how to enable the U.S. Navy to open the James River in support of General McClellan's drive toward Richmond.

8 May USS *Galena*, accompanied by the USS *Aroostook* and *Port Royal*, steamed into the James River and began bombardment of Fort Boykin on Burwell's Bay and Fort Huger on Hardin's Bluff.

USS *Monitor* and the iron-hulled USRMS *Naugatuck* (Stevens Battery), supported by the USS *Susquehanna*, *San Jacinto*, *Dacotah* and *Seminole*, began shelling the batteries on Sewell's Point. The CSS *Virginia* steamed down the

Elizabeth River from Gosport Navy Yard to contest the Union advance. While it appeared a second conflict between the two ironclads might occur, Goldsborough ordered the Federal squadron to withdraw to its anchorage beyond Fort Monroe. The CSS *Virginia* stayed out in Hampton Roads for several hours hoping to engage the *Monitor*. When no action ensued, Flag Officer Josiah Tattnall ordered the *Virginia* into the Elizabeth River.

Members of the *Monitor*'s crew were critical of their ship's failure to engage the *Virginia* as acting Assistant Paymaster William Keeler noted:

> *A good deal of fault has been found with Captain Jeffers by the officers on board for not attacking the* Merrimack *as we had her in a very favorable spot that would have given us every advantage we desired. He has always complained that he could not get permission to attack her from the Flag Officer, but we have reason to think that he had the consent of the President to "pitch into her" if a favorable opportunity offered. Still if his orders were simply to make a reconnaissance to discover if the batteries had been strengthened or re-enforced with men or guns, he accomplished his object.*

President Abraham Lincoln observed the entire event from the ramparts of Fort Wool and was disappointed with the naval action. Lincoln conducted a personal reconnaissance of the Ocean View and selected a site for a Union landing.

**9 May
2:00 p.m.**

Wool organized an embarkation of six thousand Union troops. The soldiers were loaded on canal boats to be later ferried across the Chesapeake Bay to

Ocean View, Virginia. President Lincoln had selected this landing site the night before. Brigadier General J.K.F. Mansfield commanded the first wave. General Wool was in overall command of the expeditionary force.

4:00 p.m.   Confederates held a Council of War chaired by Flag Officer George N. Hollins concerning the fate of Norfolk and the Gosport Navy Yard. The Confederate army asked the CSS *Virginia* to stay at Craney Island for ten days to cover the Confederate retreat from Norfolk.

5:00 p.m.   President Abraham Lincoln ordered USS *Monitor* to reconnoiter at Sewell's Point. The *Monitor* discovered the batteries abandoned. Lincoln ordered Wool to initiate the landing at Ocean View.

6:00 p.m.   USS *Galena* reached Jamestown Island.

10 May   The USS *New Ironsides* was launched in Philadelphia, Pennsylvania.

The *New Ironsides* was 232 feet in length with a draft of 15 feet 8 inches. This large ironclad had various thicknesses of iron plate ranging from 3 to 4.5 inches. The *New Ironsides* had a speed of six knots and her armament consisted of two 150-pounder rifles, two 50-pounder rifles, fourteen 11-inch Dahlgrens, one 12-pounder rifle and one 12-pounder smoothbore.

Union forces occupied Pensacola, Florida. The Federals captured Fort Barrancas and McRae as well as Warrington Navy Yard. Within the yard were the CSS *Fulton* and an ironclad under construction.

The Confederate River Defense Fleet, commanded by Captain James E. Montgomery, consisting of the rams and cotton-clads CSS *General Bragg*, *General Sumter*, *General Sterling Price*, *General Earl Van Dorn*, *General M. Jeff Thompson*, *General Lovell*, *General Beauregard* and *Little Rebel*, attacked a Federal squadron at Plum Point Bend, Tennessee. Union ironclads USS *Mound City* and *Cincinnati* were rammed and sunk.

7:00 a.m.   The Union army completed landing at Ocean View, Virginia, and began the march on Norfolk.

8:00 a.m.   Lieutenant John Pembroke Jones, flag lieutenant of the CSS *Virginia*, reported to Flag Officer Josiah Tattnall that the Confederate flag no longer flew over the Sewell's Point batteries.

5:00 p.m.   General Wool's troops occupied Norfolk, Virginia.

7:00 p.m.   Lieutenant J.P. Jones reported to Flag Officer Josiah Tattnall that Portsmouth was abandoned and Gosport Navy Yard was in flames.

The destruction of Gosport Navy Yard left the Confederates with few options. The *Virginia* could have been taken out to attack the Union fleet, perhaps sinking in a blaze of glory. Neither this action nor any effort to take the *Virginia* out to sea en route to another port was considered wise. Flag Officer Josiah Tattnall realized that an effort must be made to get the *Virginia* up the James River toward Richmond. The pilots advised that this could only be achieved if the huge ironclad could reduce her draft from twenty-three feet to eighteen feet so that she could cross Harrison's Bar. The crew immediately went to work throwing coal, ballast and everything else overboard except the ironclad's guns and ammunition.

"USS *New Ironsides*," lithograph, ca. 1862. *Courtesy of The Mariners' Museum.*

USS *Cincinnati,* photograph, ca. May 10, 1862. *Courtesy of John Moran Quarstein.*

11 May	Even though the *Virginia* had been lightened to twenty feet, the pilots informed Lieutenant Catesby ap Roger Jones that the *Virginia* could not get across the bar. The pilots noted that the wind was from the west rather than the east, blowing the water away from the bar and making it even shallower. Since the lightening had made the *Virginia* "no longer an ironclad and was therefore unable to engage the Federal fleet it had to be scuttled."
2:00 p.m.	The *Virginia* steamed across the mouth of the Elizabeth River from Sewell's Point to Craney Island and was grounded.
4:58 p.m.	The *Virginia* was scuttled. Ashton Ramsay reflected on the scene: "Still unconquered we hauled down our drooping colors, their laurels all fresh and green, with mingled pride and grief, gave her to the flames, and set the imminent fires roaring against the shuttled guns. The slow match, the magazine, and that last, deep, low, sullen, mournful boom told our people, now far away on the march, that their gallant ship was no more." Flag Officer Tattnall reported, "Thus perished the *Virginia* and with her, many high flown hopes of naval supremacy and success."
11:00 p.m.	President Abraham Lincoln steamed up the Elizabeth River aboard the USS *Baltimore* to view the smoldering ruins of the Gosport Navy Yard.
12 May	USS *Maratanza* steamed up the Pamunkey River to within twenty-two miles of Richmond.
	CSS *Virginia*'s crew arrived in Richmond.
	Commander John Rodgers's squadron shelled Fort Huger.
	The Confederates abandoned Fort Boykin and Fort Huger.
13 May	Lieutenant Catesby ap Roger Jones was ordered to report with the *Virginia*'s crew to Commander Ebenezer Farrand at Drewry's Bluff. The crew began the construction of two gun emplacements.
14 May	Rodgers's James River flotilla, which consisted of the USS *Galena*, *Monitor*, *Naugatuck* (Stevens Battery), *Aroostook* and *Port Royal*, arrived at Harrison's Landing, Virginia.

"Destruction of Rebel Ram *Merrimac*," Currier & Ives, lithograph, 1862. *Courtesy of The Mariners' Museum.*

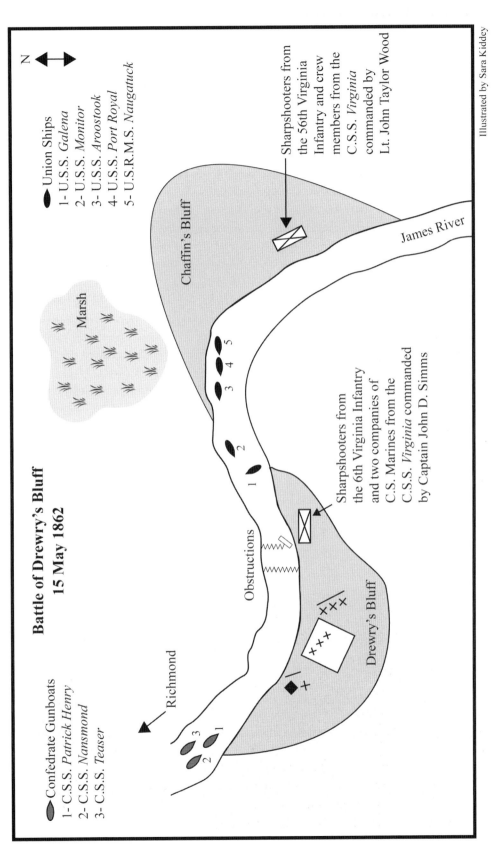

Illustrated by Sara Kiddey

The Union squadron led by Commander John Rodgers steamed up the James River to capture Richmond. Rodgers's command included two wooden gunboats and the ironclads USS *Galena*, USS *Monitor* and the USMRS *Nagauuck*. The Confederates had constructed fortifications atop a ninety-foot bluff and blocked the James River with obstructions. The Union ships were unable to contend with Confederate fire that penetrated the *Galena's* armor. The *Monitor* was unable to elevate her guns to bombard the Confederate gun emplacements. The Federals could not pass the Confederate defenses and fell back down the James River.

Confederates continued work constructing fortifications atop Drewry's Bluff.

15 May

6:30 a.m. Rodgers's flotilla left its anchorage near the mouth of Kingsland Creek and steamed toward Drewry's Bluff.

7:45 a.m. With the *Galena* in the lead, Rodgers placed his flotilla within six hundred yards of the bluff. The river was very narrow at this point and also blocked by obstructions placed by the Confederates only a few days before. Rodgers swung the *Galena*'s broadside toward the Confederate batteries. Confederate Charles H. Hasker was amazed by how Rodgers placed the *Galena* into action with such "neatness and precision." Hasker called the maneuver "one of the most masterly pieces of seamanship of the whole war." The *Galena* received two hits while completing the maneuver and quickly became the primary target of the Confederate batteries. The Confederates encountered significant problems. The ten-inch columbiad, loaded with a double charge of powder, recoiled off its platform when the first shot was fired. The mud and log casemate protecting the seven-inch Brooke gun collapsed from the first shot's vibrations.

9:00 a.m. Confederate plunging shot had begun to take effect upon the *Galena*. Lieutenant William Jeffers moved the USS *Monitor* virtually abreast of the *Galena* in an effort to draw some of the Confederate shot away from the larger ironclad. The *Monitor*'s turret, however, did not permit the ironclad to elevate her two eleven-inch Dahlgrens sufficiently to hit the Confederate batteries. The *Monitor* was struck three times by Confederate shot before she backed downstream.

10:00 a.m. The *Naugatuck*'s Parrott rifle burst and forced the vessel out of action.

11:15 a.m. An eight-inch shell crashed through the *Galena*'s bow gun port and exploded. The shell ignited a cartridge, then being handled by a powder monkey, killing three men and wounding several others. The explosion sent smoke billowing out of the ironclad's gun ports.

11:30 a.m. The *Galena* slipped her cables and retreated downriver. Confederate gunners on the bluff gave her three hearty cheers when the *Galena* broke off action. As the *Monitor* passed Confederate sharpshooters along the riverbank, Lieutenant John Taylor Wood hailed the *Monitor*'s pilothouse and shouted, "Tell Captain Jeffers that is not the way to Richmond."

11:45 a.m. The Battle of Drewry's Bluff was over. The *Galena* had suffered significant damage. She was hit forty-three times and thirteen shots had penetrated the iron plate. Her railings were shot away, the smokestack riddled and she suffered twenty-four casualties. The fight demonstrated that the *Galena* was not shot-proof. The *Monitor*'s limited gun elevation and firepower made the ironclad ineffective during the battle. The U.S. Navy had reached to within eight miles of the Confederate capital. Commander John Rodgers noted that if he had had infantry support, then Richmond would have fallen.

17 May Federal naval forces including the ironclads *Galena* and *Monitor* silenced Confederate lower James River fortifications.

USS *Galena*,
photograph, 1862.
*Courtesy of John
Moran Quarstein.*

Fort Huger was bombarded. The Federals exploded Fort Boykin's magazine.

24 May George Geer of the USS *Monitor* reflected about some of his "old salt" shipmates to his wife: "I wish you could see the body's of some of these old sailors; they are regular Picture Books. They have India ink pricked all over their body. One has a snake coiled around his leg, some have splendid done pieces of Coats of Arms of states, American Flags, and most all have the Crusifiction of Christ on some part of their body."

26 May Lieutenant Isaac Newton Brown was ordered "to take command of the CSS *Arkansas* and finish the vessel without regard to expenditure of men or money." The work proceeded on the ironclad at Yazoo City, Mississippi.

27 May USS *Milwaukee* was laid down at Carondelet, Missouri. The *Milwaukee* was a double-turret monitor designed by James Eads.

The CSS *Baltic* was launched at Selma, Alabama. The *Baltic* was converted from a river towboat. This side-wheeler was plated with four inches of iron plate. Her armament included two nine-inch Dahlgrens and two thirty-two-pounder rifles. The *Baltic* proved unfit for service in defense of Mobile Bay and was dismantled in 1864.

31 May The Battle of Fair Oaks, Virginia.

Robert E. Lee assumed command of the Confederate army outside of Richmond.

6 June	Union ironclad flotilla commanded by Flag Officer Charles Henry Davis destroyed the Confederate River defense fleet during the Battle of Memphis.
17 June	USS *Weehawken* at Secor Shipyard, Jersey City, New Jersey. *Weehawken* was an improved monitor of the *Passaic*-class. The pilothouse was located on top of the turret and a permanent smokestack was added. She was armed with one fifteen-inch Dahlgren and one eleven-inch Dahlgren.
	The Union ironclad USS *Mound City* was severely damaged during her engagement with the Confederate batteries on the White River near St. Charles, Arkansas. Confederate solid shot was fired at close range and pierced the *Mound City*'s iron plate and exploded her steam drum. The Pook *City*-class river ironclads were not shot-proof at close range.
19 June	Commander Matthew Fontaine Maury reported that electric torpedoes (mines) had been planted in the James River near Chaffin's Bluff, Virginia, by the CSS *Teaser*.
25 June	The Battle of Oak Grove, Virginia.
26 June	The Battle of Mechanicsville, Virginia.
	Union General McClellan requested naval assistance to transport supplies from White House Landing on the Pamunkey River to the James River.
27 June	Battle of Gaines's Mill, Virginia.
28 June	Flag Officer David Farragut's fleet passed Confederate batteries at Vicksburg, Mississippi.
29 June	The Battle of Savage Station, Virginia.
	Lieutenants John Mercer Brooke and Robert Dabney Minor commanded an armored railway gun (seven-inch Brooke rifle) during the Savage Station engagement. The gun was protected by an iron-plated shield and operated on the Richmond and York River Railroad.

"Commander John M. Brooke," engraving, ca. 1880.

Courtesy of The Mariners' Museum.

COMMANDER JOHN M. BROOKE.

30 June	Battle of Glendale, Virginia.
	Union General George McClellan selected Harrison's Landing as the James River base for the Army of the Potomac.
1 July	Last engagement of the Seven-Days' Battles fought at Malvern Hill, Virginia. Union gunboats, including the USS *Monitor* and *Galena*, provided artillery support for the retreating Union army.
4 July	USS *Maratanza* engaged and captured the CSS *Teaser*. The *Teaser* had been laying mines in the James River and had also served as a balloon boat to gather intelligence.
9 July	General R.E. Lee advised President Jefferson Davis that his army could not strike against the Union army at Harrison's Landing because of the Federal gunboats.
11 July	U.S. Congress passed an act to provide relief to the relatives of the officers and crew of the USS *Congress* and *Cumberland*.
14 July	Congress passed an act that ended grog rations in the U.S. Navy. According to George Geer of the *Monitor*, "the Grog is whiskey and they give a Gil cup twice each day, and it is equal to a good stiff horn each time."
15 July	CSS *Arkansas* embarked on her first cruise. The *Arkansas* engaged the Union ironclad USS *Carondelet*, gunboat USS *Tyler* and ram *Queen of the West* in the Yazoo River. During this running fight, the *Carondelet* and *Tyler* were disabled and the *Arkansas* continued to chase the *Queen of the West* into the Mississippi River. The *Arkansas* steamed through the combined fleets of Farragut and Davis, totaling over thirty vessels. Only one Union ship, the USS *Lancaster*, was seriously damaged. The *Arkansas* escaped to Vicksburg. Farragut pursued the *Arkansas*; however, darkness had fallen and the Confederate ironclad was anchored under the protection of the Vicksburg batteries. As the Union ships passed Vicksburg, the *Arkansas* was struck several times by shot. The USS *Winona* and *Sumter* suffered significant damage during the action.
16 July	David Glasgow Farragut was promoted to rear admiral in honor of his victory at New Orleans.
19 July	The court martial meeting in Richmond honorably acquitted Flag Officer Josiah Tattnall of any wrongdoing when he ordered the destruction of the CSS *Virginia*.
22 July	USS *Essex* and ram *Queen of the West* attacked the CSS *Arkansas* at anchor at Vicksburg. The *Queen of the West* was severely damaged during the action.
6 August	CSS *Arkansas*'s engines failed while the ironclad steamed down the Mississippi River to support a Confederate attack upon Baton Rouge, Louisiana. When the USS *Essex* steamed toward the disabled *Arkansas*, the Confederate ironclad's commander, Lieutenant Henry Stevens, ordered his ship scuttled.
7 August	William Keeler of the USS *Monitor* complained about the uncomfortable and unhealthy conditions aboard monitors. On July 14 he wrote, "If this sweltering weather continues it will curtail letter writing as you will find, for our state rooms are nearly as bad as the black hole of Calcutta and I find a letter is written at the cost of a large amount of perspiration." On this date, Keeler

USS *Essex*, photograph, ca. 1862. *Courtesy of The Mariners' Museum.*

reinforced his complaints and noted, "Hot, hotter, hottest—could stand it no longer, so last night I wrapped my blanket round me and took to our iron deck—if the bed was not soft it was not so insufferable hot as my pen...what with heat, mosquitoes and a gouty Captain I have nearly gone distracted." Commander Thomas Stevens was named captain of the USS *Monitor*.

9 August

George Geer of the USS *Monitor* commented about how the ironclad's commander endeavored to circumvent the U.S. Navy's new rules on liquor:

> *Our Captain is going to do something he thinks smart. The new law about liquor says no liquor shall be brot [sic] on any government vessel after the 1ˢᵗ of September, but says nothing about what is on hand at the time, so our captain has sent for three 40 gallon barrels to have on hand. That is enough to last us one year. I hope the government will catch him at it someway, and make him trouble. I hope he will get his deserts yet, before the war is over.*

16 August

Confederate Secretary of the Navy S.R. Mallory reported to the Confederate Congress that the

> *want of iron is severely felt throughout the Confederacy, and the means of increasing its production demand...prompt consideration of Congress. The Government has outstanding contracts accounting to millions of dollars, but the iron was not forthcoming...Scrap iron of all classes is being industriously collected by agents of the Government, and we are now rolling railroad iron into plates for covering ships.*

Lack of iron plate plagued Confederate ironclad construction.

USS *Catskill*, Mathew Brady, photograph, ca. 1864. *Courtesy of The Mariners' Museum.*

21 August	USS *New Ironsides* was commissioned.
23 August	CSS *Chicora* was launched at Eason Shipyard, Charleston, South Carolina. The *Chicora* was 172 feet 6 inches in length with a draft of 14 feet. Her shield had 4 inches of iron plate. The *Chicora* was armed with two 9-inch Dahlgrens and four 6.4-inch Brooke rifles.
26 August	Franklin Buchanan was promoted to admiral in the Confederate navy "for gallant and meritorious conduct in attacking the enemy's fleet in Hampton Roads and destroying the frigate *Congress*, sloop of war *Cumberland*."
30 August	The USS *Passaic* was launched at Greenpoint, New York. The *Passaic* was the first of a new class of monitors designed by John Ericsson. Ericsson endeavored to correct some of the problems encountered with the USS *Monitor*. The *Passaic*-class included eight vessels: *Comanche, Catskill, Lehigh, Montauk, Nahant, Nantucket, Passaic* and *Patapsco*. This improved monitor design was longer (two hundred feet in length) and included the pilothouse on top of the turret, a permanent smokestack and mounted at least one fifteen-inch Dahlgren in the turret.
3 September	The City of Natchez, Mississippi, unconditionally surrendered to the USS *Essex*.
4 September	USS *Indianola* launched at Brown Shipyard, Cincinnati, Ohio.
5 September	Admiral S.F. DuPont advised Secretary of the Navy Gideon Welles that the Confederates were building ironclads at Charleston, South Carolina, even though he noted that these gunboats were "well protected by their armor, but not as formidable for offensive operations against our vessels, in consequence of their deficiency in steam power." DuPont added that if the Confederates could resolve propulsion problems then there was a "necessity of sending some iron-clad vessels of our own, to render our position off Charleston tenable."
	USS *Chillicothe*, a river ironclad, was commissioned.
7 September	USS *Essex* was struck fourteen times by heavy shot while engaged with the batteries defending Port Hudson, Louisiana. Captain W.D. Porter noted that these heavy batteries "seriously interrupt the free navigation of the lower Mississippi."
11 September	Rear Admiral S.P. Lee, concerned about the reports concerning the Confederate construction of the *Merrimack II* (CSS *Richmond*), requested an ironclad to be

stationed in Hampton Roads to counter any Confederate ironclad attack. Assistant Secretary of the Navy Fox replied that the *New Ironsides* would soon be sent to Hampton Roads. Fox wrote, "With the *Ironsides* you will feel no anxiety. She is fast, and has a terrible battery, and is a match for the whole Southern navy. If the *Merrimac* Number 2 comes down, I trust they will follow her up and destroy her."

14 September USS *Lafayette* was acquired for the U.S. Navy. The *Lafayette* was purchased as an army quartermaster vessel at Fort Henry in 1861 and converted by Eads at St. Louis to a design of Captain William D. Porter. The ironclad *Lafayette* was one of the most heavily armed ships on the Mississippi River. Her armament included four eleven-inch Dahlgrens, four nine-inch Dahlgrens, four one-hundred-pounder rifles, six twenty-four-pounder howitzers and two twelve-pounder howitzers. The *Lafayette*'s unique casemate design featured two and a half inches of iron plate backed by two inches of rubber. This concept proved to be a failure.

24 September The USS *New Ironsides* arrived in Hampton Roads, Virginia.

27 September *Passaic*-class monitor *Patapsco* was launched. River ironclad *Choctaw* was launched.

30 September USS *Monitor* was ordered to Washington Navy Yard for repairs. The *Monitor* became a tourist attraction while in the yard. William Keeler wrote, "Our decks were covered and our ward room filled with ladies…There appeared to be a general turn out of the sex in the city, there were women with children and women without children, and women—hem—expecting, an extensive display of lower extremities was made going up and down our steep ladders." Louis Stodder said that after these visits, the visitors had taken souvenirs and he wrote, "When we came up to clean that night there was not a key, doorknob, escutcheon—there wasn't a thing that hadn't been carried away."

While at Washington Navy Yard the *Monitor* had her bottom cleared of marine growth, iron patches were placed over dents caused by Confederate shot, new davits and cranes were installed to hold ships and telescoping smokestacks were added.

4 October The seagoing ironclad frigate *Dunderberg* was laid down at the William H. Webb Yard, New York, New York. The *Dunderberg* was designed by John Lenthall as a reproduction of the CSS *Virginia* with sloping casemate sides and a 50-foot ram. With a length of 377 feet and four inches, she was the longest wooden hulled warship built in the United States. She was plated with four and a half inches of iron on her casemate and three and a half inches elsewhere. The *Dunderberg* had a double-bottom and collision bulkheads. The ironclad was designed to mount four fifteen-inch and eight eleven-inch Dahlgrens. The *Dunderberg* was not completed until after the war's conclusion and was therefore never accepted by the U.S. Navy. She was sold to France in July 1867 and renamed the *Rochambeau*.

October 7 *Passaic*-class monitor USS *Nahant* launched at Boston's City Point Shipyard.

9 October	*Passaic*-class monitor USS *Montauk* launched at Continental Iron Works, Greenpoint, New York.
11 October	CSS *Palmetto State* launched at Charleston, South Carolina.
25 October	Rear Admiral S.F. DuPont advised Secretary of the Navy Gideon Welles that the Confederates were building ironclads in Savannah with the intention "to open the Savannah River, then come to Port Royal, and thence off Charleston, and raise the blockade." DuPont asked Welles to detail the *New Ironsides* and *Passaic* to his command.
27 October	*Passaic*-class monitor *Sangamon* was launched at Reaney Shipyard, Chester, Pennsylvania.
	Rear Admiral S.P. Lee advised Assistant Secretary of the Navy G.V. Fox that Union control of the North Carolina Sounds could "only be maintained by ironclads adapted to navigation there."
31 October	Confederate Congress established a Naval Submarine Battery Service under the command of Lieutenant Hunter Davidson. Torpedoes were an effective method of defending the long Confederate coast with its many inlets, harbors and sounds. Union Secretary of the Navy Gideon Welles considered torpedoes "always formidable in harbors and internal waters, and…have been more destructive to our naval vessel than all other means combined."
2 November	USS *Monitor* crewmember George Geer wrote his wife about the repairs to the Union ironclad:

> *They are fixing the* Monitor *up much bettor* [sic] *than she was before. They will make a perfect little palace of her. The workmen work nights and Sundays. I can hear them hammering away as I am writing. They have named her guns, "Worden and Ericsson," and have had the names engraved on them in very large letters.*

3 November	Seaman Jacob Nicklis wrote his father about the USS *Monitor* when he arrived at the Washington Navy Yard:

> *The* Monitor *lies in the Yard at present for repairs and she will probably take some of us, as her crew ran away when they landed in the yard on account of her not being sea worthy. But since then they have altered her so I think there will be no danger.*

5 November	*Passaic*-class monitor *Weehawken* launched. The *Weehawken* was originally named the *Conestoga*. She was built by Zeno Secor & Company of Jersey City, New Jersey, and her machinery was manufactured by Morris Towne & Company of Philadelphia, Pennsylvania.
16 November	USS *Monitor* crewmember Jacob Nicklis wrote his father that "I do not like the boat because of her accommodations."
17 November	Acting Assistant Paymaster William Keeler recorded the *Monitor*'s repairs:

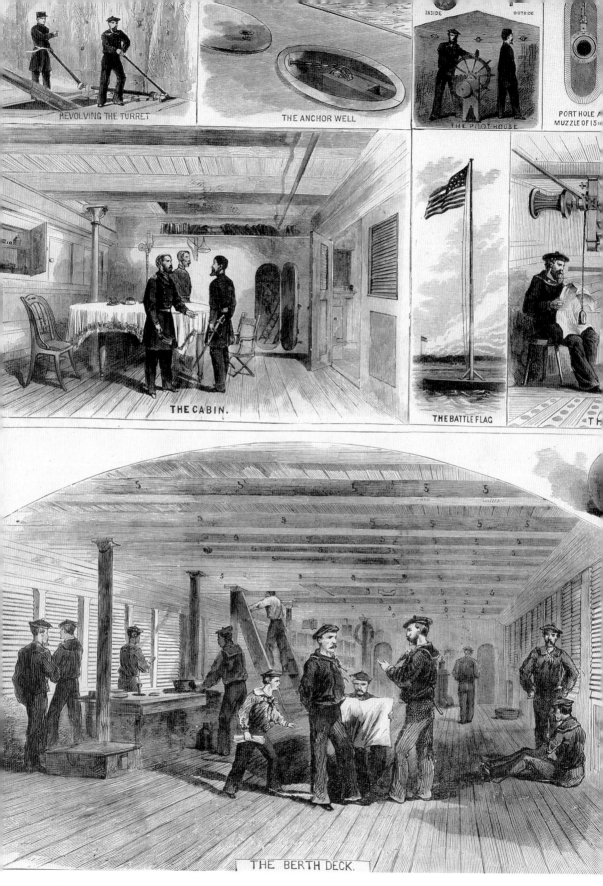

REVOLVING THE TURRET

THE ANCHOR WELL

THE PILOT HOUSE

PORT HOLE A
MUZZLE OF 15

THE CABIN.

THE BATTLE FLAG

THE BERTH DECK.

"USS *Montauk* Interior," W. T. Crane, engraving, ca. 1862. *Courtesy of The Mariners' Museum.*

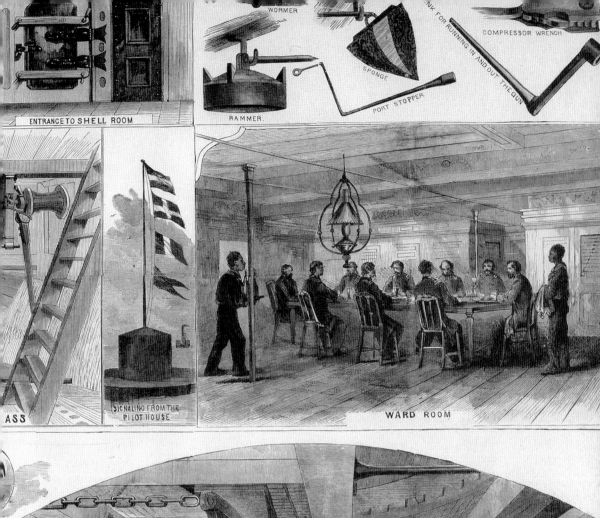

WORMER

SPONGE

PORT STOPPER

COMPRESSOR WRENCH

...NK FOR RUNNING IN AND OUT THE GUN

ENTRANCE TO SHELL ROOM

RAMMER.

...ASS

SIGNALING FROM THE PILOT HOUSE

WARD ROOM

UNDER THE TURRET.

Our vessel has undergone a variety of changes. A large telescopic smoke pipe capable of being run up some thirty feet, takes the place of the two low square box like things you see in the photograph. The fresh air funnels have been replaced by two much higher. Our old boats were all left behind and we were furnished with others better adapted to our wants and large iron cranes and davits to raise them out of the water and carry them on, instead of dragging them up to our decks to be in the way, or dragging them in the water after us.

The raged shot marks in our sides have been covered with iron patches and the places marked, "Merrimac," "Merrimac's Prow," "Minnesota," and "Fort Darling," to indicate the source from whence the blow was received. New awnings have been furnished, ventilators for our deck lights and many other little conveniences which would have added greatly to our comfort last summer could we have had them then.

22 November   CSS *Atlanta* was launched after conversion from the *Fingal* by the Tift brothers at Savannah, Georgia.

25 November   USS *Passaic* was commissioned.

6 December   Tower ironclad USS *Keokuk* was launched at Underhill Shipyard, New York.

     Passaic-class monitor USS *Nantucket* launched at Boston, Massachusetts.

8 December   President Abraham Lincoln sent a recommendation of thanks to the Congress on behalf of Commander J.L. Worden in honor of his service as commanding officer of the USS *Monitor* during the March 9, 1862 Battle of Hampton Roads.

12 December   USS *Cairo*, on an expedition up the Yazoo River with four other gunboats to clear the waterway of torpedoes, was sunk after striking two torpedoes. Lieutenant Commander Thomas O. Selfridge Jr. reported, "The *Cairo* sunk in about twelve minutes after the explosion, going totally out of sight except the top of her chimneys, in six fathoms of water." The *Cairo* was the first of over forty Union vessels sunk by torpedoes during the war.

     USS *Tuscumbia* launched at New Albany, Indiana.

16 December   *Passaic*-class monitor the USS *Catskill* was launched at Continental Iron Works, Greenpoint, New York.

17 December   The *Passaic*-class monitor the USS *Montauk* was commissioned.

18 December   Assistant Secretary of the Navy G.V. Fox wrote,

I believe there is no workshop in the country capable of making steam machinery or iron plates and hulls that is not in full blast with Naval orders. Before another year we shall be prepared to defend ourselves with reasonable hopes of success against a foreign enemy, and in two years we can take the offensive with vessels that will be superior to any England is now building.

U.S. gunboat *Cairo*, photograph, ca. 1862. *Courtesy of The Mariners' Museum.*

25 December USS *Monitor*'s officers and crew celebrated Christmas Day in Hampton Roads. The officers enjoyed a three-hour dinner. William Keeler noted, "In fact we arrived at the conclusion that the Star Spangled Banner next to us 'ironclads' was about the 'biggest thing' to be found just now outside Barnum's Museum."

USS *Monitor* was ordered to proceed to Beaufort, North Carolina, to help blockade Wilmington, North Carolina, in the Cape Fear River. This news was not well received by the crewmembers who had experienced the ironclad's voyage from New York to Hampton Roads in March. Lieutenant Samuel Dana Greene warned, "I do not consider this steamer a seagoing vessel. She has not the steam power to go against a head wind or sea, and…would not steer even in smooth weather, and going slow she does not mind her helm readily."

Union ironclads USS *Benton*, *Cincinnati*, *Baron De Kalb* and *Louisville* engaged Confederate batteries at Drumgold's Bluff and Haynes's Bluff while clearing torpedoes out of the Yazoo River.

28 December USS *Monitor* readied for her sea voyage. "The turret and sight holes were caulked," remembered Dr. Greenville Weeks, "and every possible entrance for water made secure, only the smallest opening being left in the turret top."

Seaman Jacob Nicklis wrote his father about the *Monitor*'s upcoming voyage to Beaufort, North Carolina: "They say we will have a pretty rough time going around Hatteras, but I hope that it will not be the case."

29 December *Passaic*-class monitor USS *Nahant* was commissioned.

2:30 p.m. USS *Monitor*, with the weather "clear and pleasant, and every prospect of its continuation," left Hampton Roads en route to Beaufort, North Carolina. The powerful 236-foot long-side wheeler, the USS *Rhode Island*, was detailed to tow

Officers of the USS *Monitor*, photograph, ca. 1862. *Courtesy of The Mariners' Museum.*

the ironclad. The *Monitor* was secured to the *Rhode Island* by two towlines. The *Rhode Island* and *Monitor* were to be accompanied on their voyage south by the USS *State of Georgia* towing the improved monitor, USS *Passaic*.

6:00 p.m. The USS *Monitor* passed Cape Henry, Virginia.

December 30

5:00 a.m. Commander John Bankhead reported,

> *We began to experience a swell from the southward with a slight increase of wind from the southwest, the sea breaking over the pilothouse forward and striking the base of the tower, but not with sufficient force to break over it. Found that the packing of oakum under and around the base of the tower had loosened somewhat from the working of the tower as the vessel pitched and rolled. Speed at this time was about five knots; ascertaining from the engineer of the watch that the bilge pumps kept her perfectly free, occasionally sucking. Felt no apprehension at the time.*

6:40 a.m. The USS *Monitor* made signal to the USS *Rhode Island* to stop. This action enabled adjustments to be made to the hawser connecting the two ships.

7:30 a.m. The USS *Rhode Island* and the USS *Monitor* proceeded on their course.

12:00 p.m. Winds increased during the USS *Monitor*'s voyage south, and waves began crashing over the ironclad's pilothouse. George Geer remembered that "soon the sea commenced to break over us and wash up against the tower with a fearful rush, and the sea was white with foam, but I was satesfide [*sic*] she would stand it out unless the storm should increase."

1:00 p.m. The USS *Rhode Island* reported that she arrived at Cape Hatteras lighthouse.

3:00 p.m. Winds increased to gale force and the sea had grown rough. Bilge pumps started to remove small amounts of water coming into the ironclad.

4:00 p.m. George Geer noted that the *Monitor* was "in sight of the Hatras [*sic*] lighthouse and I thought as soon as we got past the cape it would clear up."

5:00 p.m. Dinner was served to officers and crew. The *Monitor* had weathered well the rising swells. Commander Bankhead sent the *Rhode Island* a message indicating that if the *Monitor* needed help during the storm, he would signal with a red light.

6:00 p.m. Commander John Bankhead recorded that, "Toward evening the swell somewhat decreased, the bilge pumps being found amply sufficient to keep her clear of the water that penetrated through the sight houses of the pilot house, hawse hole, and base of the tower (all of which had been well calked previous to leaving)."

7:30 p.m. The storm increased in its ferocity. Waves dashed across the deck and broke against the turret and pilothouse with violent force.

Commander John Bankhead recalled that he "found the vessel towed badly, yawing very much, and with the increased motion making somewhat more water around the base of the tower. Ordered engineer to put on the Worthington pump and bilge injection and get the centrifugal pump ready and report to me immediately if he perceived any increase of water."

8:00 p.m. The *Monitor* was suddenly struck by a series of fierce squalls. The ironclad was now "in heavy weather, riding one huge wave, plunging through the next, as if shooting straight for the bottom of the ocean." The *Monitor*'s helmsman, Francis Butts, recalled the effects of the heavy gale on the *Monitor*, stating that the ironclad would drop into a wave "with such force that her hull would tremble, and with a shock that would sometimes take us off our feet."

Commander John Bankhead noted that "the sea about this time commenced to rise very rapidly causing the vessel to plunge heavily, completely submerging the pilot house and washing over and into the turret and at times into the blower pipes. Observed that when she rose to the swell, the flat under surface of the projecting armor would come down with great force, causing considerable shock to the vessel and turret, thereby loosening still more packing around its base."

9:00 p.m. The Worthington steam pump and Adams centrifugal steam pump had failed to stop the flow of seawater. The water had risen over a foot deep in the engine room when Commander Bankhead put the crew to work on the hand pumps and organized a bucket brigade. The ironclad struggled "in a sea of hissing, seething form." William Keeler recalled that "her bow would rise on a huge billow and before she could sink into the intervening hollow, the succeeding wave would strike her under her heavy armor with a report like a thunder and violence that threatened to tear apart her thin sheet iron bottom and heavy armor which it supported."

10:00 p.m. The pumps were having little effect combating the incoming water. George Geer reported that "the pump threw a stream as large as your body, and for about one hour the water did not gain. Nor did we gain on it much." Commander Bankhead ordered the red lantern displayed and tried to signal the *Rhode Island* for help. The ironclad's commander also ordered the lines cut and dropped anchor to stop the ironclad's pitching.

10:00 p.m. USS *Rhode Island* finally had noticed the *Monitor*'s urgent messages for help. Lifeboats were launched to begin rescue operations. It was a difficult task, and several of the *Monitor*'s crew were carried overboard as they tried to enter the lifeboats.

11:30 p.m. Commander John Bankhead recognized that the *Monitor* was in serious trouble and the ironclad was in danger of sinking:

> *My engines working slowly, and all the pumps in full play, but water gaining rapidly, sea very heavy and breaking entirely over the vessel, rendering it extremely hazardous to leave the turret in fact, several men were supposed to have been washed overboard at this time. While waiting for the boats to return, the engineer reported that the engines had ceased to work, and shortly after all the pumps stopped; also, the water putting out the fires and leaving no pressure of steam.*

"Sinking of the USS *Monitor*," engraving, ca. 1863. *Courtesy of John Moran Quarstein.*

31 December

12:00 a.m.   Rescuers returned to the *Rhode Island*, and survivors were disembarked. When the lifeboats were readied to save those who remained aboard the *Monitor*, one was shattered by the *Rhode Island*'s hull.

1:00 a.m.   The USS *Monitor* sank with four officers and twelve sailors aboard in 220 feet of water.

1:30 a.m.   Commander Stephen Trechard, captain of the USS *Rhode Island*, noted that the *Monitor*'s "light had unfortunately disappeared."

CHAPTER 6

IRON FEVER

T HE EVENTS OF 1862 ILLUSTRATED that ironclads were the key to naval supremacy. Ironclads appeared to be considered the critical component of the Union's effort to achieve victory along the coastline and waterways of the South. The Confederacy also recognized that it had to have ironclads if it was to have any chance of maintaining Southern independence. Accordingly, after the Battle of Hampton Roads North and South alike continued the construction of ironclads. Most of these eighty-five ironclads were based on the designs tested by the CSS *Virginia* and USS *Monitor* on March 9, 1862.

Stephen Russell Mallory recognized that the Confederacy could no longer be defended solely by prewar coastal fortifications. Mallory realized by summer 1862 that prewar harbor defensive systems were no longer effective. Union steam-powered warships could steam past fixed fortifications. Forts St. Philip and Jackson were unable to stop Farragut's fleet from steaming past. The once impenetrable masonry walls of large defensive works like Fort Pulaski and Fort Macon became easy prey to besieging rifled artillery. Consequently, Mallory sought to create a defense in depth using naval resources. Submarines, torpedoes, torpedo boats and ironclads were new technologies that Mallory hoped would tip the balance in favor of the Confederacy. Torpedoes had already proven themselves as a viable weapon when the *Cairo* was sunk. While somewhat effective as a harbor defense tool, torpedoes needed more technological advantages before they could serve as an offensive weapon able to break the blockade. The new ironclads were smaller, lighter draft vessels with lesser armament. The lighter draft enabled these vessels to operate in the shallow rivers and sounds. The production of Brooke rifles allowed these smaller ironclads to have effective firepower. The Confederacy would attempt to build over fifty ironclads, yet only twenty-two were commissioned. All Confederate ironclads were plagued by similar problems: poor propulsion systems, limited industrial infrastructure, an over-taxed transportation network and a lack of sufficient workers.

Union naval leaders recognized that Confederate ironclads could only be countered with monitors. Furthermore, ironclads were needed to counter the effects of explosive shells thereby serving as a shot-proof platform to subdue Southern in-depth harbor defenses. John Ericsson and his innovative ironclad design were placed on a pedestal following the March 9 battle. Therefore, the U.S. Navy would eventually construct forty-nine monitor-styled warships. While shot-proof and well suited for harbor operations, monitors had numerous weaknesses. Post-battle designs endeavored to enhance seaworthiness and increased firepower. The Federals attempted to compensate for this weakness by mounting two and even three turrets on some warships. Although monitors could not alone reduce coastal fortifications, monitors mounting fifteen-inch Dahlgrens proved themselves superior to Confederate ironclads.

USS *Atlanta*, photograph, ca. 1864. *Courtesy of The Mariners' Museum.*

The new monitor and casemate ironclads were tested immediately in 1863. On January 31, 1863, the CSS *Chicora* and *Palmetto State* struck at the blockading fleet outside of Charleston harbor. These two ironclads damaged four Union vessels and General P.G.T. Beauregard claimed that the *Chicora* and *Palmetto State* broke the blockade. The Federals, however, were quick to establish the blockade and soon stationed ironclads to guard Charleston. The only other Confederate effort to send an ironclad to attack the Union blockade was the ill-fated venture of the CSS *Atlanta*. Commander William Webb sought to strike at the South Atlantic Blockading Squadron's base at Beaufort, South Carolina. The concept was that the *Atlanta* could force the Federals to break off their Savannah and Charleston stations if the Beaufort supply depot was destroyed. Webb believed that the *Atlanta*, fitted with the Scottish-made engines of the *Fingal* and armed with two 7-inch Brooke and two 6.4-inch Brooke rifles as well as a spar torpedo, could successfully engage a Union monitor. The use of the *Fingal*'s hull proved troublesome as the *Atlanta* had a sixteen-foot draft, which meant the ironclad had limited area to operate in the shoals of the coastal sounds. On June 17, 1863, the *Atlanta* made a foray into Wassau Sound below Savannah and ran hard aground as she approached two *Passaic*-class monitors. The USS *Weehawken* and *Nahant* moved toward the Confederate ironclad. The *Atlanta* could not bring her guns to bare. The *Weehawken*, armed with 15-inch and 11-inch Dahlgrens, steamed to within three hundred yards of the stranded Confederate ironclad. Four of the five shots fired struck the *Atlanta*. The *Atlanta*'s casemate was broken and she was forced to surrender.

Although the fifteen-inch Dahlgren gave the *Passaic*-class monitors the power to break through the six-inch plate armored shield of the *Atlanta*, these guns did not give the Union ironclads firepower to destroy well-organized coastal defenses. Nevertheless, Secretary of the Navy Gideon Welles was determined to capture the "seat of the rebellion." Naval strategists also believed that ports like Charleston and Wilmington, North Carolina, could be closed only by occupation. The South Atlantic Blockading Squadron commander, Rear Admiral Samuel Francis DuPont, assembled a force of nine armorclads including seven monitors, and the casemate-styled ironclad *New Ironsides* and the tower ironclad *Keokuk*. DuPont was not in favor of the attack, since Charleston's complex, in-depth defenses had been created by General P.G.T. Beauregard.

Several coastal forts mounted seventy-seven heavy guns and the harbor was laced with torpedoes. If a force managed to pass these obstacles the ironclads CSS *Chicora* and *Palmetto State* could challenge the invader. DuPont's April 7 assault never reached beyond Fort Sumter. The Union ironclads managed to fire only fifty-five shots. In return, the Confederates struck the Union ironclads over four hundred times. Several monitors were severely damaged and the tower ironclad *Keokuk* sank. The engagement proved that monitors lacked the firepower to contest well-prepared coastal forts and that Union ironclads could be significantly damaged by Brooke bolts and other plunging solid shot. DuPont's defeat at Charleston prompted the Federals to employ other siege tactics to capture the "den of secession."

The Federals had cleared the Mississippi River of most Confederate warships; however, the Confederates were able to retain a section of the river from Vicksburg, Mississippi, to Port Hudson, Louisiana. U.S. Grant took personal command of the campaign. Union gunboats ranged up and down the river, but it was only when the Union army approached Vicksburg from the east that the Federals seized this river port. The beleaguered city capitulated on July 4, 1863. Vicksburg's surrender cut the Confederacy in half, while opening Northern midwestern commerce to the sea. The Mississippi River once again, according to President Abraham Lincoln, "flowed unvexed to the sea."

1863

1 January	<u>Battle of Galveston</u>. When Major General John Bankhead Magruder assumed command of the Department of Texas November 29, 1862, he made the "liberation" of Galveston a priority. Magruder organized a combined operation that included the cotton-clads *Neptune* and *Bayou City*. At dawn, these vessels attacked the USS *Harriet Lane*. The *Harriet Lane* was rammed by the *Neptune*; however, the Confederate vessel suffered greater damage from the action and sank. The *Bayou City* also rammed the *Harriet Lane* as dismounted Texas cavalrymen led by Colonel Thams Green boarded the Union gunboat. The *Harriet Lane* surrendered after her captain, Commander Jonathan M. Wainwright, was killed. As Confederate infantry began to pressure the Forty-second Massachusetts on one of the wharves, the USS *Westfield* attempted to support the Federal infantry but ran aground. The *Westfield* exploded, killing her commander, Commander William B. Renshaw. Federal resistance ended. Galveston remained the only major port under Confederate control when the war ended.
2 January	*Passaic*-class monitor the *Patapsco* was commissioned.
6 January	Five ironclads were ordered to join the South Atlantic Blockading Squadron.
7 January	Confederate Secretary of the Navy S.R. Mallory and Commander James D. Bulloch corresponded concerning the acquisition of European ironclads.

Mallory noted that he was "convinced that every ship may and should be used as a ram when opportunities are presented."

11 January Surgeon Grenville Weeks of the USS *Monitor* wrote to the sister of crewmember Jacob Nicklis:

> *I am too unwell to dictate more than a short sad answer to your note. Your brother went down with other brave souls, and only a good providence prevented my accompanying him. You have my warm sympathies, and the assurance that your brother did his duty well, and has I believe gone to a brighter world, where storms do not come.*

Union ironclads USS *Baron De Kalb*, *Louisville* and *Cincinnati*, commanded by Rear Admiral D.D. Porter, forced the surrender of Fort Hindman at Arkansas Post. Porter later reported that over 6,500 prisoners were taken and that "No fort ever received a worse battering, and the highest compliment I can pay those engaged is to repeat what the rebels said: 'You can't expect men to stand up against the fire of those gunboats.'"

13 January *Neosho*-class riverboat the USS *Osage* was launched at Carondelet, Missouri.

14 January Union force consisting of USS *Kinsman*, *Estrella*, *Calhoun* and *Diana*, under command of Lieutenant Commander Thomas McKean Buchanan, attacked Bayou Teche, Louisiana. The *Kinsman* was damaged by a torpedo and Buchanan was killed by shore fire.

The USS *Indianola* was commissioned.

17 January USS *New Ironsides* joined the South Atlantic Blockading Squadron off Charleston, South Carolina.

The *Passaic*-class monitor the *Lehigh* was launched.

18 January The *Passaic*-class monitor the USS *Weehawken* was commissioned.

21 January USS *Passaic* arrived in Port Royal Sound, South Carolina, bringing with her news of the USS *Monitor*'s sinking.

22 January USS *Commodore Morris*, commanded by Lieutenant Commander James H. Gillis, captured three vessels: the oyster sloop *John C. Calhoun*, the schooner *Harriet* and the sloop *Music*, in Chuckatuck Creek, Virginia.

27 January USS *Montauk*, captained by Commander John L. Worden, engaged Fort McAllister, located on the Ogeechee River below Savannah, Georgia. Rear Admiral S.F. DuPont had ordered this engagement to test the new *Passaic*-class ironclads. DuPont commented about the *Montauk*'s performance:

> *The monitor was struck some thirteen or fourteen times, which would have sunk a gunboat easily, but did no injury whatever to the* Montauk—*speaking well for the impenetrability of those vessels—though the distance was greater than what would constitute a fair test. But the slow firing, the inaccuracy of aim, for you can't see to aim properly from the turret...I asked myself this morning while quietly*

"John L. Worden, Commander of the *Montauk*," Ehrgott, Forbriger & Co., lithograph, ca. 1863. *Courtesy of The Mariners' Museum.*

dressing, if one ironclad cannot take eight guns—how are five to take 147 guns in Charleston harbor.

30 January Flag Officer Duncan Ingraham decided to send the ironclads CSS *Palmetto State* and CSS *Chicora* against the Union fleet off Charleston, South Carolina. General P.G.T. Beauregard advocated this attack, as he wanted to break the Union blockade before the Federals reinforced their fleet with monitors.

10:00 p.m. Ironclads prepared to leave anchorage.

11:15 p.m. CSS *Palmetto State* got underway.

11:30 p.m. CSS *Chicora* followed the *Palmetto State* across Charleston harbor toward the bar at the harbor's entrance.

31 January

4:30 a.m. CSS *Palmetto State*, commanded by Lieutenant John Rutledge, and CSS *Chicora*, captained by Commander John Randolph Tucker, crossed the bar in the early morning fog. The *Palmetto State* immediately rammed the *Mercedita*. When the Confederate ironclad struck the converted merchant ship, the *Palmetto State*'s forward seven-inch Brooke gun sent a shell that passed through the *Mercedita*'s boilers before exploding. The *Mercedita* quickly filled with steam and water. She appeared to be in a sinking condition when the *Mercedita*'s captain surrendered.

5:00 a.m. CSS *Chicora* engaged the side-wheeler USS *Keystone State*. The vessels traded broadsides. One shell from the *Chicora* struck the Union warship, setting fire to her woodwork. The *Keystone State* headed out to sea at twelve knots in an effort to extinguish the flames.

6:00 a.m. The *Keystone State* attempted to ram the *Chicora*.

6:15 a.m. The *Chicora* sent a shell that crashed through the hull of the *Keystone State* and passed through the steamer's boilers. Escaping steam spread throughout the vessel. Several other shells struck the *Keystone State*, creating two holes in her hull and starting a fire. The Union warship filled with water and lost all power.

6:30 a.m. The *Keystone State* struck her colors. One side wheel, however, continued to operate and the blockader moved out of range of the *Chicora*. Eventually, she was towed to Port Royal Sound by the USS *Memphis*.

6:50 a.m. The *Palmetto State* and *Chicora* engaged the USS *Quaker State*, *Augusta* and *Housatonic*. The *Quaker State* and *Augusta* both were hit by shells. The *Palmetto State* had her flagstaff shot away. The Union vessels steamed out to sea.

8:30 a.m. CSS *Palmetto State* and *Chicora* steamed to Sullivan's Island and anchored under the protection of the Confederate batteries.

4:00 p.m. CSS *Palmetto State* and *Chicora* crossed the bar into Charleston harbor and returned to their berth.

General P.G.T. Beauregard advised Richmond that the blockade off Charleston had been broken. Beauregard lauded Flag Officer Duncan Ingraham "and the gallant officers and men under your command for your brilliant achievement of last night, which will be classed hereafter with those of the *Merrimack* and *Arkansas*."

1 February	Union-blockading vessels reestablished their positions off Charleston harbor.
	Commander J.L. Worden steamed the USS *Montauk*, followed by three other wooden gunboats and the mortar schooner *C.P. Williams*, to within six hundred yards of Fort McAllister outside of Savannah, Georgia.
7:45 a.m.	*Montauk* opened fire.
7:53 a.m.	*Montauk*'s turret was struck by a Confederate shell. During this four-hour action, the *Montauk* was hit forty-eight times by Confederate artillery.
12:00 p.m.	USS *Montauk* broke off action.
	Rear Admiral D.D. Porter advised Secretary of the Navy Gideon Welles:

> *Vicksburg was by nature the strongest place on the river, but art has made it impregnable against floating batteries—not that the number of guns is formidable, but the rebels have placed them out of our reach...The people in Vicksburg are the only ones who have as yet hit upon the method of defending themselves against our gunboats, via, not erecting water batteries, and placing the guns some distance back from the water, where they can throw a plunging shot, which none of our ironclads could stand. I mention these facts to show the Department that there is no possible hope of any success against Vicksburg by a gunboat attack or without an investment in the rear of the city by a large army.*

"Admiral D.D. Porter," lithograph, ca. 1864. *Courtesy of The Mariners' Museum.*

4 February	The *Richmond*-class CSS *Savannah* was launched. The *Savannah* was constructed by Henry F. Willink and served in defense of Savannah, Georgia. She had four inches of iron plate protecting her casemate. The *Savannah* was armed with two 7-inch Brooke rifles and two 6.4-inch Brooke rifles.
7 February	The *Huntsville*-class ironclad CSS *Huntsville* was launched. The *Huntsville* was constructed by Henry D. Bassett, in Selma, Alabama. Similar to the CSS *Albemarle*, the engines were so defective that the *Huntsville*-class ironclads could only be used as floating batteries and served in defense of Mobile, Alabama.
	The *Huntsville*-class ironclad CSS *Tuscaloosa* was launched.
9 February	The *Passaic*-class monitor the USS *Sangamon* was commissioned.
13 February	USS *Indianola* ran past the batteries at Vicksburg to join the ram USS *Queen of the West* in blockading the Red River.
14 February	USS *Queen of the West* was taken under heavy fire by Confederate shore batteries while patrolling the Red River. The ram ran aground and was abandoned by her crew and captured by the Confederates.
18 February	*Neosho*-class river monitor the USS *Neosho* was launched. One of two vessels of the *Neosho*-class, the USS *Neosho* was a single-turret monitor conceived by James Eads, featuring a wooden hull and "turtle-back" design. The turret was armored by six-inch iron plate and contained two eleven-inch Dahlgrens.
	USS *Ozark* was launched and commissioned. The *Ozark* was a combination of a single two-gun turret and four-gun casemate.
19 February	Confederate Secretary of Navy S.R. Mallory ordered Commander William A. Webb to strike against Union ironclads stationed at Charleston by boarding them using small rowboats and steamers.
24 February	Confederate rams *William H. Webb* and *Queen of the West*, along with the steamer CSS *Beatty*, attacked the Union ironclad *Indianola* near Warrenton, Mississippi. Just after 10:00 a.m. the CSS *Queen of the West* rammed the *Indianola*; however, she only managed to cut in two a coal barge lashed to the side of the Union ironclad.

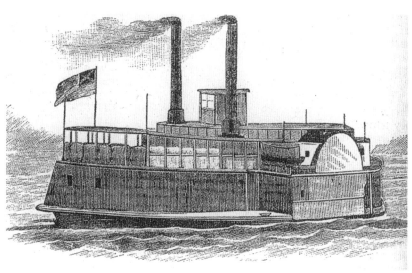

"Queen of the West," engraving, ca. 1863. Courtesy of John Moran Quarstein.

The CSS *William H. Webb* rammed the *Indianola* at full speed, which swung the *Indianola* around. The *Queen of the West* struck the ironclad again with a glancing blow and then rammed the *Indianola* astern, shattering her starboard wheelhouse. Meanwhile, the *William H. Webb* had steamed upstream, circled and then rammed the *Indianola* at full speed, crushing the starboard wheel and creating several leaks. The *Indianola* was then without power and sinking. The ironclad surrendered.

Horace L. Hunley, James R. McClintock and B.A. Whitney tested a five-man submarine in Mobile Bay, Alabama. The vessel sank, without loss of life, off Sand Island. Hunley immediately began work building another submarine, which would be known as the *H.L. Hunley*.

The *Passaic*-class monitor *Catskill* was commissioned.

25 February	The Confederates began work raising the *Indianola*. A Federal ironclad approached the *Indianola*. The Confederates panicked and ordered the *Indianola* blown up. The Federal "ironclad" was actually a barge camouflaged to look like a powerful warship. Rear Admiral D.D. Porter sent the barge downriver as a hoax in frustration over capture of the *Indianola*. The ruse worked beyond Porter's expectations.
26 February	The *Passaic*-class monitor USS *Nantucket* was commissioned.
27 February	The river ironclad USS *Lafayette* was commissioned.
28 February	USS *Montauk* attacked the CSS *Rattlesnake* (formerly the commerce raider CSS *Nashville*) while the vessel was aground in the Savannah River near Fort McAllister.
6:00 a.m.	USS *Montauk*, commanded by J.L. Worden, steamed into position to begin long-range bombardment of the *Rattlesnake*.
8:00 a.m.	*Montauk*, accompanied by the USS *Wissahickon*, *Seneca* and *Dawn*, commenced shelling the *Rattlesnake* while under heavy bombardment from Fort McAllister.
8:20 a.m.	The *Rattlesnake* was in flames.
8:30 a.m.	*Montauk* struck a torpedo while moving back down the Savannah River. The explosion fractured *Montauk*'s iron hull.
9:30 a.m.	*Rattlesnake*'s magazine ignited and the side-wheeler blew up. Worden noted that it was the "final disposition of a vessel which has so long been in the minds of the public as a troublesome pest."
3 March	*Passaic*-class monitors USS *Passaic*, *Nahant* and *Patapsco*, with three mortar schooners and the gunboats USS *Seneca*, *Dawn* and *Wissahickon*, engaged Fort McAllister near Savannah, Georgia.
11 March	USS *Chillicothe* and USS *Baron De Kalb* engaged Fort Pemberton, Mississippi, on the Tallahatchie River during the Yazoo Pass expedition. The ironclads approached to within eight hundred yards and exchanged fire with the fort. Fort Pemberton was a cotton and earthen fortification. The fort's armament included one heavy Whitworth rifle.

The *Chillicothe* was heavily damaged by two shots from the fort. One shell penetrated a three-inch iron port cover and struck a cannon while it was being loaded. The gun exploded, inflicting fourteen casualties.

"Interior View of the Turrets of the Monitor Fleet," lithograph. *Courtesy of The Mariners' Museum.*

12 March	USS *Tuscumbia* was commissioned. The *Tuscumbia* was a casemate ironclad designed by Joseph Brown and constructed in New Albany, Indiana. The *Tuscumbia* was a poorly built vessel and subject to hogging. She was 178 feet in length with a 75-foot beam and a 7-foot draft covered with six inches of iron plate. The *Tuscumbia* was powered by four engines operating side-wheels and two screw propellers. The *Tuscumbia* mounted two eleven-inch Dahlgrens forward and two nine-inch Dahlgrens aft.
13 March	USS *Chillicothe* and *Baron De Kalb* engaged Fort Pemberton on the Tallahatchie River. *Chillicothe* was struck thirty-eight times in less than ninety minutes.
14 March	USS *Tuscumbia* participated in the recapture of Fort Heiman on the Tennessee River.
	USS *Mississippi*, one of the first steam-powered warships in the U.S. Navy and Commodore Matthew Calbraith Perry's flagship in the opening of Japan in 1853, ran aground in front of Confederate water batteries at Port Hudson.
3:00 a.m.	After being struck by numerous shells, the *Mississippi* was engulfed in flames and was abandoned.
5:30 a.m.	USS *Mississippi* blew up.
16 March	USS *Chillicothe* engaged Fort Pemberton, Mississippi. The ironclad was struck eight times and was forced to break off action.
19 March	Rear Admiral S.F. DuPont advised Secretary of the Navy Gideon Welles, "I think that these monitors are wonderful conceptions, but, oh, the errors of detail, which would have been corrected if these men of genius could be induced to pay attention to the people who are to use their tools and inventions."
	Monadnock-class oceangoing monitor USS *Agamenticus* was launched. The *Agamenticus* was a wooden hulled twin turret monitor designed by John Lenthall. She was armed with four fifteen-inch Dahlgrens.
23 March	USS *Choctaw* was commissioned. She was converted from a merchant ship to an ironclad from plans by Captain William D. Porter. Armor and armament were too heavy for the hull.
26 March	The Union submarine USS *Alligator* was ordered to join Rear Admiral S.F. Dupont's squadron off Charleston, South Carolina.
28 March	John Randolph Tucker replaced Flag Officer Duncan Ingraham as commander of the Charleston Naval Squadron.
2 April	USS *Alligator* sank in a storm off the North Carolina coast.
4 April	Rear Admiral S.F. DuPont completed his plans to attack Charleston harbor. He instructed the ironclad commanders to pass the Confederate batteries on Morris Island and to concentrate their assault upon Fort Sumter. The ironclads were ordered to "carefully avoid wasting shot and will enjoin upon them the necessity of precision rather than rapidity of fire."
5 April	USS *Patapsco* and *Catskill* crossed the Charleston bar to guard the buoys that marked the channel into the harbor.
6 April	Rear Admiral S.F. DuPont established his flag in the USS *New Ironsides* in preparation for the attack on Charleston.

Flag Officer William Lynch advised Confederate Secretary of the Navy S.R. Mallory about the status of ironclads under construction in North Carolina. He said:

> *One ironclad, the* North Carolina, *building here, is very nearly ready for her crew…The other, the* Raleigh, *is now ready for her iron shield, and can in eight weeks be prepared for service, as far as the material is concerned. At Whitehall, upon the Neuse, we have a gunboat in nearly the same state of forwardness as the* Raleigh; *at Tarboro we have one with the frame up, the keel of one is laid near Scotland Neck.*

In the spring of 1862, two 150-foot ironclads had been laid down in Wilmington, North Carolina. When Gosport Navy Yard had been abandoned, three other smaller ironclads, intended for the defense of the North Carolina Sounds, were destroyed. This prompted the construction of three other ironclads. The ship building at Tarboro, North Carolina, was destroyed during a Federal raid.

7 April   Rear Admiral S.F. DuPont's long awaited ironclad attack against Charleston, South Carolina, occurred.

12:00 p.m.   A fleet of nine ironclads got underway in a line ahead column. The lead ship was the USS *Weehawken*, commanded by Captain John Rodgers.

2:30 p.m.   Union vessels advanced up north and moved to within five hundred yards of Fort Sumter. When Rodgers reached the fort, he abruptly stopped the *Weehawken*, as he noticed a line of barrels that he believed to be torpedoes. This maneuver forced the line behind the *Weehawken* into disarray. Communications between the ships broke down as the other ironclads endeavored to hold themselves in position.

3:00 p.m.   USS *Weehawken* opened fire on Fort Sumter.

3:40 p.m.   *Weehawken* was hit fifty-three times in forty minutes. A torpedo exploded near her, which lifted the monitor out of the water but did no damage. However, shot from Sumter and Moultrie had great effect upon the ironclad. The *Weehawken* began taking water through a shot hole that had been made in her deck.

The other Union ironclads steamed themselves into position beneath the guns of Fort Sumter. The *Passaic* had her eleven-inch gun disabled and her turret malfunctioned. The plates forming the upper edge of her turret were broken and the pilothouse was badly dented from shot. The *Passaic* was struck thirty-five times by shot. The *Patapsco* took forty-seven hits. DuPont's flagship, the *New Ironsides*, had become unmanageable in the heavy current and anchored over a Confederate torpedo containing two thousand pounds of gunpowder. The torpedo failed to explode.

4:00 p.m.   Captain John Rodgers steamed the *Weehawken* away from Fort Sumter. The monitor had taken a terrible beating. Rodgers determined that he could not steam through the Confederate obstructions and feared that his ironclad could become entangled if he endeavored to pass through.

The USS *Catskill* steamed to within six hundred yards of Fort Sumter. The *Catskill* was struck by twenty shots, which broke the deck plates and forward deck planking. The monitor began taking on water. The *Montauk* maneuvered with great difficulty and was struck fourteen times by Confederate shot. The *Nantucket* followed the *Catskill* and was battered by fifty-one shots. Her turret was jammed. The *Nahant* took thirty-six hits. The impact of one shot damaged the steering gear, as three other shots disabled the turret.

4:30 p.m.   USS *Keokuk* steamed ahead of the crippled *Nahant* to a position six hundred yards off Fort Sumter. The Confederates focused their cannonade upon this ironclad. The *Keokuk* was struck ninety times in thirty minutes. This under-armed and poorly armored warship was holed beneath the waterline by almost twenty projectiles and was in a sinking condition when she withdrew from action.

5:30 p.m.   Dupont steamed the *New Ironsides* to the head of the line and ordered a withdrawal.

DuPont's attack on Charleston was a dismal failure. The *Passaic*-class monitors were unable to maintain an effective rate of fire to challenge the Confederate fixed fortifications. The heavy ordnance, including smoothbores and Brooke rifles, proved to be a match for the stationary monitors. The Confederates had placed range markers in the harbor, which enhanced their aim. Most of the 439 shots from Fort Sumter and Fort Moultrie struck their targets. The monitors were not to be totally shot-proof from plunging Confederate shot, the turrets were easily jammed and pilothouses were prominent targets. One shot struck the *Nahant*'s pilothouse. Nuts from iron bolts sheered off, mortally wounding the helmsman and injuring the pilot. The *Keokuk* was to be a total failure. Designed by John Ericsson's former partner C.W. Whitney, the *Keokuk* featured an experimental armor scheme with a "sandwich" of one-inch iron plates enclosing a two-inch inner layer of wood bolted together and placed vertical strips to a thin wooden framework. This wood and iron was then covered by a half-inch layer of boilerplate. The two towers were not turrets, but mounted eleven-inch Dahlgren pivot guns designed to use three fixed gunports. The *Keokuk* left the April 7 engagement in a sinking condition.

Admiral DuPont reported to the secretary of the navy after the attack:

> When I withdrew the ironclad vessels from action on the evening of the 7th, I did so because I learned it too late in the day to attempt to force a passage through the obstructions which we had encountered, and I fully intended to resume offensive operations the next day; but when I received the reports of commanders of the ironclads as to the injuries those vessels had sustained and their performance in action I was fully convinced that a renewal of the attack could not result in the capture of Charleston, but would, in all probability, end in the destruction of a portion of the ironclad fleet and might leave several of them sunk within reach of the enemy (which opinion I afterwards learned was fully shared in by all their commanders). I therefore determined not to renew the attack.

Dupont advised that Charleston could not be taken by just a naval attack and would require major support from the U.S. Army.

8 April   USS *Keokuk* floundered off Morris Island, South Carolina.

Major General David Hunter advised Rear Admiral S.F. DuPont that "No country can ever fail that has men capable of facing what your ironclads had yesterday to endure."

11 April   General P.G.T. Beauregard requested that the Confederate States navy endeavor to launch an attack on the Union ironclads stationed inside the Charleston bar with spar-torpedo rowboats.

14 April   Commander Charles F.M. Spotswood commented about his service on the floating iron battery CSS *Georgia* guarding the approach to Savannah: "Anything that floats at sea will suit me…for being shut up in an Iron Box (for she is not a vessel) is horrible, and with no steam power to move her, in fact she is made here to a pile pier…She is not a fit command for a Sergeant of Marines." The CSS *Georgia* was 250 feet in length and armored with four inches of iron plate. She was armed with four 6.4-inch Brooke rifles and two 10-inch Brooke smoothbores. The *Georgia* had a speed of three knots and could serve only as a floating battery.

CSS *Missouri* was launched at Shreveport, Louisiana. The *Missouri* never saw action and served to protect the Red River. The ironclad was 183 feet in length with a draft of 10 feet 3 inches. Her power plant were engines taken from the

Grand Era. This center wheel system gave this casemated ironclad a speed of 5.3 knots. The *Missouri* was armed with one 11-inch Dahlgren, one 9-inch Dahlgren and two 32-pounder smoothbores.

15 April The *Passaic*-class monitor USS *Lehigh* was commissioned.

24 April General P.G.T. Beauregard requested a Whitworth rifle to mount on Morris Island to cover the crew removing the guns off the sunken USS *Keokuk.*

29 April Union ironclads USS *Benton, Tuscumbia* and *Pittsburg* engaged Confederate batteries at Grand Gulf, Mississippi. Even though the Union ironclads silenced one of the Confederate batteries, they suffered serious damage. The *Tuscumbia* was struck eighty-one times by shot. The ironclad was repaired; however, due to mechanical and structural problems the *Tuscumbia* did not see any further action.

1 May Confederate Congress, as requested by the Secretary of the Navy Stephen Russell Mallory, enacted legislation to create a Provisional Navy of the Confederate States.

2 May Captain John Rodgers of the USS *Weehawken* advised Secretary of the Navy Gideon Welles about the performance of monitors during the assault upon Charleston harbor:

> *The punishment, which the monitors are able to withstand, is wonderful—but it cannot be denied that their gun gear is more liable to accident than was foreseen. Battles are won by two qualities, ability to endure, and ability to injure. The first we possess in an unrivaled degree—the latter one more sparingly.*

7 May Confederates recovered the two eleven-inch Dahlgren smoothbores from the USS *Keokuk* wreck.

The *Charleston Mercury* noted that the guns "will be mounted for our defense, valuable acquisitions, no less than and some trophies of the battle of Charleston harbor."

13 May The USS *Neosho* was commissioned.

27 May The USS *Cincinnati* was sunk by Vicksburg batteries. The credit is generally given to the Confederate rifled gun known as "Whistling Dick."

30 May CSS *Atlanta*'s forward engine broke down while steaming down the Savannah River. The Confederate ironclad ran aground.

31 May USS *Carondelet* supported U.S. Army operations below Vicksburg near Perkins Landing, Mississippi.

6 June Rear Admiral S.P. Lee, commander of the North Atlantic Blockading Squadron, requested that the USS *New Ironsides* was needed to enforce the blockade of the Cape Fear River. Lee believed that two ironclads were required to effectively close the two entrances to this blockade runners' haven.

8 June Confederate Secretary of the Navy S.R. Mallory advised Confederate Naval Agent Commander James Bulloch that "We need ironclads, ironclads, ironclads."

CSS *Atlanta*,
photograph.
*Courtesy of The
Mariners' Museum.*

16 June CSS *Atlanta*, commanded by Commander William A. Webb, steamed down the Savannah River to a position five miles from Wassau Sound in preparation for her strike against the Union ironclads blockading Savannah.

17 June CSS *Atlanta*, with the wooden steamers CSS *Isondiza* and *Resolute*, engaged USS *Weehawken* and *Nahant* in Wassau Sound below Savannah, Georgia.

4:10 a.m. *Atlanta* left the Wilmington River and entered Wassau Sound.

4:20 a.m. USS *Weehawken* got underway.

4:30 a.m. *Atlanta* fired a shell at the *Weehawken* from a range of one and a half miles. Webb's intended tactics were to use his spar torpedo to sink the *Weehawken* and then engage the *Nahant* with his Brooke rifles. He was highly optimistic of victory.

4:35 a.m. *Atlanta*, with a sixteen-foot draft, ran aground on a sandbar. She backed free, but due to shallow water the *Atlanta* failed to respond to her helm and ran aground again, listing slightly.

5:00 a.m. USS *Weehawken* approached to within three hundred yards of the *Atlanta* and then opened fire. The monitor was armed with one fifteen-inch and one eleven-inch Dahlgrens. The guns were fired five times and four shots struck the *Atlanta* with devastating results. The first fifteen-inch shot struck the *Atlanta*'s starboard side and cracked her casemate. Almost fifty men were injured. A second shot hit the Confederate ironclad's knuckle and the third glanced off the port shutter of the starboard battery just as the closure was being opened. Half of the gun crew was wounded as a result. The final shot hit the pilothouse, blowing off its top and wounding two of the pilots.

5:15 a.m. The *Atlanta* surrendered. The loss of the *Atlanta* shocked the Confederacy and proved that Confederate casemated ironclads were not a match for monitors.

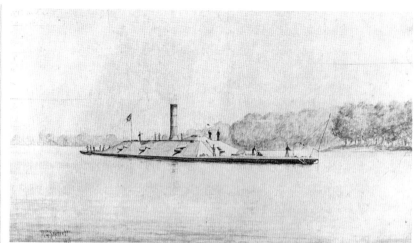

The fifteen-inch Dahlgren had the hitting power to break and penetrate the Confederate armor. John Rodgers received a vote of thanks from Congress and was promoted to commodore for his leadership.

24 June Rear Admiral John Dahlgren was detached from duty as chief of the Bureau of Ordnance and ordered to replace Admiral DuPont as commander of the South Atlantic Blockading Squadron.

26 June Rear Admiral Andrew Hull Foote died from the wound he received at Fort Donelson, Tennessee.

29 June The converted USS *Roanoke* was recommissioned as an ironclad. The screw frigate was cut down to her gundeck and covered with four and a half inches of iron. The *Roanoke* was fitted with a ram bow. She had three turrets. The *Roanoke* was a failure, as the weight of her armor was too great for the hull. The ship rolled excessively and had too great of a draft for coastal operations.

30 June Flag Officer Josiah Tattnall ordered Commander William W. Hunter to assume command of the ironclad CSS *Savannah*.

The CSS *Savannah* was commissioned.

1 July CSS *Albemarle* was launched at Edwards Ferry, North Carolina. The *Albemarle* was designed by Chief Naval Constructor John Luke Porter and built by Gilbert Elliot. She was 152 feet in length with a draft of 9 feet. Plated with 4 inches of iron, the *Albemarle* had an armament of two pivot mounted 6.4-inch Brook rifles. The *Albemarle* was damaged at launch and taken to Halifax, North Carolina, for completion.

4 July City of Vicksburg, Mississippi, surrendered.

Admiral Dahlgren assumed command of the South Atlantic Blockading Squadron.

The CSS *North Carolina* was launched at the Laird Brothers Shipyard, Birkenhead, Great Britain. The *North Carolina* was one of the "Laird-Rams" contracted by Confederate agent Commander James D. Bulloch. She was built under the code name *El Monassir*, supposedly for the Egyptian government.

Flag officer Josiah Tattnall, photograph, ca. 1865. *Courtesy of John Moran Quarstein.*

The *North Carolina* was a bark-rigged warship with ten inches of armor plate protecting her sides and two turrets. Each turret contained two nine-inch rifles and was constructed of five inches of armor plate. The ram was confiscated by the British government in October 1863.

Commander Issac Newton Brown was detailed to the command of the CSS *Charleston* in Charleston, South Carolina.

9 July	Port Hudson, Louisiana, surrendered.
10 July	Monitors USS *Catskill*, *Montauk*, *Nahant* and *Weehawken* bombarded Confederate batteries on Morris Island, South Carolina. This action provided cover for the landing of Union troops under the command of Brigadier General Quincy Adams Gilmore. The USS *Osage* was commissioned.
11 July	Ambassador Charles Francis Adams protested the construction of ironclads in Great Britain intended for the Confederacy.
13 July	A naval expedition, led by the ironclad USS *Baron De Kalb*, captured Yazoo City, Mississippi. The *Baron De Kalb* struck a mine and sank in fifteen minutes.
16 July	Commander James Bulloch issued a contract to Naval Constructor Lucien Armand to build two ironclads for the Confederacy at Bordeaux, France.
18 July	Union ironclads USS *Montauk*, *New Ironsides*, *Catskill*, *Nantucket*, *Weehawken* and *Patapsco* bombarded Confederate batteries on Morris Island, South Carolina. This action covered the failed attack of the Fifty-fourth Massachusetts Infantry on Fort Wagner.
24 July	Union ironclads USS *New Ironsides*, *Weehawken*, *Patapsco*, *Montauk*, *Catskill* and *Nantucket* bombarded Fort Wagner on Morris Island, South Carolina. The USS *Onondaga* was commissioned. The *Onondaga* was a twin turret monitor designed by G.W. Quintard. The monitor mounted two fifteen-inch Dahlgrens.
1 August	The USS *Canonicus* was launched at City Point Yard, Boston. The *Canonicus* was the first of the *Canonicus*-class and these monitors were larger than the *Passaic*-class. The *Canonicus* mounted two fifteen-inch Dahlgrens.
4 August	Boat crews from the CSS *Chicora* and *Palmetto State* captured an unfinished Union battery at Vincent's Creek on Morris Island, South Carolina.
5 August	USS *Commodore Barney* was severally damaged when a one-thousand-pound electric torpedo exploded near her at Dutch Gap, Virginia.
7 August	General P.G.T. Beauregard requested the transfer of the CSS *H.L. Hunley* from Mobile Bay, Alabama, to Charleston, South Carolina.
11 August	Increased pressure on Charleston, South Carolina, by the Union fleet prompted General P.G.T. Beauregard to station the ironclads CSS *Chicora*, *Charleston* and *Palmetto State* off Fort Ripley in Charleston harbor.
15 August	Submarine *H.L. Hunley* arrived in Charleston, South Carolina. Beauregard referred to the submarine "as the most formidable engine of war for the defense of Charleston now at his disposition and accordingly is anxious to have it ready for service."

17 August	Union ironclads USS *Weehawken*, *Catskill*, *Nahant*, *Montauk*, *Passaic*, *Patapsco* and *New Ironsides* bombarded Fort Wagner on Morris Island, South Carolina. Captain G.W. Rodgers of the USS *Catskill* was killed during the actions.
21 August	Confederate torpedo boat *Torch* attacked the USS *New Ironsides* but was unable to make contact with her torpedo and broke off action.
23 August	USS *Weehawken*, *Nahant*, *Montauk*, *Passaic* and *Patapsco* bombarded Fort Sumter as the USS *New Ironsides* engaged Fort Wagner.
24 August	CSS *Hunley* armament was modified. The submarine was originally designed to tow a floating copper cylinder torpedo with firing triggers. The concept was for the submarine to dive under an enemy vessel, surface on the other side and continue on course until the torpedo struck the target and exploded. Instead, the *Hunley* was fitted with a bow-mounted spar torpedo.
29 August	CSS *H.L. Hunley*, after several successful dives, sank with the loss of five seamen while moored next to the steamer *Etiwan*. The *Hunley* was raised and received a new crew.
	The CSS *Mississippi* was launched in Birkenhead, Great Britain, and was known as the *El Tousson*. Seized by the British government in October 1863, she would be completed as the HMS *Wivern*.
1 September	Commander Catesby ap Roger Jones, commander of the Confederate Naval Gun Foundry at Selma, Alabama, shipped munitions to Mobile Bay, Alabama.
2 September	Union ironclads bombarded Fort Sumter. During the past six months Fort Sumter had been pounded by Union army and navy cannon fire and the fort's sea face was reduced to rumble.
6 September	Under the protection of the ironclads CSS *Charleston*, *Chicora* and *Palmetto State* the Confederates abandoned their batteries on Morris Island, South Carolina.
7 September	Rear Admiral J.A. Dahlgren demanded the surrender of Fort Sumter. The fort had been so devastated by Union bombardments that Sumter's appearance "from seaward was rather that of a steep, sandy island than that of a fort." General P.G.T. Beauregard replied to Dahlgren, "to take it if he could."
8 September	During an operation against Fort Sumter, the USS *Weehawken* grounded. The USS *New Ironsides* positioned herself between the *Weehawken* and Fort Moultrie on Sullivan's Island. The *New Ironsides* was struck fifty times by shot and the *Weehawken* was eventually refloated with the aid of tugs.
9 September	The Union navy assaulted Fort Sumter with a small boat attack with four hundred sailors and marines. The Confederates, who had the signal book from the sunken USS *Keokuk*, were aware of the assault. The CSS *Chicora* supported the defense of Fort Sumter. The attack was repulsed.
12 September	The CSS *Missouri* was commissioned.
	The *Canonicus*-class monitor the USS *Tecumseh* was launched.
17 September	Reports of the CSS *Albemarle*'s construction prompted Secretary of the Navy Gideon Welles to advise Secretary of War Edwin Stanton that the control of the North Carolina Sounds would be jeopardized if a Confederate ironclad came down the Roanoke River into the Sounds.

"John A.B. Dahlgren," lithograph, ca. 1855. *Courtesy of The Mariners' Museum.*

19 September	Horace Hunley requested command of the CSS *H.L. Hunley*.
22 September	Flag Officer J.R. Tucker detailed Lieutenant William T. Glassell to command the torpedo boat CSS *David*.
5 October	CSS *David* exploded a sixty-pound torpedo against the hull of the USS *New Ironsides*. The Union ironclad was severally damaged and forced to leave blockade duty off Charleston, South Carolina, for repairs.
6 October	The USS *Patapsco* deployed inventor John Ericsson's anti-obstruction torpedo net. Even though tests indicated that the device worked, it appeared only useful against fixed obstructions in calm seas. The device interfered with the *Patapsco's* maneuverability and appeared "too complicated."
15 October	CSS *H.L. Hunley* sank during a practice dive under the CSRS *Indian Chief*. All hands, including Horace Hunley, were lost. General P.G.T. Beauregard detailed Lieutenant George Dixon, CSA, to take command of the *Hunley* and recondition the submarine. Beauregard further ordered that the *Hunley* not dive again.
18 October	Rear Admiral J.A. Dahlgren advised Secretary of the Navy Gideon Welles that the monitors assigned to the South Atlantic Blockading Squadron played a major role in the capture of Morris Island, South Carolina. Dahlgren noted that the monitors fired over eight thousand rounds and were struck by enemy shot nearly nine hundred times.
20 October	Commander James Bulloch advised Secretary of the Navy S.R. Mallory that the ironclads under construction at Liverpool, Great Britain, known as Hulls 294 and 295, had been seized by the British government. The "Laird Rams" were added to the Royal Navy's growing fleet of ironclads.
5 November	Union ironclads bombarded Fort Sumter. Rear Admiral John Dahlgren noted that the "only original feature left is the northeast face, the rest is a pile of rubbish."
16 November	USS *Lehigh* was grounded while protecting Union troops on Cumming's Point near Charleston, South Carolina. While under heavy fire from Fort Moultrie, the USS *Nahant* assisted the *Lehigh* to free herself from the shoal.
18 November	*Kalamazoo*-class monitor the USS *Passaconaway* was laid down at the Portsmouth Navy Yard, New Hampshire. The *Passaconaway* was a double turret monitor mounting four fifteen-inch Dahlgrens. The hull was designed by Benjamin H. Delano and her machinery by John Baird. While conceived for ocean cruising, none of the *Kalamazoo*-class was launched or commissioned.
25 November	Commander John Mercer Brooke advised Secretary of the Navy S.R. Mallory, "The deficiency of the heavy ordnance has been severely felt during this war. The timely addition of a sufficient number of heavy guns would render our ports invulnerable to the attacks of the enemy's fleets, whether ironclad or not."
30 November	Secretary of the Navy S.R. Mallory noted in his annual report the two major problems faced by the Confederate ironclad construction program: lack of skilled labor to build ships and the inability to obtain sufficient iron plate.
	The ironclad ram CSS *Fredericksburg* was launched at the Richmond Navy Yard. The *Fredericksburg* was 188 feet in length and was armed with four guns.

"USS *Weehawken*,"
Parsons-Endicott
& Co., lithograph,
ca. 1864. *Courtesy
of The Mariners'
Museum.*

6 December   USS *Weehawken* sank while tied to a buoy inside the bar at Charleston harbor. While loading ammunition, the tide washed down an open hatch and the *Weehawken* rapidly filled with water. The monitor foundered with the loss of twenty-four officers and men.

11 December   Confederates shelled the wreck of the USS *Indianola* to stop Federal efforts to refloat the ironclad.

14 December   General P.G.T. Beauregard ordered Lieutenant George Dixon to take the *H.L. Hunley* and to "sink and destroy any vessel of the enemy with which he can come in conflict."

16 December   *Canonicus*-class monitor the USS *Saugus* was launched at Harlan Shipyard, Wilmington, Delaware.

24 December   Commander Catesby ap Roger Jones reported to Admiral Franklin Buchanan that the guns being cast at the Selma Naval Gun Foundry for the CSS *Tennessee* would soon be delivered to Mobile Bay, Alabama.

26 December   The USS *Dictator* was launched.

CHAPTER 7

QUESTIONS OF IRON AND TIME

ONCE THE MISSISSIPPI RIVER HAD been secured for the Union, the Federals turned their attention to closing the remaining Southern ports. Ports like Wilmington, North Carolina, became a blockade runner's haven. Early in the war nine of ten runners ran through the blockade. The odds decreased to three out of four making successful trips by 1864. Despite the risks caused by the Union blockade, sleek gray-painted fast side-wheelers continued to keep this tenuous lifeline open for the Confederacy. The runners slipped in and out of Southern ports going to Nassau or Bermuda, where they exchanged cotton for war material and other manufactured goods. A fleet of 1,650 runners made an estimated 8,000 round trips. Over 600,000 small arms were brought into the Confederacy during the war. If the Union could stop this flow of material, the Federals would have weakened the South economically and lessened her ability to wage war.

By 1863 Savannah and Charleston, while not captured, had been effectively closed by Union naval action. Charleston had the most in-depth defensive schemes in the world. The combination of torpedoes, submarines, heavy rifled guns, ironclads and torpedo boats saved Charleston from capture; however, the concentration of Union besieging forces made the port not very accessible to blockade runners. The two remaining havens were Mobile, Alabama, and Wilmington, North Carolina.

The Confederacy had been very diligent in North Carolina. Not only did the Confederates intend to defend Wilmington with the largest earthen fortification in the world, Fort Fisher, two ironclads, the CSS *North Carolina* and *Raleigh,* had been constructed. The *North Carolina* was poorly built and had a worm-eaten bottom, which required the vessel to be constantly pumped to avoid sinking. Two other ironclads, CSS *Neuse* and *Albemarle,* had been constructed upriver away from the Union controlled Sounds. Since the Federals had no ironclads within these inland seas, the Confederates hoped to regain control of this rich region. The ironclads, the Confederates believed, could give them naval superiority and the Federals swept into the sea. The CSS *Albemarle* was the first to emerge. Commanded by James W. Cooke, the *Albemarle* attacked the Federal squadron at Plymouth, North Carolina, in conjunction with a land assault led by Brigadier General Richard Hoke.

The *Albemarle* rammed and sank the USS *Southfield.* The gunboat USS *Miami* fled the scene. The *Albemarle*'s presence enabled Hoke to reoccupy the town of Washington, North Carolina, on the Pamlico River. The Confederates appeared ready to liberate all of eastern North Carolina because of their ironclads.

Blockade runner *R.E. Lee*, photograph. *Courtesy of the Virginia War Museum.*

Hoke, just promoted to major general in honor of his victory at Plymouth, wished to besiege the last Union stronghold, New Bern, on the Neuse River. Unfortunately for the Confederates, the ironclad built up the Neuse River was unable to participate in Hoke's campaign. The CSS *Neuse*, commanded by Lieutenant Benjamin Loyall, endeavored to steam down the Neuse River toward New Bern; however, the *Neuse* ran hard aground. She would not be freed from the sandbar until mid-May. Meanwhile, the *Albemarle* was ordered to support Hoke's assault on New Bern, North Carolina. Commander Cooke would have to take his ironclad from Plymouth across the Albemarle, Croatan and Pamlico Sounds, and then up the Neuse River to New Bern. The *Albemarle* left Plymouth on May 5 and encountered an entire Union gunboat squadron commanded by Captain Melancton Smith that afternoon in Albemarle Sound. The Federals most powerful craft were four double-ender gunboats. These vessels simultaneously attacked and surrounded the *Albemarle*, pumping shot into the ironclad. This action caused no damage to the *Albemarle* as the Union "guns might as well have fixed blank carriages." The USS *Sassacus* rammed the *Albemarle*, causing significant damage to the ironclad. As the *Sassacus* held firm in the *Albemarle*'s side, a shell exploded in the *Sassacus*'s boiler. The vessels then drifted apart. The battle continued until darkness. All of the Union double-enders were damaged; however, they had stopped the *Albemarle*'s cruise. The *Albemarle* limped back to Plymouth, where she would stay.

The *Albemarle* would eventually be destroyed by a torpedo under her hull placed by the daring Lieutenant William Cushing on October 27, 1864. The Union quickly reoccupied eastern North Carolina.

The last major port serving the Confederacy on the Gulf of Mexico, Mobile, Alabama, became a major target for Rear Admiral David Farragut's Gulf Coast Blockading Squadron in the summer of 1864. The Confederacy had done everything it could do to defend this vital part. Several ironclads had been constructed. Unfortunately, the CSS *Baltic* was an unsuccessful warship and only the CSS *Tennessee* was operational. Coastal fortifications, the most significant being Fort

"Battle of Mobile Bay," Xanthus Smith, pencil sketch, ca. 1864. *Courtesy of The Mariners' Museum.*

Morgan mounting forty-seven powerful guns on Mobile Point, and torpedo fields defending the harbor entrance were Mobile Bay's strongest assets. Nothing, however, could stop Farragut from attacking on August 5, 1864. When the Union squadron of nineteen vessels including eight steam-screw sloops and four monitors attempted to force entry through Mobile Bay's narrow entrance, disaster struck. The monitor USS *Tecumseh* hit a torpedo and sank in ninety seconds. The dramatic loss of the *Tecumseh* stopped the entire Union squadron directly under the guns of Fort Morgan. Unless something was done, the Federals would suffer even greater losses. At this moment, Admiral Farragut yelled his legendary command, "Damn the torpedoes! Full speed ahead!" The Federal fleet passed the Confederate fort and torpedo only to be assaulted by the powerful CSS *Tennessee*. The *Tennessee*, commanded by Admiral Franklin Buchanan, attacked the entire Union fleet and was forced to surrender. Even though the city of Mobile would not surrender until the war's conclusion, the bay was effectively closed to blockade runners.

Now the only major Southern link to the outside world was Wilmington, North Carolina. General R.E. Lee noted that if Wilmington fell, then he would be forced to abandon Richmond. The Federals recognized this strategic situation and organized a joint army-navy operation under Admiral D.D. Porter and Major General Benjamin Franklin Butler. The operation was a dismal failure for the Union.

The year 1864 ended for the Confederates with only Wilmington, North Carolina, remaining for blockade runners. Savannah, Georgia, had been captured by General William Tecumseh Sherman's army. The Confederate ironclad squadron was destroyed to prevent its capture. Confederate ironclads were unable to make a lasting difference stopping Federal control of the Southern coastline. Only in the North Carolina Sounds could the Confederacy boast of an ironclad success and this was short-lived. Elsewhere, the overwhelming Union industrial and shipbuilding strength was too much for the Confederacy to counter. The CSS *Tennessee*, by design and construction, simply could not defeat four monitors in combat. The Union "Anaconda" was apparently ready to consume its prey by the end of 1864.

2 January	General R.E. Lee advised Confederate President Jefferson Davis:

> *The time is at hand when an attempt can be made to capture the enemy's forces at New Bern…I can spare troops for the purpose, which will not be the case as spring approaches…A bold party could descend the Neuse at night, capture the gunboats and drive the enemy from their works…the gunboats, aided by the ironclads building on the Neuse and Roanoke, would clear the waters of the enemy.*

7 January	Rear Admiral John Dahlgren issued an alert to his vessels warning of a Confederate torpedo attack.
15 January	Major General Richard Taylor, concerned about an impending Federal strike up the Red River in Louisiana, hoped that the ironclad CSS *Missouri* would be able to descend the river to help thwart any Union advance.

Commander James W. Cooke, CSN, was ordered to assume command of the CSS *Albemarle* at Halifax, North Carolina.

Commodore H.H. Bell confided to Commander Robert Townsend of the USS *Essex*,

> *The rams and ironclads on the Red River and in Mobile Bay are to force the blockade at both points and meet here* [New Orleans], *whilst the army is to do its part. Being aware of these plans, we should be prepared to defeat them. The reports in circulation about their ironclads and rams being failures may be true in some degree; but we should remember that they prevailed about the redoubtable* Merrimack *before her advent.*

16 January	Confederate Secretary of the Navy Mallory ordered Flag Officer John K. Mitchell, commander of the James River Squadron, to use his squadron of ironclads, CSS *Fredericksburg* and CSS *Richmond*, to make a sortie against the Union supply base at City Point, Virginia.
17 January	Rear Admiral D.G. Farragut requested several monitors to join his squadron in support of his planned attack upon Mobile Bay, Alabama. "I must have ironclads enough to lie in the bay to hold the gunboats and rams in check in the shoal water."
22 January	South Atlantic Blockading Squadron maintained its watch on Charleston, South Carolina, with four ironclads.
2 February	Confederate boat expedition led by Commander John Taylor Wood captured and destroyed the USS *Underwriter* in the Neuse River near New Bern, North Carolina.
4 February	Union monitors USS *Lehigh*, *Nahant* and *Passaic* destroyed the blockade runner *Presto* near Fort Moultrie on Sullivan's Island, South Carolina.
5 February	CSS *Chicora*'s boilers were condemned. Flag Officer J.R. Tucker ordered that the *Chicora* serve as a floating battery.

8 February USS *Milwaukee* was commissioned. The *Milwaukee* was the first in a class of monitors designed by James Eads to operate on the Western waterways. Commander Catesby ap Roger Jones wrote Admiral Franklin Buchanan:

> *The revolving turret enables the monitor class to bring their guns to bear without reference to the movements or turning of the vessel. You who fought the* Virginia *know well how to appreciate that great advantage. You doubtless recollect how often I reported to you that we could not bring one of her ten guns to bear. In fighting that class, it is very important to prevent the turret from revolving, which I think may be done either with the seven inch or 6.4 inch rifles or 64-pounder, provided their projectiles strike the turret at or near its base where it joins the deck…If the turret is prevented from revolving, the vessel is less than efficient that one with the same guns having the ordinary parts, as the monitors ports are so small that the guns can not be trained except by the helm.*

USS *Patapsco*'s cutter captured the blockade-runner schooner *Swift* off Cabbage Island, Georgia.

10 February *Milwaukee*-class double-turret monitor USS *Chickasaw* commissioned. The *Chickasaw* featured one Ericsson turret and one Eads-designed turret. Each turret contained two eleven-inch Dahlgrens and was plated with eight inches of iron. The *Milwaukee*-class monitors were 229 feet in length and had a 6-foot draft with a speed of nine knots. All of this class was built at Carondelet, Missouri.

16 February CSS *Tennessee II* was commissioned. This ironclad was constructed at Bassett Shipyard in Selma, Alabama. The *Tennessee* was 209 feet in length with a 14-foot draft. Her casemate was plated with 6 inches of iron forward, 5 inches broadside and aft. The casemate contained two 7-inch Brooke rifles and four 6.4-inch Brooke rifles, as well as a ram. The *Tennessee* was underpowered, as her engines had been taken from a riverboat steamer.

Rear Admiral John A.B. Dahlgren ordered one hundred torpedoes to counteract Confederate torpedo activities.

Lieutenant Robert Dabney Minor inspected progress on the construction of the CSS *Neuse*. Minor advised Secretary of the Navy S.R. Mallory:

> *Lieutenant Commander Sharp has a force of one hundred and seventy men employed upon her, including…nineteen men from the Naval Station on the Peedee, four from Wilmington and 105 detailed temporary [sic] by Brigadier General Hoke from his brigade now in camp in this vicinity…As you are aware the steamer has two layers of iron on the forward end of her shield, but none on either broadside, or on the after part. The carpenters are now bolting the longitudinal pieces on the hull, and if the iron can be delivered more rapidly, or in small quantities with some degree of regularity, the work would progress in much satisfactory manner. The boiler was today lowered*

in the vessel and when in place, the main deck will be laid in…The river I am told is unprecedently low for the season of the year…Mr. A.F. Tift left here for Augusta, Georgia on Monday to hurry forward the remainder of the iron plates—two carloads of which arrived prior to his departure…I believe the steamer will be ready for service by the 18th of next month.

17 February   Confederate submarine *H.L. Hunley*, commanded by Lieutenant George E. Dixon, CSA, rammed her spar torpedo into the starboard side of the USS *Housatonic*. The torpedo exploded and the *Housatonic* sank immediately. The *Housatonic*'s destruction was the first successful attack of a submarine upon a warship. The *Hunley* later sank with her entire crew while returning to base.

18 February   USS *Ozark* was commissioned. The *Ozark* was a purpose-built single-turreted monitor with a wooden casemate. The turret was an Ericsson type and mounted two eleven-inch Dahlgrens. The ironclad had problems from the very beginning as the warship was unpowered and could only make five to six knots rather than the nine specified in the War Department contract. A secondary armament system was added of one ten-inch smoothbore and three nine-inch Dahlgrens mounted on exposed positions on the *Ozark*'s deck. A wooden casemate was added to partially protect these guns. The *Ozark* was a failure due to her structural flaws, lack of protection and weak engine system.

22 February   USS *Whitehead* steamed up the Roanoke River to investigate rumors of the construction of an ironclad by the Confederates at Halifax. The *Whitehead* could not proceed beyond Rainbow Bluff, North Carolina, because of torpedoes and the existence of Fort Branch.

27 February   Lieutenant David Porter McCorkle, CSN, advised Commander Catesby ap Roger Jones that the "*Muscogee* draws too much water; she has to be altered. It will be a long time before the *Muscogee* will be ready." The *Muscogee*, later known as the CSS *Jackson*, was built at the Columbus Navy Yard. She was 223 feet 6 inches in length with a draft of 8 feet. The casemate was armored with 4 inches of iron and housed four 7-inch Brooke rifles and two 6.4 inch Brooke rifles—designed with center wheel machinery but she drew too much water and had to be rebuilt. She was never completed.

28 February   Lieutenant Robert Dabney Minor reported to Secretary of the Navy S.R. Mallory about the progress on the CSS *Albemarle*.

With the exception of some little connections work to be completed [the ironclad] may be considered as ready. Steam will probably be raised on Friday next. The iron is all on the hull…the carpenters are now bolting the first layers of plate on the shield, and as long as iron is available the work will progress. The rudder is on place. Shell room and magazine prepared. Officer quarters arranged and berth deck ready for either hammocks if allowed the ship or banks if the canvas cannot be obtained…The ship is now afloat and when ready for service will

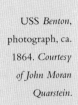

I think draw between seven to eight feet…The guns, carriages, and equipment have not yet arrived, but are expected on the 4th of March.

6 March	A Confederate "David" attacked the USS *Memphis* in the North Edisto River near Charleston, South Carolina. The "David" was damaged when the two vessels collided; however, it escaped. Since the torpedo failed to explode, the *Memphis* was not damaged.
9 March	Rear Admiral D.D. Porter had assembled his river ironclads, USS *Essex, Benton, Choctaw, Chillicothe, Ozark, Louisville, Carondelet, Eastport, Pittsburg, Mound City, Osage* and *Neosho*, at the mouth of the Red River prepared to support Major General Nathaniel Banks's campaign.
	Two 6.4-inch Brooke guns were installed on the CSS *Neuse*.
10 March	CSS *Columbia* was launched at the James Eason Shipyard in Charleston, South Carolina. This smaller casemate design ironclad was developed by William A. Graves. The *Columbia* mounted six guns and was protected by six inches of iron.
12 March	Rear Admiral D.D. Porter's gunboats steamed into the Red River, Louisiana, in support of Major General N. Banks's campaign to move up the Red River to occupy Shreveport, Louisiana. USS *Kickapoo* was launched at Allen Shipyard, St. Louis, Missouri. The *Kickapoo* was a twin-turret *Milwaukee*-class ironclad.
14 March	Union ironclads *Eastport* and *Neosho* bombarded and supported the capture of Fort De Russy on the Red River.
	Gilbert Elliott paid $2,500 for his construction of the CSS *Albemarle*.
16 March	Lieutenant Commander Charles W. Flusser, commander of the Union gunboats at Plymouth, North Carolina, on the Roanoke River, advised Rear

	Admiral S.P. Lee that the CSS *Albemarle* had been armored and would soon be operational.
18 March	CSS *Nashville* was commissioned. The side-wheeler *Nashville* was 270 feet in length. George W. Gift noted that he was "perfectly delighted with her...she is a tremendous monster...The *Tennessee* is insignificant along side of her." The *Nashville* had a casemate designed to mount three seven-inch Brooke rifles. The ironclad received her armor from the CSS *Baltic*.
20 March	Chief Naval Constructor John Luke Porter surveyed the CSS *Baltic*. Lieutenant Charles Carroll Simms of the *Baltic* advised Catesby ap Roger Jones that Porter "has made a very unfavorable report on the condition of the ship and recommended that the iron be taken from her and put upon one of the new boats that were built...Between you and I the *Baltic* is rotten as punk and is about as fit to go into action as a mud scow."
23 March	USS *Monadnock* launched at Charleston Navy Yard, Boston. The first of the *Monadnock*-class of double-turreted monitors launched, this oceangoing *Monitor*-class was designed by John Lenthall, chief of the U.S. Bureau of Naval Construction. Rear Admiral D.D. Porter stated that Lenthall was "the ablest naval architect in any country." The *Monadnock*'s armament featured four fifteen-inch Dahlgrens. This class featured a wooden hull and her two Ericsson vibrations engines enabled this monitor to make nine knots. The *Monadnock* eventually had a 3½-foot wood bulwark built on deck and a foremast when she steamed around Cape Horn after the war's conclusion.
24 March	USS *Onondaga* was commissioned. The *Onondaga* was a twin-turret monitor with an iron hull built at Continental Iron Works, Greenpoint, New York. This monitor was armed with two 15-inch Dahlgrens and two 150-pounder Parrott muzzle loaded rifles. The *Onondaga* was armored with 11.75 inches of iron plate on her turrets, 5.5 inches of iron plate on her armor belt and one inch of iron on her deck.
26 March	Major General John J. Peck advised Major General Benjamin F. Butler about the CSS *Albemarle*, noting that "I feel entirely sanguine that the ironclad in the Roanoke will be destroyed if she attacks Plymouth."
29 March	Rear Admiral D.D. Porter encountered difficulty with the low water level in the Red River. The rapids at Alexandria, Louisiana, were passed by the USS *Eastport*.
3 April	Rear Admiral D.D. Porter's river ironclads escorted Major General A.J. Smith's corps from Alexandria to Grand Ecore, Louisiana.
7 April	Rear Admiral D.D. Porter divided his squadron. Porter continued his advance up the Red River with only the ironclads USS *Osage*, *Neosho* and *Chillicothe*.
9 April	Torpedo boat CSS *Squib* (*Infanta*) attacked the USS *Minnesota*. The *Squib* was a *David*-class steam-powered torpedo boat built at Richmond, Virginia. Launched in 1864, the *Squib* was 46 feet in length with a 3½-foot draft and armed with an 18-foot spar torpedo. The *Squib* was commanded by Lieutenant Hunter Davidson. Davidson steered the *Squib* through the entire Union fleet in

"David D. Porter," lithograph, ca. 1864. *Courtesy of The Mariners' Museum.*

Hampton Roads, Virginia, and exploded a torpedo against the hull of the USS *Minnesota*. Despite the heavy gunfire brought against the Confederate Torpedo boat, the *Squib* was able to escape. The torpedo's fifty-three pounds of powder did minor damage to the *Minnesota*'s hull.

10 April Rear Admiral D.D. Porter's ironclad's movement up the Red River was blocked by an obstruction created by an old steamer, *New Falls City*, near Loggy Bayou, Louisiana.

11 April CSS *Squib* attacked U.S. warships in Hampton Roads, Virginia. The torpedo boat was driven off by heavy cannon fire.

12 April Rear Admiral D.D. Porter's ironclads began their retreat down the Red River. The ironclads were attacked at Blair's Landing, Louisiana, by Confederate dismounted cavalry and artillery commanded by Major General Thomas Green. Green, well fortified with rum, led an impetuous charge on the Union gunboats. Lieutenant Commander Thomas O. Selfridge Jr. reported that "I waited till they got into easy shelling range, and opened upon them a heavy fire of shrapnel and canister. The rebels fought with unusual pertinacity for over an hour, delivering the heaviest and most concentrated fire of musketry that I have ever witnessed." The devastating cannon fire from Porter's ironclads decided "this curious affair...a fight between infantry and gunboats." General Green was killed during the Confederate attack. The engagement also witnessed the first use of a periscope. Developed by Chief Engineer Thomas Doughty of the USS *Osage*, the device allowed gunners to effectively aim their cannon from within the *Osage*'s turret. Previously, guns were aimed through peepholes, which restricted vision and weakened an ironclad's fire control.

13 April The *Canonicus*-class ironclad USS *Catawba* was launched at the Swift Shipyard in Cincinnati, Ohio. The *Catawba* was not completed until the war's conclusion and was never commissioned.

14 April Rear Admiral D.D. Porter's ironclads were nearly stranded at Grand Ecore, Louisiana. The water level of the Red River refused to rise, in part due to Confederate efforts to divert the water.

15 April USS *Eastport* struck a torpedo in the Red River eight miles below Grand Ecore, Louisiana, and sank. USS *Quinsigamond* was a *Kalamazoo*-class double-turreted monitor designed by Benjamin F. Delano for ocean cruising. She was never launched or commissioned. The hull was constructed of poorly seasoned wood, which rotted on the stocks. The *Quinsigamond* was broken up in 1869.

16 April USS *Canonicus* was commissioned. The *Canonicus* was the first of her class to become operational. The *Canonicus*-class was an enlarged *Passaic*-class. USS *Canonicus* was 235 feet in length with a 13½-foot draft. Her turret was protected by 10 inches of iron plate and housed two 15-inch Dahlgren smoothbores.

17 April Brigadier General Richard Hoke's division attacked Federal troops at Plymouth, North Carolina.

CSS *Albemarle*, photograph, ca. 1865. *Courtesy of The Mariners' Museum.*

CSS *Albemarle* was commissioned. The *Albemarle* was 152 feet in length with a 9-foot draft. She featured an octagonal casemate on a flat hull and was armed with two 6.4-inch Brooke rifles mounted on pivot carriages.

18 April

CSS *Albemarle* required emergency repairs to her rudder head and a drag shaft coupling.

10:00 p.m.

Albemarle was anchored above Plymouth. River obstructions were surveyed and it was realized that the *Albemarle* could cross without damage due to a freshet.

19 April

12:00 a.m.

CSS *Albemarle* began her approach down the Roanoke River to Plymouth, North Carolina.

3:00 a.m.

CSS *Albemarle* passed Fort Grey on Warren's Neck. The fort sent a few shells at the *Albemarle* to no effect. The Confederate ironclad then crossed the obstructions and came abreast of Plymouth. Commander James Cooke sighted the two Union gunboats positioned at the river's mouth. Lieutenant Commander Charles Flusser had two of his most powerful gunboats, USS *Miami* and *Southfield*, prepared to meet the ironclad. Flusser had lashed the two double-ender gunboats together with hawsers with the idea to force the ironclad between his vessels and pound the Confederate ram into submission with their heavy guns.

3:30 a.m.

As the *Albemarle* approached the Union gunboats, Cooke noted the rope linking the *Miami* and *Southfield*. Cooke steered his ironclad toward the Roanoke's south shore and then swerved his vessel toward the Union gunboats. At full throttle the *Albemarle* glanced off the *Miami*'s port bow and plunged her ram into the *Southfield*. The *Southfield* began sinking immediately. Even though Cooke had ordered his ironclad's engines reversed just before impact, the *Albemarle* was wedged ten feet into the *Southfield*. The *Albemarle* could not free herself as the Union vessel quickly sank. Consequently, her bow was pulled under as water poured into the forward gunports. Somehow the *Albemarle* broke free.

3:05 a.m.   While lodged in the sinking *Southfield*, the *Albemarle* was struck by several heavy shells from the USS *Miami*. One of the *Miami*'s shells bounced off the sloped sides of the *Albemarle* and rebounded onto the deck of the *Miami* at the feet of Lieutenant Commander Flusser. The gallant Flusser was killed instantly.

3:10 a.m.   The *Miami* steamed downstream, as the *Albemarle* ineffectively shelled the escaping Union gunboat. The *Albemarle* exchanged long-range shells with two other Union gunboats, USS *Whitehead* and *Ceres*, without effect.

5:11 a.m.   At sunrise, the CSS *Albemarle* anchored one mile below Plymouth.

20 April

12:01 a.m.   CSS *Albemarle* began shelling Union fortifications defending Plymouth, North Carolina. Battery Worth and Fort Williams were targets throughout the morning.

10:00 a.m.   Brigadier General Henry W. Wessels surrendered Plymouth to Confederate Brigadier General Robert F. Hoke. Hoke was victorious, in part, due to support provided by CSS *Albemarle*. Hoke was voted the thanks of the Confederate Congress and promoted, effective April 20, to major general.

12:30 p.m.   Major General J.J. Peck telegraphed Major General B.F. Butler advising the Department of North Carolina commander that "the ram is heavy and formidable and none of the gunboats here can stand against its power. The *Southfield* is sunk and the rest disabled."

22 April   CSS *Neuse*, her armor incomplete, was ordered to participate in a joint Confederate attack upon New Bern, North Carolina. Lieutenant R.N. Bacot wrote of the *Neuse*'s maiden voyage:

> *I have bad news to tell you this time. Even more than I anticipated when I wrote last week…there was scarcely enough* [water] *for us to cross the obstructions; we nevertheless started down last Friday and had proceeded about a half mile when we grounded on a sand bar…The stern of the vessel is afloat, but the bow is four feet out of the water. We will have to wait for a freshet again…I assure you our disappointment was great when we found we could not get off; the troops were here and ready to join us in an attack on New Bern and we were all expecting to rake the city and sink the gunboats without much trouble and to have a fine time afterwards…it does seem hard to be so sorely disappointed after expecting so much.*

24 April   General P.G.T. Beauregard, commander of the Department of North Carolina, telegraphed General Braxton Bragg, military advisor to President Jefferson Davis, "Can you send me an engineer officer who can contrive some plan to get the gunboat afloat? I feel she will be materially injured if not floated soon. The water has fallen seven feet in the last four days and is still falling."

26 April   Rear Admiral D.D. Porter's squadron fought a running engagement with Confederate batteries and sharpshooters as his vessels steamed down the Red River toward Alexandria, Louisiana.

USS *Eastport*, severely damaged near Grand Ecore, Louisiana, on April 15, 1864, by a torpedo, was destroyed to prevent capture.

27 April   *Milwaukee*-class double-turret monitor USS *Winnebago* was commissioned.

Rear Admiral D.D. Porter made a second attempt to pass Confederate batteries on Deloach's Bluff, Louisiana, near the mouth of the Cane River. The ironclad USS *Neosho* supported the other Union gunboats as they passed the Confederate positions. The *Neosho*, according to Porter, withstood "the heaviest fire ever witnessed." Once at Alexandria, Porter was able to reunite with the rest of his ironclad squadron.

28 April   Rear Admiral D.D. Porter recognized that his fleet was indeed stranded above the falls at Alexandria with the Confederates converging upon them. Porter wrote Secretary of the Navy Gideon Welles, "I find myself blockaded by a fall of three feet of water, three feet four inches being the amount now on the falls; seven feet being required to get over, no amount of lightening will accomplish the objective…In the meantime, the enemy is splitting up into parties of 2,000 and bringing in the artillery…to blockade points below here." Porter was placed in a critical position. It appeared that he would have to decide between either surrender or the destruction of his ironclads.

29 April   Lieutenant Colonel Joseph Bailey suggested to Admiral Porter that a large dam of logs be constructed across the river to back up the water level to the minimum of seven feet. The dams would then be broken and Porter's ships would ride the crest of the rushing water to safety.

30 April   Work commenced on constructing the Alexandria Falls dams.

CSS *Raleigh* was commissioned at Wilmington, North Carolina. The *Raleigh* was a *Richmond*-class casemate ironclad designed by Chief Naval Constructor John Luke Porter. All of this class were underpowered, slow, top-heavy, difficult to steer and protected by insufficient armor. The *Raleigh* was 172 feet 6 inches in length with four 6.4-inch Brooke rifles.

5 May   USS *Chimo* was launched at the Adams Shipyard, Boston.

USS *Chimo* was the first *Casco*-class monitor launched. She, like her sister ships, was a design failure. The single-turret with turtleback deck monitor was designed by Chief Engineer Alban Stimers with a light draft to operate in shallow waters like the North Carolina Sounds. Unfortunately critical design errors and poorly conceived modifications resulted in only a three-inch freeboard without the addition of the turret. Consequently, the *Chimo* never had her turret mounted and was completed as a torpedo boat.

2:00 p.m.   CSS *Albemarle*, accompanied by the gunboats *Cotton Plant* and *Bombshell*, entered the Albemarle Sound en route to support the Confederate attempt to capture New Bern, North Carolina.

4:00 p.m.   Commander James W. Cooke of the *Albemarle* sighted the Union squadron in Albemarle Sound off Sandy Point. The Union squadron was commanded by Captain Melancton Smith. While the squadron contained the gunboats USS *Ceres*, *Commodore Hull* and *Whitehead*, it also featured powerful side-wheelers USS

Chief Engineer Alban C. Stimers, photograph, ca. 1862. *Courtesy of The Mariners' Museum.*

"CSS *Albemarle,* Rammed by USS *Sassaus,*" J.O. Davidson, engraving, ca. 1880. *Courtesy of John Moran Quarstein.*

Mattabesett, Sassacus and *Wyalusins.* Each of these vessels carried at least ten guns, including four nine-inch Dahlgrens and two one-hundred-pounder Parrott rifles.

4:40 p.m.   Captain Melancton Smith ordered his three heavier ships to steam past the CSS *Albemarle* and *Bombshell* "giving them a broadside at every opportunity."

4:45 p.m.   The *Mattabesett,* commanded by Commander Melancton Smith, was the first to engage the Confederate ram. The broadside punished the *Albemarle.* One shot, according to crewmen John Patrick, "knocked a hole in as, but not all the way through, splinters of wood flew about." It was the third or fourth shot that struck the *Albemarle*'s stern 6.4-inch Brooke rifle, blowing off 23 inches of the gun's muzzle. The Confederates continued to fire the rifle, as when the *Mattabesett* passed she was severely struck by shells from the *Albemarle.* One shell dismounted one of the *Mattabesett*'s guns and "every man at that gun was either killed or wounded."

4:55 p.m.   *Mattabesett* passed *Albemarle* and engaged the CSS *Bombshell.*

5:00 p.m.   *Sassacus* and *Wyalusing* passed the *Albemarle* sending broadsides against the sloped iron sides of the Confederate ram to no effect. The *Sassacus* encountered the *Bombshell* and forced that gunboat to haul down her colors.

5:05 p.m.   The USS *Sassacus*'s brief engagement with the *Bombshell* had placed the gunboat over three hundred yards away from the *Albemarle.* Her commander, Commander Francis A. Roe, decided to ram the *Albemarle.*

5:08 p.m.   *Sassacus* rammed the *Albemarle* just abaft her starboard beam where the ironclads casemates' rear joined the hull. The *Sassacus* kept up full power, which drove the *Albemarle*'s starboard down so that water rushed in the gun port. Cooke shouted to his men, "Stand to your guns, and if we must sink let us go down like brave men." The *Albemarle* sent a round through the *Sassacus*'s hull, which had already been damaged by the ram's iron-plated knuckle cutting into the gunboats bow as the ships passed each other.

5:13 p.m.   Cooke ordered the *Albemarle* to turn "hard a port." The ironclad's stern swung wide to port and the *Albemarle* broke away from the *Sassacus.*

5:15 p.m.	The bow Brooke rifle was pivoted to the starboard forward port and fired at the *Sassacus* at point blank range. The muzzle blast scorched the Union vessel's paint. The *Albemarle*'s second shot tumbled through the *Sassacus* and pierced her boilers. Steam and boiling water blew through the *Sassacus*. The vessel broke off action and drifted out of range.
5:30 p.m.	The USS *Miami*, fitted with a spar torpedo, attempted to torpedo the *Albemarle*, but could not get into position. The *Miami* was struck by shot from the *Albemarle*. Her rudder was badly damaged; the *Miami* fell back from her close encounter with the *Albemarle*.
5:55 p.m.	USS *Wyalusing* engaged the *Albemarle*.
6:30 p.m.	USS *Commodore Hull* engaged the *Albemarle* and attempted to run a seine across her bow so that it might foul her screw. The effort failed.
6:45 p.m.	The *Albemarle*, running out of fuel for her engine and somewhat damaged by over three hours of combat, headed toward the Roanoke River.
7:30 p.m.	The *Albemarle* entered the Roanoke River. The Battle of Albemarle Sound was over. The engagement was a tactical draw; however, the *Albemarle* was unable to participate in the attack upon New Bern, North Carolina. The city remained under Union control. Lieutenant Commander Francis Roe of the USS *Sassacus* called the *Albemarle* "more formidable than the *Merrimack* or the *Atlanta*, for our solid 100-pounder rifle shot flew into splinters upon her iron plates."

Chief Engineer Ashton Ramsay of the Charlotte Navy Yard lamented the lack of skilled workmen in the Confederacy when he wrote John Mercer Brooke: "I understand from you the ironclad *Virginia* [No. II] at Richmond is now in readiness for action except her gun carriages and wrought iron projectiles, which are being made at these works. If we had a full force of mechanics this work would have been finished in one-half the time."

6 May	The *Monadnock*-class double turret monitor USS *Tonawanda* was launched at Philadelphia Navy Yard.

The USS *Commodore Jones* was destroyed by a huge two-thousand-pound electronic torpedo in the James River.

8:00 p.m.	CSS *Raleigh*, commanded by Lieutenant John Pembroke Jones, steamed over the bar at New Inlet, North Carolina, and engaged the USS *Britannia*.
11:45 p.m.	The *Raleigh* exchanged shots with the USS *Nansemond*.
7 May	
5:00 a.m.	*Raleigh* engaged the USS *Howquah* and *Nansemund*. A shot from the *Raleigh* went through the *Howquah*'s smokestack.
6:00 a.m.	USS *Mount Vernon* and *Kansas* engaged the *Raleigh*.
7:00 a.m.	*Raleigh* broke off action and crossed the bar at New Inlet. As the ironclad steamed up the Cape Fear River to Southfield, North Carolina, she grounded. All attempts to float the *Raleigh* failed and the ironclad was left like "a monstrous turtle, stranded and forlorn." Eventually, the *Raleigh*'s back broke and the demise of this ironclad was blamed on faulty construction.

Lieutenant John Pembroke Jones, photograph, ca. 1864. *Courtesy Hampton History Museum.*

9 May	Work was underway trying to float the CSS *Tennessee* over the Mobile River bar using "camels."
	Rear Admiral David G. Farragut requested that ironclads be assigned to his squadron. Farragut advised Secretary of the Navy Gideon Welles, "ironclads against wooden vessels…a most unequal contest it will be, as the *Tennessee* is represented as impervious."
11 May	Ironclads USS *Mound City*, *Pittsburg* and *Carondelet* were hauled across the under rapids near Alexandria, Louisiana, and then passed through the dams to safety.
12 May	Ironclads USS *Ozark*, *Louisville* and *Chillicothe* passed the rapids in the Red River near Alexandria, Louisiana.
13 May	Ironclads USS *Ozark*, *Louisville* and *Chillicothe* passed the dams and were the last of the Rear Admiral D.D. Porter's ironclads to reach safety.
14 May	The *Milwaukee*-class double turret monitor USS *Chickasaw* was commissioned.
15 May	Lieutenant Robert Dabney Minor wrote his wife about the pressure to take the Richmond Squadron ironclads into action:

> *There is an insane desire among the public to get the ironclads down the river, and I am afraid that some of our higher public authorities are yielding to this pressure of public opinion—but I for one am not and in the squadron we know too much of the interest at stake to act against our judgment even if those high in authority wish to hurry us into an action unprepared and against vastly superior forces.*

17 May	*Canonicus*-class monitor USS *Mahopac* was launched at Secor Shipyard, Jersey City, New Jersey. The *Mahopac* was 223 feet in length with an 11-foot-6-inch draft. Her turret was protected by 10 inches of iron plate and she was armed with two 15-inch Dahlgren smoothbores.
18 May	CSS *Virginia II* was commissioned and joined the Richmond Squadron. The *Virginia II* was 197 feet in length with a 9-foot-6-inch draft. Her casemate was protected by 6 inches of iron plate on her forward shield and 5 inches on the sides. The *Virginia II* was fitted with a ram and was armed with one 11-inch Dahlgren, one 8-inch Brooke rifle and two 6.4-inch Brooke rifles.
21 May	USS *Atlanta* shelled and dispersed Confederate cavalry attacking Fort Powhatan on the James River near Wilson's Wharf, Virginia. The *Atlanta*, formerly a Confederate ironclad, was repaired and placed into service as a part of the Union James River Squadron.
25 May	Boat crew from the USS *Mattabesett* attempted to destroy the CSS *Albemarle* at Plymouth, North Carolina. The effort failed.
30 May	Rear Admiral S.P. Lee requested that more ironclads be assigned to defend Union positions along the James River against any attack made by the Confederate ironclads protecting Richmond.
1 June	Rear Admiral John Dahlgren, commander of the South Atlantic Blockading Squadron off Charleston, South Carolina, noted "of the seven monitors left,

two here are out of order, and the *Passaic* no better. The Rebels have four, wonder if they will come out and try their luck."

2 June   USS *Louisville* was damaged while engaging a Confederate battery near Columbia, Arkansas.

3 June   Ironclads USS *Neosho* and *Chillicothe* forced the Confederates to abandon a battery at Simmes Port, Louisiana.

4 June   *Casco*-class monitor the USS *Tunxis* was launched.

6 June   *Canonicus*-class monitor USS *Manhattan* was commissioned.

19 June   USS *Kearsarge* engaged CSS *Alabama* off Cherbourg, France. Heavy chains protected the *Kearsarge*'s sides and her engines. The *Alabama* sank and the *Kearsarge* suffered minimal damage due to the protection provided by their iron chains.

12 June   Flag Officer J.K. Mitchell's squadron, including two ironclads, CSS *Virginia II* and the CSS *Fredericksburg*, shelled Union monitors and gunboats at Trent's Reach. The action was brief as both the *Fredericksburg* and *Virginia II* had mechanical problems.

USS *Onondaga* engaged Confederate batteries at Howlett's and traded shells with Confederate ironclads at Trent's Reach.

CSS *Stonewall* was launched at Armand Shipyard, Bordeaux, France, under the code name *Sphinx*. The *Sphinx* was impounded by the French government and then sold to Denmark as the *Staerkodder*. The Danes rejected the ironclad, and she was renamed the *Olinde*. Commander James Bulloch was able to repurchase the vessel, renaming her the CSS *Stonewall*. The *Stonewall* had an overall length of 186 feet, 9 inches and a draft of 14 feet and 3 inches. She was protected by an armor belt of 4.5 inches with forward armor of 5.5 inches. The *Stonewall* was designed as a ram; however, she also mounted one 11-inch rifle and two 70-pounder Armstrong rifles. The *Stonewall* was the only European-constructed ironclad Commander James Bulloch was able to acquire for the Confederacy.

Canonicus-class monitor USS *Oneonta* was launched at Swift Shipyard, Cincinnati, Ohio.

23 June   USS *Tecumseh*, commanded by Commander Tunis A.M. Craven, was ordered to Farragut's Gulf Coast Blockading Squadron.

24 June   Lieutenant William Cushing, with fifteen men from the USS *Monticello*, reconnoitered up the Cape Fear River in North Carolina. Cushing discovered that the CSS *Raleigh* had been "indeed, destroyed, and nothing now remains of her above the water."

30 June   Newly constructed double-turret monitors USS *Winnebago* and *Chickasaw* were ordered to join Farragut's Gulf Coast Blockading Squadron.

2 July   Monitors USS *Lehigh* and USS *Montauk* steamed up the Stono River near Charleston, South Carolina, to disrupt construction of Confederate batteries.

USS *Puritan* was launched at Continental Iron Works, Greenpoint, New York. The *Puritan* was the largest of Ericsson's monitors. Originally designed with two turrets, this monitor was redesigned in 1865 with one turret, but it was never completed. The *Puritan* was 340 feet in length with a 20-foot draft. She mounted two 20-inch Dahlgrens.

6 July *Milwaukee*-class USS *Kickapoo* was commissioned.

9 July Rear Admiral S.P. Lee advised Secretary of the Navy Gideon Welles that the best way to destroy or capture the CSS *Albemarle* was by a torpedo attack. Lee noted that Lieutenant William Cushing was "entirely willing to make an attempt to destroy the ram, and I have great confidence in his gallantry."

13 July USS *Onondaga* shelled Confederate batteries at Dutch Gap, Virginia. The *Passaic*-class monitor USS *Catskill* captured the blockade runner *Prince Albert*.

18 July Rear Admiral David G. Farragut described his plan to attack Mobile Bay, Alabama: "I propose…fourteen vessels, two and two, as at Fort Hudson, low steam; flood tide in the morning with a light southwest wind; ironclads on the eastern side, to attack the *Tennessee*, and gunboats to attack rebel gunboats as soon as past the forts."

 USS *Onondaga* shelled Confederate batteries at Dutch Gap, Virginia.

30 July Responding to questions about the CSS *Albemarle*'s future offensive operations in the North Carolina Sounds, Secretary of the Navy S.R. Mallory wrote, "She was not designed as a floating battery merely, and while her loss must not be lightly hazarded, the question of when to attack must be left to the judgment of the naval officer in command, deciding on in view of the relationships she bears to the defenses of North Carolina."

4 August Union troops under the command of Major General Gordon Granger landed on Dauphin Island to besiege Fort Gaines. The supporting six gunboats shelled Fort Powell at Grant's Pass.

 USS *Tecumseh* joined Farragut's fleet outside of Mobile Bay, Alabama.

5 August

5:30 a.m. The Union fleet got underway in two columns. The main column consisted of seven large ships with gunboats lashed to their sides: *Brooklyn* and *Octorna*, *Hartford* and *Metacomet*, *Richmond* and *Port Royal*, *Lackawanna* and *Seminole*, *Monongahela* and *Kennebec*, *Ossipee* and *Itasca* and *Oneida* and *Galena*. To starboard of these vessels the monitors formed a second column: *Tecumseh*, *Manhattan*, *Winnebago* and *Chickasaw*.

5:45 a.m. When he saw the Union fleet approach, Admiral Franklin Buchanan called the crew of the CSS *Tennessee* onto her gun deck and gave them a brief speech: "Now, men, the enemy is coming, and I want you to do your duty. If I fall, lay me on the side and go on with the fight."

 The *Tennessee*, followed by the gunboats CSS *Gaines*, *Selma* and *Morgan*, steamed toward the approaching Federal fleet.

6:30 a.m. Union ships engaged Fort Morgan. The *Tecumseh* fired the first shot with her fifteen-inch Dahlgren.

7:00 a.m. Union ships entered the narrow channel next to Fort Morgan. Cannon fire became very intense.

Battle of Mobile Bay
5 August 1864

Where the C.S.S. *Tennessee* was rammed.

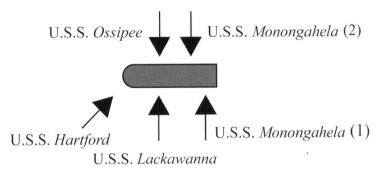

U.S.S. *Ossipee*   U.S.S. *Monongahela* (2)

U.S.S. *Hartford*   U.S.S. *Monongahela* (1)

U.S.S. *Lackawanna*

The Confederate fleet had been unable to stop Farragut's move into Mobile Bay. The *Tennessee* was too slow and the other Confederate steamers were no match for the Federal vessels. When the Union ships anchored in Mobile Bay, Admiral Franklin Buchanan steamed the *Tennessee* out and attacked the entire Federal fleet. The *Tennessee* would be rammed by Union wooden steam sloops and blasted by the 15-inch Dahlgrens of the Union monitors.

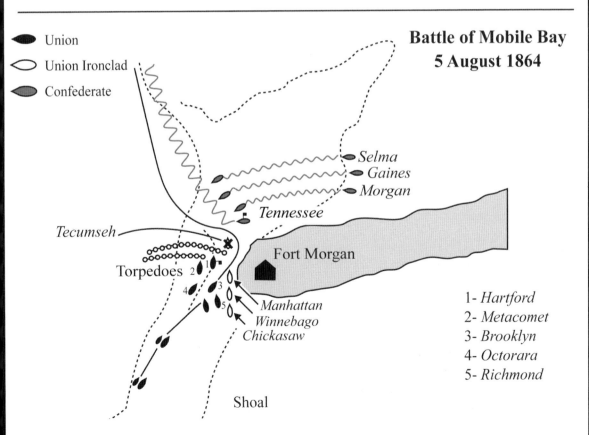

**Battle of Mobile Bay
5 August 1864**

Union
Union Ironclad
Confederate

Selma
Gaines
Morgan
Tennessee
Tecumseh
Torpedoes
Fort Morgan
Manhattan
Winnebago
Chickasaw
Shoal

1- *Hartford*
2- *Metacomet*
3- *Brooklyn*
4- *Octorara*
5- *Richmond*

Admiral David Glasgow Farragut organized his fleet in two columns to force the entrance to Mobile Bay, Alabama.

Illustrated by Sara Kiddey

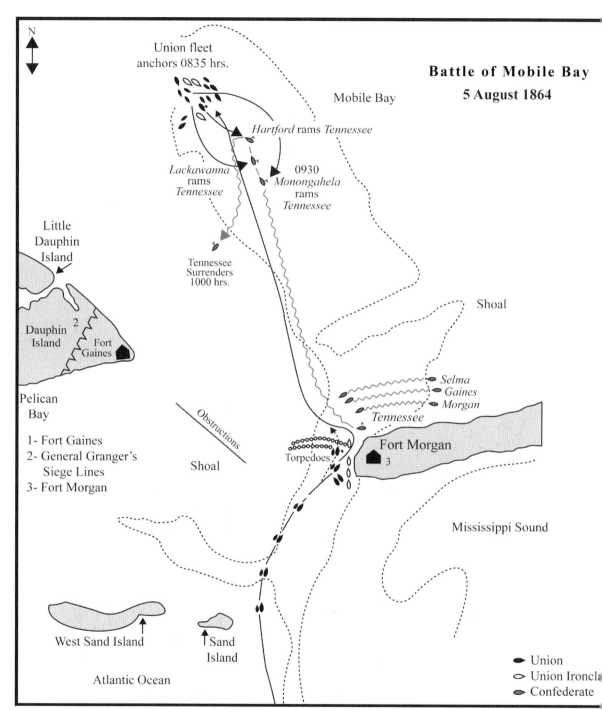

N

Union fleet
anchors 0835 hrs.

Mobile Bay

**Battle of Mobile Bay
5 August 1864**

Hartford rams *Tennessee*

Lackawanna
rams
Tennessee

0930
Monongahela
rams
Tennessee

Little
Dauphin
Island

Shoal

Tennessee
Surrenders
1000 hrs.

Dauphin
Island

2

Fort
Gaines

Selma
Gaines
Morgan

Tennessee

Pelican
Bay

1- Fort Gaines
2- General Granger's
   Siege Lines
3- Fort Morgan

Obstructions

Torpedoes

Fort Morgan

3

Shoal

Mississippi Sound

West Sand Island

Sand
Island

⬤ Union
◯ Union Ironcla
⬤ Confederate

Atlantic Ocean

Illustrated by Sara Ki

The Union monitors entered the bay close to Fort Morgan. The lead monitor, the USS *Tecumseh*, struck a torpedo and
sand. This violent action caused the Union line to fall into confusion and halt in front of Fort Morgan's heavy guns.
As the USS *Brooklyn* was stopped, Farragut ordered the *Hartford* into the torpedo field with the powerful exclamation,
"Damn the torpedoes! Full speed ahead!" This action moved the Federal fleet past Fort Morgan into Mobile Bay.

USS *Hartford*, photograph. *Courtesy of The Mariners' Museum.*

7:15 a.m. USS *Brooklyn* stopped her engines to avoid passing the slower monitors. Captain James Alden did not wish to engage the *Tennessee* without being supported by a monitor. Simultaneously, Captain Tunis Craven of the *Tecumseh* headed his monitor toward the approaching *Tennessee*. This course took the *Tecumseh* away from the channel into the torpedo field.

7:30 a.m. USS *Tecumseh* struck a torpedo and quickly began to sink. "The stern lifted high in the air with the propeller still revolving and the ship pitched out of sight like an arrow twanged from the bow." The *Tecumseh* sank in ninety seconds. All but 21 of the 113-man crew went down with the ironclad.

7:45 a.m. The dramatic destruction of the *Tecumseh* caused the entire Union line to pause in confusion. The *Brooklyn* stalled and the fleet began to be pounded by Fort Morgan's heavy guns. Captain Alden of the *Brooklyn* signaled to Admiral Farragut on the *Hartford*, "Torpedoes ahead!" Farragut replied with his legendary command, "Damn the torpedoes! Full speed ahead!" The USS *Hartford* then steamed past the *Brooklyn* through the minefield into the bay. The Union squadron followed. Only the *Oneida* was severely damaged during this phase of the action by a shell through her boiler.

8:00 a.m. As the Union ships passed Fort Morgan, the *Tennessee* tried to ram them. The *Hartford*, *Richmond* and *Brooklyn* were all able to avoid the Confederate ironclad.

The CSS *Selma* raked the *Hartford* with shells until engaged by the USS *Metacomet*. The *Selma* quickly surrendered. The *Gaines* was severely damaged by shellfire and was scuttled. The *Morgan* joined the *Tennessee* under the guns of Fort Morgan.

8:30 a.m. Farragut anchored his fleet in the bay and ordered the men to breakfast.

9:00 a.m. CSS *Tennessee* steamed toward the Union fleet. Farragut was surprised by this action and commented, "I did not think Old Buck was such a fool." Buchanan intended to strike at the entire Union squadron, his 6 guns against 157 guns. Farragut ordered the *Monongahela* and *Lackawanna* to "run down the ram." Both ships rammed the *Tennessee* and each of these vessels was badly damaged in the collision. The Confederate ironclad steamed on toward the *Hartford*. The two ships passed each other port bow to port bow. Shot from the *Hartford* bounced harmlessly off the *Tennessee*'s iron casemate, whereas the Confederate ironclad sent a shell through the *Hartford*. As the *Hartford* turned to ram the *Tennessee* she was struck midship by the *Lackawanna*. The *Hartford*'s hull was partially split above the waterline, and Farragut kept his flagship in action.

9:40 a.m. The three remaining monitors moved into position to pound the Confederate ironclad with heavy shot. As Lieutenant A.D. Wharton of the *Tennessee* remembered the impact of a fifteen-inch shot from the USS *Manhattan*:

When a hideous monster came creeping up on our port side, whose slowly revolving turret revealed the cavernous depths of a mammoth gun. "Stand clear of the port side!" I shouted. A moment after, a thundering report shook us all, while a blast of dense sulphorus smoke covered our port holes, and 440 pounds of iron, impelled by 60 pounds of powder, admitted daylight through our side, where, before it struck us, there had been over two feet of solid wood, covered with five inches of solid iron. This was the only fifteen-inch shot that hit us fair. It did not come through; the inside netting caught the splinters, and there were no casualties from it. I was glad to find myself alive after that shot.

The double turret *Chickasaw* then approached and sent shot from her eleven-inch guns at the *Tennessee*, which jammed the port shutters, cut the exposed steering chains and wounded and killed several men. Buchanan was struck by a bolt on his leg and handed command to Commander James D. Johnston.

10:00 a.m. The *Tennessee* was then dead in the water, her smokestack shot away and unable to fire back at the Union ships. Johnston surrendered. The Battle of Mobile Bay was over.

9 August Fort Morgan, commanded by Brigadier General Richard L. Page, refused to surrender. Page replied to the Federals, "I am prepared to sacrifice life, and will only surrender when I have no means of defense." The Federals initiated a naval bombardment of the masonry fort. The captured ironclad *Tennessee* was towed into action, and with a Union crew shelled Fort Morgan.

13 August Confederate ironclads CSS *Virginia II*, *Richmond* and *Fredericksburg* shelled Union positions near Dutch Gap, Virginia.

16 August The monitor *Canonicus* shelled Confederate positions near Dutch Gap, Virginia.

17 August CSS *Virginia II* and *Richmond* forced Federals to abandon their position on Signal Hill near Chaffin's Bluff, Virginia.

23 August Fort Morgan, Mobile Bay, Alabama, surrendered.

27 August USS *Milwaukee* was commissioned.

10 September Lieutenant Alexander F. Warley was ordered to command CSS *Albemarle*.

13 September Captain James W. Cooke was detailed to assume command of Halifax Navy Yard, North Carolina.

15 September Rear Admiral David G. Farragut commanded the monitors USS *Chickasaw* and *Winnebago* to guard the city of Mobile, Alabama. Mobile remained under Confederate control and was protected by three ironclads: CSS *Nashville*, *Tuscaloosa* and *Huntsville*. The *Tuscaloosa* and *Huntsville* were floating batteries.

22 September *Canonicus*-class monitor USS *Mahopac* was commissioned.

29–30 September Ironclads from the James River Squadron supported the Confederate defense of Chaffin's Bluff.

1 October Despite the support of the James River Squadron ironclads, the Confederates were unable to recapture Fort Harrison near Chaffin's Bluff, Virginia.

4 October USS *Monadnock* was commissioned.

19 October *Casco*-class monitor/torpedo boat USS *Naubac* was launched at Perrine Shipyard, Jersey City, New Jersey.

"Battle of Mobile Bay," J.O. Davidson, lithograph, ca. 1880. *Courtesy of The Mariners' Museum.*

"Battle of Mobile Bay," oil painting. *Courtesy of The Mariners' Museum.*

22 October	Rear Admiral D.D. Porter advised his command in the North Carolina Sounds that they engaged the CSS *Albemarle*:

> *There is but one chance for wooden vessels in attacking an ironclad. You will make a dash at her with every vessel you have, and "lay her onboard," using canisters to fire into her ports, while the ram strikes her steering apparatus and disables her. You will see that every vessel is provided with proper grapnels, to hold on by while going along side, and a boarding party will be appointed to lash the vessels together. Even if half your vessels are sunk you must pursue this course.*

26 October

2:00 p.m. Lieutenant William B. Cushing entered the Roanoke River with the mission of destroying the CSS *Albemarle*. The daring Cushing had volunteered to torpedo the *Albemarle*. Rear Admiral D.D. Porter had approved this expedition; however, he had advised Commander William H. Macomb, "I have directed Lieutenant Cushing to go down in a steam launch, and if possible destroy this ram with torpedoes. I have not great confidence in his success, but you will afford him all the assistance in your power, and keep boats ready to pick him up in case of failure."

10:30 p.m. Cushing's steam picket boat No. 1 ran aground. Lieutenant Cushing had selected two thirty-foot steam launches as durable boats for his expedition. These vessels were purchased in New York and were fitted with a fourteen-foot spar torpedo as well as a bow mounted twelve-pounder-brass boat howitzer. The Confederates in Wicomico Bay, Virginia, had captured steam Picket Boat No. 2 and the other had arrived in the North Carolina Sounds on October 24, 1864.

27 October

2:00 a.m. Steam Picket Boat No. 1 freed from the sandbar. Cushing's mission was delayed due to tide and time.

8:30 p.m. Cushing and fourteen men got underway. The launch towed a cutter containing seven men. These men were brought along to silence any Confederate lookouts stationed on the wreck of the *Southfield*.

11:28 p.m. Cushing's expedition entered the Roanoke River.

28 October

3:00 a.m. Cushing hoped to capture the *Albemarle* "live"; however, as his launch steamed toward the wharf a sentry discovered Cushing's approach. A bonfire was lit and a fusillade of shots rang out. Cushing cast off the cutter and ordered full steam. He noticed an anti-torpedo log boom surrounding the *Albemarle* and circled the launch so that he could gain momentum. The launch steamed through a hail of fire at full speed, crashing over the log barrier. Cushing lowered the spar, released the torpedo under the *Albemarle* and exploded the device just as a shot from the *Albemarle*'s 6.4-inch Brooke rifle smashed the launch, throwing

CSS *Albemarle*, photograph, ca. 1864. *Courtesy of John Moran Quarstein.*

Cushing's men into the river. The *Albemarle* immediately began to sink in eight feet of water with a gaping hole in her port quarter. Lieutenant Warley, commander of the *Albemarle*, later reported, "The water gained on us so fast that all exertions were fruitless, and the vessel went down in a few moments, merely leaving her shield and smokestack out." The *Albemarle* became the only Confederate ironclad sunk by enemy action. The loss of the ironclad forced the Confederates to abandon Plymouth, North Carolina.

5 November · Monitor USS *Patapsco* destroyed a blockade runner off Fort Moultrie, at Sullivan's Island, South Carolina.

11 November · USS *Dictator* was commissioned.

14 November · USS *Comanche* was launched. The *Comanche* had been built by Secor in Jersey City, New Jersey, and then shipped in parts to San Francisco, where she was reassembled by Union Iron Works.

26 November · *Casco*-class monitor USS *Napa* was launched at Naslan in Wilmington, Delaware.

29 November · Double-turret monitor USS *Onondaga* and the single-turret monitor USS *Mahopac* engaged Howlett's Battery on the James River.

4 December · USS *Casco* was commissioned.

6 December · Monitors USS *Sangus*, *Onondaga*, *Mahopac* and *Canonicus* shelled Howlett's Battery on the James River below Richmond, Virginia. USS *Saugus*'s turret was disabled by a seven-inch Brooke bolt.

USS *Neosho* engaged Confederate batteries on the Cumberland River near Bell's Mills, Tennessee. The *Neosho* was reinforced by the USS *Carondelet*. Cannon fire from these ironclads disabled several Confederate gun positions.

16 December · USS *Neosho* and *Carondelet* supported Major General George Thomas's offensive against General John Bell Hood's Army of Tennessee outside Nashville, Tennessee.

18 December · Secretary of the Navy S.R. Mallory requested that the CSS *Savannah* not be scuttled or surrendered in the aftermath of Savannah's capture by Major General William Tecumseh Sherman's army. "Under any circumstances,

it is better for the vessels, for the navy, for a cause and country, that these vessels should fall in the conflict of battle…than that they should be tamely surrendered to the enemy or destroyed by their own officers. If fall they must, let them show neither weakness of submission nor of self-destruction, but inflict a blow that will receive defeat from discredit."

Canonicus-class monitor USS *Manayunk* was launched at Snowden Mason, Pittsburgh, Pennsylvania.

20 December The unfinished ironclad CSS *Milledgeville* was set afire. The *Milledgeville* was 175 feet in length with six inches of iron protecting her casemate. Designed to mount six guns, the *Milledgeville* was never commissioned. The Confederates also destroyed a large ironclad ram still in the stocks. The floating battery *Georgia*'s guns were spiked and the "non-descript marine monster was scuttled within a log crib near Elba Island, Georgia."

21 December Commander Thomas W. Brent had tried to clear a path through a torpedo field to allow the CSS *Savannah* to escape out to sea and thence to Charleston, South Carolina. The torpedoes were too securely mounted, and Brent decided to scuttle the *Savannah*.

22 December *Passaic*-class monitor USS *Tippecanoe* was launched at Greenwood Shipyard, Cincinnati, Ohio. The *Tippecanoe* was 224 feet in length with a 17½-foot draft.

CSS *Jackson* was launched at Columbus Navy Yard, Columbus, Georgia. Formerly known as the *Muscogee*, the ship was originally designed with center wheel machinery. This system proved to be a failure, and the ironclad was rebuilt as a modified *Albemarle* type with twin screws. While the *Jackson* was never commissioned, she was armed with four 7-inch and two 6.4-inch Brooke rifles.

23 December A joint army-navy expedition began its investment at Fort Fisher, defender of the entrance to the Cape Fear River, North Carolina. The powder boat USS *Louisiana* ran aground 250 yards off Fort Fisher.

Fifteen-inch Rodman at Fort Monroe, Virginia. *Courtesy of John Moran Quarstein.*

THE FIFTEEN-INCH COLUMBIAD.

24 December	
1:40 a.m.	*Louisiana* exploded; however, Fort Fisher was not damaged by the blast.
11:30 a.m.	The Union fleet, commanded by Rear Admiral D.D. Porter, began its massive bombardment of Fort Fisher. Porter had over forty ships mounting more than sixty ships, including four monitors and the USS *New Ironsides*. Over ten thousand rounds were fired at the fort during the day.
25 December	
10:30 a.m.	Bombardment renewed.
1:30 a.m.	Troops commanded by Major General Godfrey Weitzel landed. When the Federals realized that the fort had suffered only minimal damage, twenty-three casualties and two disabled guns, the attack was cancelled.
6:00 p.m.	Union soldiers began reembarking in surfboats. Bad weather forced seven hundred troops to be left on the beach.
27 December	Union soldiers were recovered from the beach near Fort Fisher, and the Federal expedition returned to Hampton Roads.
	Fort Fisher commander Colonel William Lamb telegraphed Richmond, "This morning, December 27, the foiled and frightened enemy left our shore."
30 December	General U.S. Grant replaced Major General B.F. Butler as commander of the Fort Fisher expedition with Major General Alfred Terry. Grant advised Rear Admiral D.D. Porter, "Please hold on where you are for a few days and I will endeavor to be back again with an increased force and without the former commander."

CHAPTER 8

SINK BEFORE SURRENDER

THE CONFEDERATE IRONCLADS WOULD WITNESS each of their home ports captured by a combination of Union land and naval forces. Even though Stephen Russell Mallory had hoped that squadrons in Richmond, Savannah and elsewhere would make one final effort to attack Union blockaders and besiegers, he would be greatly disappointed. A few half-hearted attempts were made by Confederate ironclad squadrons to "go down game." However, these forays had no tactical or strategic benefit. Dynamic and daring leadership was lacking and the lethargy of defeat permeated the crews. As each port fell, the Confederate ironclads were blown up in a "spectacle...beyond description." The last Confederate ironclad, CSS *Missouri*, did not surrender until June 3, 1865.

The Confederate ironclads had been able to defend their harbors from capture by Union naval forces. This ironclad stalemate was broken only when the Federal navy began to utilize land forces to invest and eventually capture the major Confederate ports. Savannah and Charleston, under threat by Union monitors since 1863, fell due to the advance of Major General William Tecumseh Sherman's army. Confederate ironclads were destroyed as these troops entered the cities.

The Union navy learned by its operations at Charleston and other well-defended ports that it needed the cooperation of the U.S. Army to achieve complete success. The joint amphibious assault under Rear Admiral David Dixon Porter and Major General Alfred Terry took Fort Fisher guarding the Cape Fear River approach to Wilmington, North Carolina. The fall of Fort Fisher closed the last harbor by which supplies from Europe could reach General R.E. Lee's army defending Richmond. The defense of Richmond had become so desperate that Flag Officer J.K. Mitchell took three ironclads down the James River in a dash against the Union supply depot at City Point, Virginia. When two of the Confederate ironclads ran aground, Union shore batteries and the fifteen-inch Dahlgrens of the USS *Onondaga* pounded them. This last engagement between ironclads was anticlimactic.

April witnessed the end of the last two ironclad squadrons. Lee's retreat from Petersburg prompted the destruction of the James River Squadron. Shortly thereafter, on April 12, 1865, two of the Mobile ironclads, *Huntsville* and *Tuscaloosa*, were destroyed. Flag Officer Ebenezer Farrand took the rest of his small squadron up the Alabama River and into the Tombigbee, where the still incomplete CSS *Nashville* was surrendered.

All of the Confederate efforts to purchase a European ironclad came to fruition in 1865. Commander James Bulloch was able to acquire the *Sphinx*, then known as the *Staerkodder*,

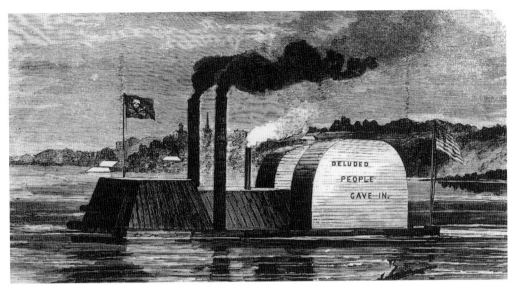

"Deluded People Gave In—Porter's Smoke Pot Ironclad," engraving, ca. 1863. *Courtesy of John Moran Quarstein.*

from Denmark. This sluggish and unseaworthy French-built ironclad was commissioned into Confederate service in January 1865 as the CSS *Stonewall* and placed under the command of Captain Thomas Jefferson Page. The vessel did not arrive in American waters until the war was over.

4 January	Flag Officer J.K. Mitchell noted that the James River Squadron ironclads "will be expected to take a part, not only in opposing the advance of the enemy, but held in readiness to move and act in any direction whenever an opportunity offers to strike a blow."
	USS *Marietta* launched at Tomlinson, Pittsburgh, Pennsylvania. It was a flat-bottomed iron-hulled, single-turret river ironclad with two funnels abreast. The *Marietta*'s turret was plated with six inches of iron and contained two eleven-inch Dahlgrens.
5 January	USS *Indianola* was raised from the Mississippi River where the ironclad had been sunk by Confederates to prevent her capture.
7 January	Captain Thomas Jefferson Page assumed command of the CSS *Stonewall* in Copenhagen, Denmark.
8 January	Major General Alfred Terry and eight thousand Union soldiers embarked from Bermuda Hundred, Virginia, en route to Cape Fear, North Carolina.
12 January	CSS *Columbia* ran onto a sunken wreck near Fort Moultrie on Sullivan's Island, South Carolina. Extensive efforts to refloat her failed, and the ironclad was abandoned.
13 January	Rear Admiral D.D. Porter initiated the second naval bombardment of Fort Fisher. At dawn the Union ironclads, USS *New Ironsides*, *Saugus*, *Canonicus*, *Monadnock* and *Mahopac*, steamed to within one thousand yards of the fort and opened fire.

3:00 p.m.   Under Porter's covering fire, four Union divisions were landed.

During the evening Union monitors continued the bombardment of the fort's land force.

14 January   At daylight the Union fleet reopened its cannonade of the fort. An estimated one hundred shells a minute were fired at Fort Fisher. By nightfall, the Union commanders planned the assault on the fort.

15 January   Union fleet continued bombardment of Fort Fisher until midday.

2:00 p.m.   Bombardment ended.

2:30 p.m.   Union forces attacked the fort. A naval contingent of two thousand sailors and Marines assaulted Fort Fisher's northwest bastion as four thousand troops from Terry's command attacked the land face batteries. The naval assault was repulsed, however; according to Fort Fisher's commander Colonel William Lamb, "Their gallant attempt enabled the army to enter and obtain a foothold, which they otherwise could not have done."

10:00 p.m.   Fort Fisher surrendered. The port of Wilmington, North Carolina, was effectively closed to blockade runners.

USS *Patapsco*, commanded by Lieutenant Commander Stephen P. Quackenbush, struck a torpedo in Charleston harbor and sank immediately with the loss of sixty-four officers and crew.

16 January   Secretary of the Navy S.R. Mallory advised Flag Officer J.K. Mitchell of the James River Squadron:

> *I regard an attack upon the enemy and the obstructions of the river at City Point, to cut off Grant's supplies, as a movement of the first importance to the country and one which should be accomplished if possible.*

Mitchell had recently learned that the obstructions placed in the James River had been weakened by high water and only one monitor guarded the river near Dutch Gap.

Rear Admiral D.D. Porter noted the destruction of the last Confederate fort defending the Cape Fear River, commenting that "the death knell of another fort is booming in the distance. Fort Caswell with its powerful batteries is in flames and being blown up, and thus is sealed the door through which this rebellion is fed."

20 January *Casco*-class monitor USS *Chimo* was commissioned.

The *Chimo* was finished as a torpedo boat and was detailed to serve as a station ship at Point Lookout, North Carolina.

Marietta-class river ironclad USS *Sandusky* was launched at Tomlinson, Pittsburgh, Pennsylvania.

21 January Secretary of the Navy S.R. Mallory urged Flag Officer J.K. Mitchell to pass Union obstructions at Trent's Reach and attack City Point, Virginia: "You have an opportunity, I am convinced, rarely presented to a naval officer, and one which may lead to the most glorious results to your country." Mitchell asked General R.E. Lee "to give me your views and wishes as to my cooperation with the army down the river in the event of our being successful."

23 January
6:00 p.m. Flag Officer J.K. Mitchell ordered his squadron to steam down the James River to Trent's Reach. The three ironclads had wooden vessels firmly lashed to their sides: the gunboat *Hampton* and torpedo boat *Hornet* to the *Fredericksburg*, gunboat *Beaufort* and tender *Drewry* to the *Richmond* and the gunboats *Nansemond* and *Torpedo* to the *Virginia II*. The CSS *Fredericksburg* led the squadron down the narrow river. The Confederate plan, according to Lieutenant John Randolph Eggleston, was

> *nothing less than the division of Grant's army into three parts and the destruction of his water base at City Point. We were to go through their obstructions and after running through the pontoon bridge some fifteen miles below would have left one ironclad to cruise up and down the river and prevent them from communicating with each other. The other two would have gone down to City Point...and their obstructed the channel with sunken vessels so that it would have been impossible for them to have remained there under the fire of the ironclad that would have been left...while the other ironclad would have been free to run up the Appomattox.*

The Federals had been warned of this sortie; however, most of the Union ironclads were still involved with the operation to capture Wilmington, North Carolina. The Fifth Division of the North Atlantic Blockading Squadron, under the command of Commander William Parker, consisted of the twin turret monitor *Onondaga* and several wooden gunboats, including the screw-steamer *Daylight* and the side-wheelers *Eutaw*, *Hunchback*, *Massasoit*, *Miami*, *William Putnam* and *Commodore Barney*. The *Onondaga* had the heaviest ordnance of any monitor:

two 15-inch Dahlgren smoothbores and two 150-pounder rifles. The *Onondaga* was stationed near the Union obstructions at Trent's Reach.

8:00 p.m. Confederate squadron steamed abreast of Union fortification Fort Brady on Signal Hill. The Federals discovered the rams approaching and opened fire with their heavy one-hundred-pounder Parrotts. The Confederate ironclads did not respond; however, Confederate batteries across the James River provided counter-battery fire and disabled one of the Union battery's Parrott rifles.

The ironclads continued down the river under constant fire from Union artillery and sharpshooters.

9:00 p.m. Confederate squadron reached the western end of Trent's Reach. CSS *Scorpion* inspected the channel through the Union obstructions.

24 January

12:15 a.m. CSS *Richmond* was discovered aground near the obstructions.

1:30 a.m. CSS *Fredericksburg* and the gunboat *Hampton* crossed the obstructions.

1:45 a.m. Flag Officer J.K. Mitchell learned about the CSS *Virgina II*'s grounding. The CSS *Torpedo*, *Drewry*, *Scorpion* and *Hornet* all ran aground striving to free the *Virginia II*. Mitchell ordered the CSS *Fredericksburg* back across the obstructions to protect the two stranded ironclads. Several gunboats were eventually floated. Mitchell directed the wooden vessels and torpedo boats to "take up their anchorage before daylight opposite Battery Dantzler, under cover of a wooden point, which would secure them from the observation of the enemy, or at least afford some protection from his fire." Mitchell initially ordered the CSS *Fredericksburg* to help cover the other ironclads; however, Flag Officer Mitchell decided that it would be best for the *Fredericksburg* to stay out of Union battery range when daylight came.

6:55 a.m. Lieutenant John McIntosh Kell, commander of the stranded CSS *Richmond*, ordered the grounded wooden gunboat *Drewry* abandoned.

7:00 a.m. Union gunners in Battery Parsons saw the grounded Confederate vessels just 1,500 yards away and began firing their 100-pounder Parrott rifle at the *Drewry*.

7:10 a.m. The third shell from Battery Parsons caused the *Drewry* to explode. The *Drewry*'s destruction could be heard eighteen miles away in City Point, Virginia. The shock from the explosion sent the torpedo boat *Scorpion* drifting downstream out of control. The *Scorpion* was later captured by the Federals.

10:45 a.m. After being struck by over seventy projectiles the *Virginia II* floated free and began to steam upriver. At this moment, the USS *Onondaga*, supported by the gunboats *Hunchback* and *Massassoit* as well as the torpedo boat *Sputen Duyvil*, steamed to within a half-mile of the obstructions. Commander Parker had moved the *Onondaga* downriver when he learned of the approach of the Confederate ironclads. When General U.S. Grant learned about the stranded Confederate ironclads and the possibility that one of these ironclads still might be able to attack the huge unprotected Union supply base at City Point, he ordered Commander Parker to strike at the Confederate squadron.

The *Onondaga*'s first shot from her fifteen-inch Dahlgren struck the *Virginia II*'s port quarter, broke through the four-inch armor and broke the wood backing.

11:00 a.m. The second shot from the *Onondaga* broke though the *Virginia II*'s casemate, killing one man and wounding two others. A Confederate petty officer noted that it "became evident very soon that the *Virginia* was no match for Ericsson's little tub."

11:15 a.m. As the *Virginia II* steamed out of the *Onondaga*'s range, the Union turned her attention to the CSS *Richmond*. The *Richmond* had already been heavily hit by shot and shell from Battery Parsons when the *Onondaga* sent one shot that knocked off the *Richmond*'s stern port shutter.

9:00 p.m. Flag Officer Mitchell met with his commanders and decided to make another attempt to cross the obstructions. En route, Mitchell discovered that the Federals had positioned a "brilliant Drummond light" to illuminate the obstructions and aid Union battery fire during the evening.

10:30 p.m. Mitchell broke off the movement and ordered his ships back to Chaffin's Bluff.

CSS *Stonewall* rendezvoused with the blockade runner *City of Richmond* in Quiberon Bay, France. The *Stonewall* received some coal from the *City of Richmond*.

25 January Captain T.J. Page wrote to Secretary of the Navy S.R. Mallory, "You must not expect too much of me; I fear that the power and effect of this vessel have been too much exaggerated. We will do our best."

28 January Confederate submarine torpedo boat *St. Patrick*, commanded by Lieutenant John T. Walker, attacked the USS *Octorara* off Mobile Bay, Alabama. The torpedo failed to explode. The *St. Patrick* was a steam-powered torpedo boat that was operated by hand crank when submerged. She was fifty feet in length and was operated by a six-man crew. The *St. Patrick* was built by J.P. Halligen in Selma, Alabama.

CSS *Stonewall* left Quiberon Bay for Ferrol, Spain.

CSS Stonewall, photograph, ca. 1865. Courtesy of The Mariners' Museum.

1 February	*Casco*-class monitor *Suncook* was launched at Boston. This monitor was immediately laid up upon completion.
6 February	When Rear Admiral D.D. Porter learned that another ironclad ram was being constructed on the Roanoke River near Halifax, North Carolina, he advised Commander William N. Macomb, commander of the Union squadron in the North Carolina Sounds, to fit a spar:

> *To the bow of every gunboat and tug, with a torpedo on it, and run at the ram, all together. No matter how many of your vessels get sunk, one or the other of them will sink the ram if the torpedo is coolly exploded. Have your large rowboats fitted with torpedoes also, and…put your large vessels alongside her, let the launches and small torpedo boats run in and sink her…You can sling a good siege anchor to an outrigger spar, and let it go on her deck, and by letting go your own anchor keep her from getting away until other vessels pile in on her. Five or six steamers getting alongside of a ram could certainly take her by boarding. If you can get on board of her, knock a hole in her smokestack with axes, or fire a Howitzer through it, and drop shrapnel down into the furnaces…*
>
> *Set torpedoes in the river at night, so that no one will know where they are. Obstruct the river above Plymouth and get what guns are there to command the approaches. Get a net or two across the river, with large meshes, so that when the ram comes down the net will dog her propeller…It is strange if we with all our resources cannot extinguish a rebel ram.*

8 February	Flag Officer Samuel Barron was directed to return to the Confederacy. This order ended Confederate efforts to secure European-built ironclads.
10 February	The monitor USS *Lehigh* supported troop movements up the Stono and Folly Rivers near Charleston, South Carolina.
11 February	USS *Niagara* reached Corunna, Spain, in search of the CSS *Stonewall*.
	Secretary of the Navy Gideon Welles advised the commanders of the West Coast and East Coast Blockading Squadrons that the CSS *Stonewall* would soon arrive in American waters: "Her destination is doubtless some point on our coast, and it behooves you to be prepared against surprise, as she is represented to be formidable and capable of inflicting serious injury."
14 February	Commander William Parker was court-martialed for his failure to engage the Confederate ironclads closely with the USS *Onondaga* during the Battle of Trent's Reach. Even though he was cleared on a technicality, Rear Admiral D.D. Porter still believed he was guilty of "an error in judgment." Porter advised Parker's replacement, Lieutenant Commander Homer Blake, that had Parker acted with any resolution on February 14, "we should now be in possession of the whole Rebel Navy and on our way to Richmond. The *Onondaga* I consider a match for the whole Rebel fleet, and I fell mortified that

I failed to impress the late commander of the Division with the importance of acting coolly and energetically if any occasion offered."

15 February   USS *Niagara* arrived in Ferrol, Spain.

17 February   Charleston, South Carolina, was abandoned by the Confederate army. That evening all of the shipyards, torpedo boats and one ironclad on the stocks were destroyed.

18 February   Flag Officer John Randolph Tucker ordered the destruction of the ironclads CSS *Chicora, Palmetto State* and *Charleston*. The *Charleston Daily Courier* reported: "The explosions were terrific. Pieces of the iron plate, red hot, fell on the wharves and set them on fire…Tremendous clouds of smoke went up forming beautiful wreaths."

Flag Officer J.K. Mitchell was replaced by Rear Admiral Raphael Semmes as commander of the James River Squadron.

22 February   When Rear Admiral Raphael Semmes learned about the fall of Wilmington, North Carolina, he commented, "We had lost our last blockade-running port. Our ports were now all hermetically sealed. The anaconda had, at last, wound his fatal folds around us."

5 March   The monitor USS *Sangamon* arrived in Hampton Roads, Virginia, and was immediately sent up the James River to guard against any offensive movement by the Confederate James River Squadron during the spring freshets.

9 March   General Braxton Bragg ordered the evacuation of Kinston, North Carolina. The *Neuse* was detailed to cover the Confederate army's retreat and "if practicable, before sacrificing, to move down the river by way of diversion, and to make the loss…as costly to the enemy as possible."

13 March   *Casco*-class monitor USS *Shawnee* was launched at Curtis Tildery in Boston.

14 March   CSS *Neuse* was set afire; however, a loaded gun discharged, blowing a hole below her waterline, and the ironclad quickly sank in shallow water.

17 March   *Casco*-class monitor USS *Naubuc* was commissioned.

20 March   CSS *Albemarle* was raised by the Federals.

21 March   *Casco*-class monitor USS *Modoc* was launched at Perrine, Jersey City, New Jersey.

24 March   CSS *Stonewall* left Ferrol, Spain, and attempted to engage the steam screw frigate USS *Niagara* and the steam screw sloop of war *Sacramento*. Commodore T.T. Craven, commander of the *Niagara*, advised that the

> *Stonewall is a very formidable vessel, about 175 feet long, brig-rigged, and completely clothed in iron plates of five inches in thickness. Under her topgallant fire castle is her casemated Armstrong 300-pounder rifled gun. In a turret abaft her main mast are two 120-pounder rifled guns, and she has two smaller guns mounted in broadside. If as fast as refuted to be, in smooth water she ought to be more than a match for three such ships as the* Niagara.

Craven refused to engage the *Stonewall* as he advised Secretary of the Navy Gideon Welles,

> *At this time the odds in her favor were too great and too certain, in my humble judgment, to admit of the slightest hope of being able to inflict upon her even the most trifling injury, whereas, if we had gone out, the* Niagara *would most undoubtedly have been easily and promptly destroyed. So thoroughly a one-sided combat I did not consider myself called upon to engage.*

Craven would be court-martialed and found remiss in his duties for not attacking the *Stonewall*. Flag Officer T.J. Page of the CSS *Stonewall* was surprised by the Federal inaction, noting, "To suppose that these two heavily armed men of war were afraid of the *Stonewall* is to me incredible."

28 March   The twin-turret monitor USS *Milwaukee* struck a torpedo in Alabama's Blakely River and sank. No lives were lost.

29 March   The monitor USS *Osage* struck a torpedo in the Blakely River and sank in three minutes. The *Osage* lost four men, and eight were wounded in the explosion.

2 April
4:00 p.m.   Secretary of the Navy S.R. Mallory ordered the destruction of the Confederate James River Squadron when Richmond was abandoned. Mallory later reflected on his command:

> *The James River Squadron, with its ironclads, which had laid like chained bulldogs under the command of Rear Admiral Semmes to prevent the ascent of the enemy's ships, would, in the classic flush of the times, "go up" before morning; and the naval operations of the Confederacy east of the Mississippi would cease.*

CSS *Nashville* and *Huntsville* steamed up the Tennessee River midway between Spanish Fort and Fort Blakely and shelled besieging troops of Union General Frederick Steele.

3 April
2:00 p.m.   The CSS *Fredericksburg*, *Richmond* and *Virginia* II were burned to prevent their capture. The unfinished CSS *Texas* was left undamaged. Semmes moved the crews of these ironclads away from Drewry's Bluff aboard wooden gunboats

> *by the glare of the burning ironclads. They had not proceeded far before an explosion, like the shock of an earthquake, took place, and the air was filled with missiles. It was the blowing up of the* Virginia, *my late flagship. The spectacle was grand beyond description. Her shell-rooms had been full of loaded shells. The explosion of the magazine threw all these shells, with their fuses lighted, into the air. The fuses were of different lengths, and as the shells exploded by twos and threes, and by the dozen, the pyrotechnic effect was very fine. The explosion shook the houses in Richmond, and must have waked the echoes of the night for forty miles around.*

10 April   *Casco*-class monitor USS *Klamath* was launched at Cincinnati, Ohio.

12 April   City of Mobile, Alabama, surrendered. Confederate ironclads CSS *Huntsville* and *Tuscaloosa* were destroyed. Flag Officer Ebenezer Farrand escaped up the Tombigbee River with the CSS *Nashville*.

17 April   Columbus, Georgia, was captured by Union forces. CSS *Jackson* was destroyed.

Several individuals suspected of involvement in the assassination of President Abraham Lincoln were imprisoned aboard the monitors USS *Montauk* and *Saugus*.

26 April   *Casco*-class monitor USS *Nausett* was launched at Boston.

27 April   The body of President Lincoln's assassin, John Wilkes Booth, was delivered to the Washington Navy Yard by the USS *Montauk*.

3 May   Stephen Russell Mallory resigned his appointment as Confederate Secretary of the Navy.

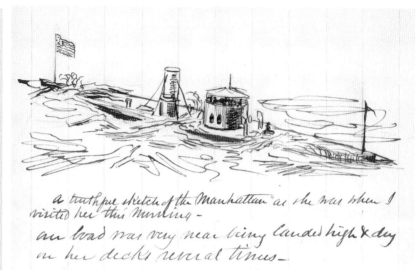

a truthful sketch of the Manhattan as she was when I visited her this morning — an boad was very near being landed high & dry on her decks several times —

4 May	*Casco*-class monitor USS *Waxsaw* was launched at Denmead Shipyard, Baltimore, Maryland.
	Flag Officer Ebenezer Farrand offered to surrender "all Confederate naval forces, officers, men and public property yet afloat under his command and now blockaded…in the Tombigbee River."
8 May	*Casco*-class monitor USS *Yazoo* was launched at Cramp Shipyard, Philadelphia, Pennsylvania.
	CSS *Missouri* steamed down from Shreveport, Louisiana, and reached the rapids above Alexandria, Louisiana. The *Missouri* anchored in mid-river to help defend the Red River against any Union expedition.
10 May	Flag Officer Ebenezer Farrand surrendered the ironclad CSS *Nashville* and the wooden gunboats *Baltic*, *Morgan* and *Black Diamond* near Nanna Hubba Bluffs on the Tombigbee River.
11 May	CSS *Stonewall* arrived in Havana, Cuba. Flag Officer T.J. Page learned that the war was virtually over.
19 May	Flag Officer T.J. Page delivered the CSS *Stonewall* over to the governor general of Cuba for $16,000. The money was the exact amount needed to pay off the officers and crew. The *Stonewall* was given over to the U.S. Navy and eventually sold to Japan. She became known as the *Azuma* and served in the Imperial Japanese Navy until 1908.
24 May	*Passaic*-class monitor USS *Comanche* was commissioned at San Francisco, California. The *Comanche*'s existence helped deter the Confederate commerce raider CSS *Shenandoah* from any attempt to attack San Francisco.
27 May	Rear Admiral Cornelius K. Stribling surveyed the CSS *Stonewall* in Havana, Cuba. Stribling did "not consider her so formidable a vessel as had been represented. In a seaway she would be powerless, and unless her speed was greater than that of her opponent and her ram could do no harm."

3 June	Lieutenant Jonathan H. Carter surrendered the CSS *Missouri* to Lieutenant William E. Fitzhugh of the USS *Ouachita*. While the *Missouri* never fired her guns in combat, she was the last Confederate ironclad to surrender.
23 June	Rear Admiral Samuel Francis DuPont died in Philadelphia, Pennsylvania.
27 June	*Casco*-class monitor USS *Naupuc* was decommissioned.

CHAPTER 9

VICTORY AND VISION

THE CIVIL WAR MARKED A turning point in history. The conflict introduced modern war to the world. War reached beyond the battlefield and placed powerful pressures upon the homefront to produce the muskets, manpower and material needed to attain victory. Total war required all of a nation's assets to be devoted to the war effort. Northern and Southern homefronts alike were distorted and modified as a result of this experience. The social, political and economic impact of the Civil War altered American society and changed the way wars would be fought in the future.

The War Between the States revolutionized American thinking. The war ended slavery, expanded educational opportunities and ended sectional differences. It also reinforced the rise of industrialization. The experience of huge armies marching across the landscape maintained by forced conscription required extensive logistical support. Factories mass-producing uniforms, food, weapons, equipment and ships prospered. Industrialization prompted the development and improvement of various new technologies. Once these technical tools were introduced onto the battlefield, combat changed beyond comprehension and attrition warfare ensued. Consequently, war became a battle of resources and invention. The nation with the greatest resources available would be the victor.

Few facets of the Civil War more closely reinforce the technology and attrition theme than does the war on the water. The war witnessed an overnight change to naval tactics. Boarding tactics and "fighting instructions" became archaic and forgotten due to steam power, ironclads, revolving turrets, torpedoes and rifled cannons. These tools reinforce the attrition thesis and left an incredible mark on future ship and ordnance design.

Secretary of the Navy Gideon Welles was able to create naval policy that followed the concepts of Lieutenant General Winfield Scott's Anaconda Plan. It was an effective blueprint for victory. The Union navy enacted the Anaconda Plan through its decisive blockade and capture of Southern ports. Federal fleet actions resulted in the Union control of the Mississippi, which divided the Confederacy while simultaneously closing each outlet to European goods. The fall of Fort Fisher proved the Union navy's effectiveness as Colonel William Lamb recounted, "For the first time in the history of sieges the land defenses of the works were destroyed, not by any act of the besieging army, but by the concentrated fire, direct and enfilading, of an immense fleet plowed into them without intermission, until…the slopes of the works were rendered practicable for assault."

The Federals had brought the largest fleet assembled in American waters. Union ironclads and wooden steam-powered frigates provided the mobility to direct superior firepower at any and every defensive point. Fort Fisher was overwhelmed and the fort's capture basically marked the end of Confederate resistance. General R.E. Lee recognized that without the flow of supplies

"USS *Carondelet* & CSS *Arkansas*," engraving, ca. 1863. *Courtesy of John Moran Quarstein.*

entering Wilmington, Richmond could not be held. The Union navy proved its critical role in the economic, financial and psychological defeat of the Confederacy.

The Confederacy entered the war with significant naval disadvantages. The long coastline and vast tracks of territory traversed by navigable streams provided the U.S. Navy with numerous opportunities to disrupt Confederate commerce and military operations. Since the South had no navy at the war's beginning, the task to counter the Federals' overwhelming advantages fell onto the shoulders of Confederate Secretary of the Navy Stephen Russell Mallory. Mallory initially misjudged the capability of Southern ironclads to break the Union blockade and threaten Union cities as well as the ability of coastal forts to defend against Federal naval assault. Steam power and rifled guns proved at Port Royal Sound, New Orleans, and the North Carolina Sounds that some comprehensive system of defense in depth was needed. Flag Officer J.K. Mitchell noted that "the enemy, with his large naval establishment and unlimited transportation, has, in all his expeditions against us, appeared in such overwhelming force as to render successful resistance on the part of ours utterly out of the questions."

Mallory however, was not swayed by such defeatism and strove to remake the Confederate homefront navy into a force able to counter the Federal fleet. Ironclads were constructed for harbor defense, torpedoes were deployed and torpedo boats were created. These weapons proved able to protect Southern harbors from water attack. While Confederate ironclads never became the ultimate weapon that Mallory had envisioned, his efforts forced the agrarian South to deploy the new technologies of the submarine and mine warfare. Mallory was justified when he wrote after the war:

> *I am satisfied that, with the means at our control and in view of the overwhelming force of the enemy at the outset of the struggle, our little navy accomplished more than could have been hoped for.*

Even though torpedoes and submarines were unique weapons that would continue to play an important role in naval warfare, it was Mallory's drive to create ironclads that truly changed naval warfare. John Newland Maffitt noted that to "the Confederates belongs of testing in battle the invulnerability of ironclads and of revolutionizing the navies of the world. The *Merrimack* did that." The CSS *Virginia*'s sortie on March 8, 1862, as credited by crewmember E.V. White, "wrought an entire change in naval architecture and in defensive fortifications throughout the world. Wooden frigates had almost ceased to be of any value. The blow that sunk the *Cumberland* demolished also the fleets of England and France." While the Confederacy had clearly proved the power of iron over wood, the revolution continued with the Union's counterstroke. The USS *Monitor*'s timely appearance in Hampton Roads and her combat with the *Virginia* on March 9 established a new era in shipbuilding. Even though there were numerous flaws in the *Monitor*'s design, the revolving armored turret, with its concentration of guns able to fire in any direction, would dominate naval shipbuilding for the next seventy-five years. Warships would continue to evolve; however, they would continue to feature iron construction, low profile, speed, maneuverability and cannons with tremendous hitting power. The March 9, 1862 Battle of Hampton Roads defined the modern warship.

The *Monitor*'s success in Hampton Roads prompted the construction of another sixty Union ironclads. The U.S. Navy grew beyond expectations during the war. Of all the ships built, purchased and leased, it was the fleet of ironclads that enabled the Union to achieve victory while simultaneously creating a vision for future navies to follow. The Union may have constructed a few very durable and effective casemated warships; monitors became the backbone of naval operations.

While the U.S. Navy continued to rely on Civil War–era monitors for the next thirty years, European navies experimented with various ironclad designs. Central battery, casemate and turreted seagoing warships were produced. Each design had its strengths and weaknesses. The lower freeboard monitor concept of the Civil War was transformed into seagoing cruiser's mounting turrets. Advances in propulsion systems, steel construction and watertight rifled guns helped to complete the transition from broadside to turret by the late nineteenth century.

The Civil War also successfully introduced mines, torpedoes and submarine warfare. Each of these tools was able to sink enemy warships. Continued advances during the latter part of the nineteenth century enhanced these weapons and they would have a profound impact upon naval warfare during the twentieth century. As envisioned by the Confederacy, small warships like torpedo boats and submarines were easier to produce and proved to be great equalizers. A small nation could use these weapons to create a larger fleet. Nevertheless, naval power could not depend upon these tools. Nations needed oceangoing battle cruisers designed to protect and control their commerce and overseas interests.

As European nations explored how to improve Civil War–era weapons, the U.S. Navy seemed content to rely on its fleet produced during the war. Wooden frigates and monitors armed with breech-loading rifles and smoothbores were quickly outclassed by their European counterparts. The greatest naval establishment of 1865 soon lagged behind nations like Chile. The U.S. Navy endeavored to modernize following the October 30, 1873 *Virginius* affair; however, the

Gun deck, CSS *Virginia*, John Luke Porter, plan, 1861. *Courtesy of The Mariners' Museum.*

USS *Miantonomoh*, photograph, ca. 1880. *Courtesy of The Mariners' Museum.*

reconstruction of the *Miantonomoh*-class of monitors resulted in scandal and did not solve the rise of U.S. imperialism.

The real modern U.S. Navy began with the construction of the three cruisers *Atlanta*, *Boston* and *Chicago*. During the next fifteen years the U.S. Navy strove to keep pace with European warship advancements. Battleships like the *Maine*, *Indiana* and *Kentucky* began to bring the United States on par with its European rivals.

During all of this ship modernization, the U.S. Navy continued to maintain and construct monitors. Some Civil War–era monitors like the USS *Puritan* were broken up and rebuilt as improved monitors. Others stayed in ordinary and were actually recommissioned for the Spanish-American War and then scrapped in the postwar era. The last *Canonicus*-class monitor, the USS *Canonicus*, was recommissioned and participated in the April 1907 Jamestown Naval Review in Hampton Roads, Virginia. The venerable relic operated under her own power. She was the last of Civil War monitors and was sold for scrap in February 1908. The U.S. Navy's "new monitors" continued in service. All but the USS *Cheyenne* (formerly USS *Wyoming* BM-10) were decommissioned and sold for scrap after World War I. The *Cheyenne* was decommissioned in 1926 and was not stricken from the Naval Vessel Register until 1937. The monitor was sold for scrap in 1939. One ironclad still remained afloat in American waters, the *Amphitrite*. The ironclad was sold in 1920 and moved to South Carolina and then Florida, where she served as a floating hotel. The *Amphitrite* was chartered by the U.S. government to house workers building a new air station near Elizabeth City, North Carolina. After another stint as a floating restaurant at Sandy Point, Maryland, near the Chesapeake Bay Bridge, the *Amphitrite* was towed to Baltimore, Maryland, where the Patapsco Steel Corporation scrapped her in 1952.

Naval warfare evolved for over 3,500 years before the tremendous explosion of new tactics and technology during the nineteenth century. All of these great changes in ordnance, naval architecture and propulsion were tremendous. The evolutions from sail to steam, shot to shell and wood to iron all came together during the American Civil War. The Confederacy's need to protect its coastline and trade prompted Secretary of the Navy Stephen Russell Mallory to seek a new weapon to challenge the North's larger wooden navy. The result was the combination of several old and new technologies epitomized by sloped armor plating, rifled guns, steam power and a ram. Ancient and modern tools were unified into a warship that dominated all wooden warships in Hampton Roads. The North's ability to apply superior technology checkmated the Confederate ironclad on March 9, 1862. These two ironclads, CSS *Virginia* and USS *Monitor*, closed out the era of sailing wooden warships and introduced the modern iron battleships. The *Virginia*–*Monitor* legacy would dominate naval warfare until steel-turreted, heavy-gunned battleships were superseded by air power. The March 8–9, 1862 Battle of Hampton Roads was a powerful point of change. The events leading up to and following this momentous engagement detail how historical events all become mere steppingstones for the future.

1865

17 July	*Casco*-class monitor USS *Suncook* was launched at Globe Iron Works in Boston, Massachusetts.
22 July	The seagoing ironclad frigate ram *Dunderberg* was launched at William N. Webb Yard in New York, New York. The *Dunderberg* was designed by John Lenthall and was a replication of the CSS *Virginia*'s sloped armored casemate. She was fitted with a fifty-foot ram. The *Dunderberg* was the longest wooden ship ever built; however, she was never commissioned by the U.S. Navy. She was purchased by France and renamed the *Rochambeau*.
24 July	The USS *Ozark* was decommissioned. She was sold for scrap on November 29, 1865.
10 August	*Casco*-class USS *Nausett* was commissioned.
18 August	*Casco*-class USS *Shawnee* was commissioned.
18 September	The twin-turret monitor USS *Miantonomoh* was commissioned at the Brooklyn Navy Yard in New York. Designed by John Lenthall, the *Miantonomoh* displayed 3,401 tons; she was 250 feet in length and armed with four 15-inch Dahlgren smoothbores. The *Miantonomoh* was considered an "oceangoing monitor," but during her cruise to Europe she was towed most of the way.

"USS *Miantonomoh,* photograph, ca. 1880. *Courtesy of The Mariners' Museum.*

27 September	*Canonicus*-class USS *Manayunk* was delivered to the U.S. Navy.
10 October	The famous "laird rams," *North Carolina* (*El Monassir*) and *Mississippi* (*El Tousson*), were completed and commissioned as the HMS *Wivern* and HMS *Scorpion*. The *Wivern* served as a coastal defense and depot ship at Hong Kong until broken up in 1922. The *Scorpion* served as a coastal defense ship at Bermuda. She was sunk as a target ship off Bermuda in 1901.
21 October	The *Casco*-class *Waxsaw* was completed at F&W Denmead & Sons, Baltimore, Maryland.
28 October	*Casco*-class *Wassau* was completed at George W. Lawrence Yard in Thomaston, Maine.
17 November	Construction was suspended on all of the *Kalamazoo*-class double-turret monitors. The four monitors were *Kalamazoo*, *Passaconaway*, *Quinsigamond* and *Shackamaxon*. These monitors were designed for ocean cruising; however, their hulls were built of poorly seasoned wood and they rotted on the stocks.
18 November	*Casco*-class *Koka* was delivered to the U.S. Navy.
15 December	*Casco*-class *Yazoo* was completed at Cramp Shipyard, Philadelphia, Pennsylvania.

1866

15 January	HMS *Royal Sovereign* was used to conduct experiments to assess the resistance of Coles-designed turrets to heavy shot. Three shots were fired at close range against the after turret (10 inches iron-front, 5.5 inches iron-sides and back) of the *Royal Sovereign* from one of the 9-inch guns carried by the HMS *Bellerophon*. The shots did not disable the turret. The *Royal Sovereign* was originally laid down as a 121-gun wooden ship-of-the-line; however, construction was stopped and conversion into an ironclad was begun on April 4, 1862. The *Royal Sovereign* was the first British turreted ironclad.
19 January	*Casco*-class *Cohoes* was delivered to the U.S. Navy.
15 February	*Canonicus*-class monitor the *Tippecanoe* was delivered to the U.S. Navy. This monitor would not be commissioned until January 24, 1876.
12 March	*Casco*-class monitors the *Etlah* and the *Shiloh* were delivered to the U.S. Navy.
11 April	HMS *Bellerophon* was commissioned. The *Bellerophon* was a central battery ironclad battleship mounted with a ram. The central battery differed from the broadside concept as it featured a small number of heavy-caliber guns centrally mounted. The steel hull was built on the new "bracket-frame" concept. The ship's watertight compartments and double-hull design were built into the *Bellerophon* to guard against the ram and torpedo.
6 May	*Casco*-class monitors the *Yuma* and the *Klamath* were delivered to the U.S. Navy.
7 May	*Casco*-class monitor the *Umpqua* was completed at Snowden & Mason in Pittsburgh, Pennsylvania.
20 July	The most decisive naval engagement of the Seven Weeks' War was fought between the Italian and Austrian fleets for control of the Adriatic Sea. The Italian fleet, commanded by Admiral Count Carlo Pellion di Persano, which consisted of eleven armored ships, steamed against the Austrian-controlled

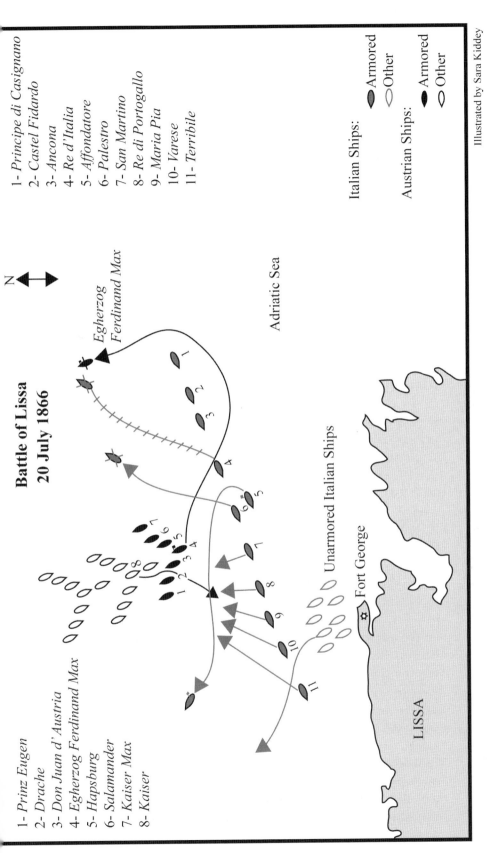

Battle of Lissa
20 July 1866

N

Egherzog Ferdinand Max

Adriatic Sea

Unarmored Italian Ships

Fort George

LISSA

1- *Prinz Eugen*
2- *Drache*
3- *Don Juan d' Austria*
4- *Egherzog Ferdinand Max*
5- *Hapsburg*
6- *Salamander*
7- *Kaiser Max*
8- *Kaiser*

1- *Principe di Casignano*
2- *Castel Fidardo*
3- *Ancona*
4- *Re d'Italia*
5- *Affondatore*
6- *Palestro*
7- *San Martino*
8- *Re di Portogallo*
9- *Maria Pia*
10- *Varese*
11- *Terribile*

Italian Ships:
● Armored
○ Other

Austrian Ships:
● Armored
◇ Other

Illustrated by Sara Kiddey

Admiral Tegethoff recognized that the Italian fleet contained more ironclads and guns than his command. Tegethoff decided to use the ram as his primary weapon. The Austrian admiral's arrow formation gave impetus to his attack. The Italian line was broken and two ironclads were lost in a dramatic manner: the *Re d'Italia* was rammed and sunk in a few minutes and the *Palestro* was set on fire and, as a result, exploded.

island of Lissa. The Austrian fleet, commanded by the dynamic Rear Admiral Wilhelm Von Tegetthoff, moved to stop this Italian strike force. Tegetthoff's command contained only seven armored ships. Since his vessels did not possess heavy modern shellguns, he believed in the ram and thought the ship itself would be the chief weapon.

10:00 a.m. Tegetthoff neared Lissa. His ships were in two divisions. The Italians, recognizing this threat, broke off their landing operation. Persano formed his command into armored and unarmored divisions. The Italians steamed northeast from Lissa in an irregular line ahead.

11:00 a.m. Tegetthoff approached in three arrowhead lines, the seven armored ships in the van, and broke through the Italian line. All of the Austrian ships were committed to the battle and a melee ensued. Tegetthoff's flagship, *Ergherzog Ferdinand Max*, rammed and sunk the *Re d'Italia*. A wooden, steam-powered ship-of-the-line, the *Kaiser*, rammed the *Re diPorto Gallo*; however, the Austrian ship suffered greater damage and broke off action. Shellfire severely damaged the Italian armored frigates *Affondatore* and *Palestro*.

2:30 p.m. The *Palestro* exploded and the Italians retreated. The *Affondatore* sank later due to damage incurred at Lissa.

Lissa was the first sea battle between ironclad warships. Naval artillery did not seem as effective against ironclads as did the ram. The dramatic ramming and sinking of the *Re d'Italia* influenced ship design for the next three decades. The ram became standard equipment in battleship construction.

30 June USS *Monadnock* was decommissioned. This double-turret monitor had proven her seaworthiness by steaming around Cape Horn en route to the Pacific Coast.

16 December USS *New Ironsides* was destroyed by fire.

1867

2 March USS *Onondaga* was sold to France.

15 October CSS *Albemarle* was sold for scrap at Gosport Navy Yard, Portsmouth, Virginia.

1868

2 April USS *Oneota* had been delivered to the U.S. Navy, but she was never commissioned. She was sold to Peru and renamed *Manco Capac*.

Another *Canonicus*-class monitor, USS *Catawba*, was simultaneously sold to Peru and renamed *Atahualpa*.

24 April CSS *Stonewall* was sold to Japan. Renamed *Azuma*, she served in the Imperial Navy until 1908.

25 May HMS *Monarch* was commissioned. The *Monarch* was the first oceangoing sail-rigged, steam-powered warship to carry all of her guns in turrets.

2 December Her Majesty's Victorian Ship (HMVS) *Cerberus* was launched. The *Cerberus* was the first British warship powered only by steam. This twin-turret breastwork monitor was a departure from American Civil War–era monitors. The breastwork was a centrally built superstructure on which turrets were mounted, one at each end. This layout gave a clear field of fire over the stern and bow.

Breastwork monitors like the *Cerberus* retained a low-freeboard main desk; however, the higher armored deck amidships afforded greater protection for the funnel, turret bases and airshafts as well as keeping these areas clear of the sea. The *Cerberus* was 225 feet in length and mounted four ten-inch muzzle-loading rifles.

1869

27 March   HMS *Captain* was launched. The *Captain* was a controversial design of Cowper Coles with only a six-foot-seven-inch freeboard and a full-sail rig. She had two turrets containing four twelve-inch muzzle-loading rifles and also carried two seven-inch muzzle-loading rifles.

4 May   CSS *Atlanta* was sold to Haiti. Renamed the *Triumph*, she sank off Cape Hatteras, North Carolina, en route to Haiti.

15 May   The twin-turret monitor the USS *Tonawanda* was renamed the USS *Amphitrite*.

10 August   The USS *Tippecanoe* was renamed the USS *Wyandotte*. She was not commissioned until 1876.

1870

4 January   The USS *Miantonomoh* sank the tug USS *Maria* in a collision off Martha's Vineyard, Massachusetts.

28 July   The twin-turret monitor *Miantonomoh* was decommissioned.

7 September   HMS *Captain* heeled over under the force of wind upon her sails and capsized with the loss of 480 lives. Ironclad advocate and turret designer Cowper Coles went down with the *Captain*. The disaster was due to a design flaw, which did not provide adequate freeboard for the ironclad while operating under sail in heavy seas.

4 November   Ship action took place during the Franco-Prussian War off Havana, Cuba, between the French ironclad *Bouvet* and the Prussian ironclad *Meteor*. The *Bouvet* mounted one sixteen-centimeter rifle and four twelve-centimeter guns while the *Meteor* had one sixteen-centimeter and two twelve-centimeter guns.

The two ironclads circled each other until closing to a range of three hundred yards when the *Bouvet* rammed the *Meteor*. The *Meteor* was able to position herself only to receive a glancing blow. Nevertheless, the *Meteor* lost her main mast and her propeller was fouled. A shot from the *Meteor* disabled the *Bouvet's* boiler and the vessels broke off action.

1871

9 April

HMVS *Cerberus* arrived in Melbourne, Victoria, Australia. The *Cerberus* became the flagship of the Victorian navy. She was incorporated into the Royal Australian Navy in 1911 and used as a store ship. Renamed the Her Majesty's Australian Ship *Platypus II*, she served as a submarine store ship. The *Cerberus* was sold for scrap in 1924. She was sunk on September 26, 1926, at Half Moon Bay in Blackhawk, Victoria, where she still remains today.

1872

25 March

HMS *Thunderer* was launched. The *Thunderer* was a *Devastation*-class battleship. This class contained the first true capital ship built by any nation and began the transformation of the monitor-type ship into the oceangoing battleship. The *Thunderer* was 285 feet in length and mounted four 12-inch muzzle-loading rifles in two centerline turrets. Her armor belt was 12 inches and supported by 18 inches of teak.

1873

30 October

A former Confederate blockade runner built in Scotland, the *Virginius* was captured by Spanish authorities trying to smuggle arms to rebels in Cuba. The Spanish executed the ship's captain, 1841 Annapolis graduate Joseph Fry. The ensuing diplomatic crisis forced the United States to mobilize for war. It took three months for Admiral D.D. Porter to assemble a fleet of Civil War relics. A British journalist noted about the U.S. Navy that there "never was such a hapless, broken down, tattered, forlorn apology for a Navy as that possessed by the United States."

1874

23 June

U.S. Navy ordered Civil War–era monitors to be reconstructed. The *Amphitrite*, *Terror*, *Miantonomoh*, *Monadnock* and the never completed *Puritan* were to be rebuilt following the Virginius affair. Construction on all of these monitors, except the *Miantonomoh*, was later suspended.

1875

27 April

HMS *Inflexible* was launched to counter the construction of the Italian central citadel battleships *Diablo* and *Enrico Dandolo*. The *Inflexible* mounted four sixteen-inch rifles in two centerline turrets to fire ahead, mounted a ram and underwater torpedo tubes. She was the first ship to have electric lights and had the thickest armor of any ship then afloat.

11 November

The last British armor-clad with a full-sail rig, HMS *Shannon*, was launched.

5 December

The Civil War–era twin turret *Miantonomoh* had been broken up in 1874 and the new monitor (BM-5) was launched at John Roach & Son, Chester, Pennsylvania.

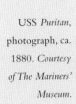

USS *Puritan*, photograph, ca. 1880. *Courtesy of The Mariners' Museum.*

1877

1 January   USS *Dictator* was decommissioned.

17 September   HMS *Shannon* was commissioned.

8 October   *Canonicus*-class monitor *Saugus* was decommissioned.

1878

26 January   The first successful self-propelled torpedo attack occurred when the Russian torpedo boat *Constantine* sank a Turkish patrol boat.

1879

8 October   During the war between Chile and Peru for control of nitrate deposits, in an action off Point Angamos, the armored ships *Almirante Cochrane* and *Blanco En Calada* (built in Britain and each armed with six nine-inch Armstrong rifles) engaged the Peruvian ironclad *Huascar*. The *Huascar* had two ten-inch Armstrong rifles mounted in her turret and was commanded by Captain Miguel Grau. Grau had been raiding the Chilean coast when five Chilean warships commanded by Patrico Lynch caught up with and engaged the *Huascar*. During the next ninety minutes, the two Chilean ironclads pounded the Peruvian ironclad into submission.

1880

7 January   Peruvian monitor *Manco Capac* (formerly USS *Oneota*) was blown up by her crew at Arica, Peru, to prevent capture by the Chilean navy.

16 January   Peruvian monitor *Atahualpa* (formerly the USS *Catawba*) was scuttled at Callao, Peru, to prevent capture by the Chilean navy.

USS *Puritan*, photograph, ca. 1880. *Courtesy of The Mariners' Museum.*

1882

6 October   USS *Miantonomoh* was commissioned in an uncompleted condition.

22 November   HMS *Collingwood* was launched. The *Collingwood* was mounted with four twelve-inch breech-loading rifles in fore and aft barbette mounts as well as six six-inch rifles mounted in a central broadside battery to repel torpedo boats.

6 December   The never completed *Puritan* was "repaired" and launched under the direction of Secretary of the Navy George Robeson. The reconstruction project featured very little of the original *Puritan*. The rebuilt *Puritan* (BM-1) had two turrets and a breastwork superstructure as typified by other "new monitors."

1883

3 March   The U.S. Congress authorized the construction of three modern cruisers, the *Atlanta*, *Boston* and *Chicago*.

13 March   USS *Miantonomoh* (BM-5) was decommissioned.

24 March   USS *Terror* (BM-4), a totally rebuilt version of the Civil War-era monitor USS *Agamenticus*, was launched.

"USS *Amphitrite,
Puritan,
Montgomery* and
Ericsson," Frederic
Shiller Cozzens,
chromolithograph,
ca. 1898. *Courtesy
of The Mariners'
Museum.*

7 June	USS *Amphitrite*, the lead ship in her class of twin-turret and twin-screw new monitors, was launched.
23 August	During the Tonkin War's Battle of Foo Chow, French torpedo boats numbers 45 and 46 sunk the Chinese flagship in one minute.
19 September	USS *Monadnock* (BM-3), a rebuilt version of the Civil War–era monitor, was launched. The reconstruction of Civil War–era monitors was an effort to disguise the fact that the U.S. Navy was building new ships rather that just repairing old vessels.
27 September	USS *Dictator*, originally designed by John Ericsson as *Protector*, was sold and broken up. USS *Roanoke*, formerly a sister ship to the USS *Merrimack* and reconfigured as a three turret monitor, was sold and broken up.

1886

3 August	The U.S. Congress authorized the construction of the USS *Maine*.

1889

18 November	The USS *Maine* was launched. This armored cruiser was part of an effort to modernize the U.S. Navy. She had a primary battery of four ten-inch guns.

1891

15 March	*Canonicus*-class monitor USS *Saugus* was sold.
17 June	USS *Olympia*, a protected cruiser, was laid down at Union Iron Works, San Francisco, California.

1894

17 September	Battle of Yalu River. Japanese fleet destroyed the Chinese fleet during this decisive Sino-Japanese War naval engagement.

1895

23 April	The USS *Amphitrite* (BM-2) was commissioned.
1 December	Pre-*Dreadnought* battleship HMS *Majestic* was commissioned.

1896

20 February	USS *Monadnock* (BM-3) was commissioned.

USS *Kearsarge*, photograph, ca. 1898. *Courtesy of The Mariners' Museum.*

15 April	USS *Terror* (BM-4) was commissioned.
10 December	USS *Puritan* (BM-1) was commissioned.

1898

15 February	USS *Maine* was destroyed by internal explosion in Havana Harbor, Cuba. Following the *Maine's* destruction, several Civil War–era monitors were recommissioned, including the *Catskill, Lehigh, Nahant, Passaic, Sangamon* and *Wyandotte* (*Tippecanoe*) for coastal defense against any attack by the Spanish fleet.
24 March	USS *Kearsarge* and *Kentucky* launched at Newport News Shipbuilding. The battleships were part of the revitalization of the U.S. Navy in the 1890s. The two previous classes of battleships, *Indiana* and *Iowa*, combined good armor with heavy armament.
25 April	The United States declared war on Spain.
1 May	<u>Battle of Manila Bay</u>. Commodore George Dewey's squadron of protected cruisers destroyed an inferior Spanish fleet.
3 July	Rear Admiral William T. Sampson's fleet of five battleships and two protected cruisers destroyed a Spanish fleet commanded by Admiral Pascual Cervera at Santiago Bay, Cuba. Commodore Winfield Scott Scheley's *Brooklyn* opened the engagement and the Spanish ships were overwhelmed by the heavy twelve-inch guns of the American battleships.

The U.S. Navy's new monitors all had active service during the Spanish-American War. The *Monadnock* steamed across the Pacific to operate on blockade duty in the Manila area. The *Puritan, Miantonomoh, Terror* and *Amphitrite* all served in the U.S. Navy's blockade of Cuba and Puerto Rico. The *Amphitrite* with the battleship *Iowa* shelled San Juan, Puerto Rico, on May 12, 1898. The after-blast of the monitor's ten-inch guns destroyed the ship's gig

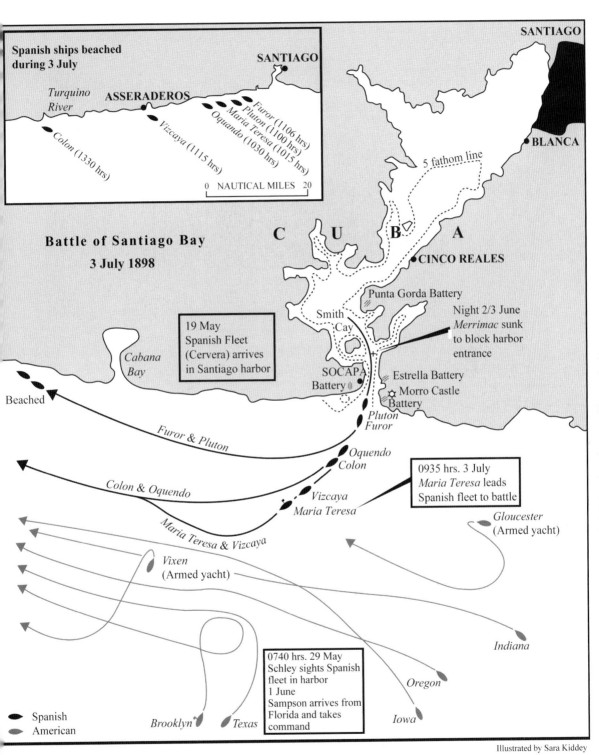

Spanish ships beached during 3 July

Turquino River

ASSERADEROS

SANTIAGO

Furor (1106 hrs)
Pluton (1100 hrs)
Maria Teresa (1015 hrs)
Oquendo (1030 hrs)

Vizcaya (1115 hrs)

Colon (1330 hrs)

0   NAUTICAL MILES   20

SANTIAGO

• BLANCA

5 fathom line

C   U   B   A

• CINCO REALES

Punta Gorda Battery

Night 2/3 June
Merrimac sunk
to block harbor
entrance

Battle of Santiago Bay
3 July 1898

Smith
Cay

19 May
Spanish Fleet
(Cervera) arrives
in Santiago harbor

Cabana Bay

SOCAPA
Battery

Estrella Battery

☆ Morro Castle
Battery

Beached

Pluton
Furor

Furor & Pluton

Oquendo
Colon

0935 hrs. 3 July
Maria Teresa leads
Spanish fleet to battle

Colon & Oquendo

Vizcaya
Maria Teresa

Maria Teresa & Vizcaya

Gloucester
(Armed yacht)

Vixen
(Armed yacht)

Indiana

0740 hrs. 29 May
Schley sights Spanish
fleet in harbor
1 June
Sampson arrives from
Florida and takes
command

Oregon

Iowa

Brooklyn   *Texas*

● Spanish
● American

Illustrated by Sara Kiddey

The Spanish fleet attempted to break through the American blockade to escape Santiago. The American fleet used its superior speed and gunnery to track down and destroy each of the Spanish ships.

and railings on the superstructure. The monitor's poor ventilation caused the death of one gunner's mate from heat.

1899

17 January — *Canonicus*-class monitor *Wyandotte* (*Tippecanoe*) was decommissioned and sold.

22 March — *Passaic*-class monitor *Camanche* was sold.

10 October — *Passaic*-class monitor *Passaic* was sold.

14 November — The New Navy monitor *Arkansas* (BM-7) was laid down at Newport News Shipbuilding, Newport News, Virginia.

1900

8 September — The New Navy monitor *Wyoming* was launched at Union Iron Works, San Francisco, California. The "New Navy" monitors were 255 feet in length and had a draft of 12 feet 6 inches. These monitors featured a breastwork to house superstructure and one turret containing two 12-inch breech-loading rifles. Additional armament included four 4-inch guns and two 6-pounders.

10 November — The New Navy monitor USS *Arkansas* was launched.

24 November — The New Navy monitor USS *Connecticut* (BM-8) was launched.

1901

30 November — The New Navy monitor USS *Florida* (BM-9) was launched at Crescent Shipyard in Elizabeth Port, New Jersey.

4 December — The *Passaic*-class monitor *Catskill* was sold.

1902

24 March — *Canonicus*-class monitors *Manayunk* and *Manhattan* were sold.

25 March — *Canonicus*-class monitor *Mahopac* was sold.

28 October — The New Navy monitor USS *Arkansas* (BM-7) was commissioned.

8 December — The New Navy monitor USS *Wyoming* (BM-10) was commissioned.

1903

5 March — The New Navy monitor *Connecticut* (BM-8) was renamed the *Nevada*.

18 June — The New Navy monitor *Florida* (BM-9) was commissioned.

1904

9 February — Japanese surprise attack against the Russian fleet at Port Arthur. Japanese destroyers damaged three Russian ships with torpedoes.

14 April — *Passaic*-class monitors *Montauk* and *Lehigh* were sold.

16 April — *Passaic*-class monitor *Nahant* was sold.

10 August — Battle of Yellow Sea. Vice Admiral Togo Heihachiro's combined fleet defeated the Russian fleet commanded by Admiral Vitgeft. Vitgeft was killed in the action and the Russians failed to escape Port Arthur.

1905

27 May — Battle of Tsushima. Japanese destroyed the Russian Baltic Fleet. Tsushima was the first naval battle in which the radio was used in action.

1906

10 February — HMS *Dreadnought* was launched. The *Dreadnought* was the first battleship to have a uniform main battery (ten twelve-inch guns) and made all other battleships obsolete.

USS *Nahant*, photograph, ca. 1900. *Courtesy of The Mariners' Museum.*

7 May   USS *Virginia* was launched at Newport News Shipbuilding. The *Virginia* was outdated the moment she was launched.

8 May   The monitor USS *Terror* was decommissioned.

18 December   The U.S. Navy's response to the HMS *Dreadnought*, the USS *South Carolina*, was laid down at William Cramp and Sons, Philadelphia, Pennsylvania. The *South Carolina* had a main battery of eight twelve-inch guns.

1907

7 June   *Canonicus*-class monitor USS *Canonicus* moved under her own power while participating in the Jamestown Naval Review. The *Canonicus*'s turret displayed shot damage received by this monitor during her service in the James River in 1864.

The rebuilt and recently recommissioned *Miantonomoh* also participated in the Jamestown Exposition, commemorating the tercentenary of the first permanent English settlement in America.

21 December   The USS *Miantonomoh* was decommissioned.

1908

19 February   The last Civil War–era monitor, the USS *Canonicus*, was sold for scrap.

1 July   The New Navy monitor *Wyoming* was renamed the USS *Cheyenne* (BM-10).

1909

2 March   The New Navy monitor *Arkansas* was renamed USS *Ozark* (BM-7).

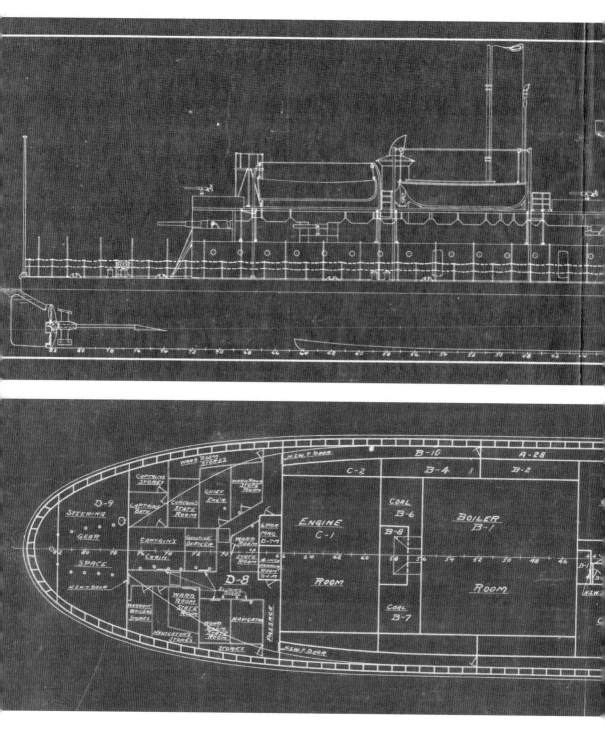

USS *Arkansas*, blueprint, ca. 1899. *Courtesy of The Mariners' Museum.*

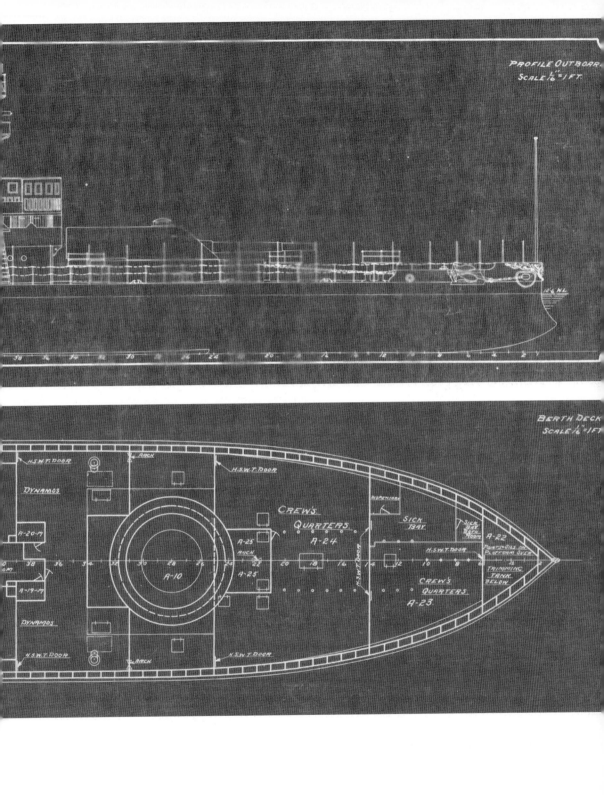

PROFILE OUTBOARD.
SCALE ½"=1FT.

BERTH DECK
SCALE ⅛"=1FT.

HMS *Dreadnought*, photograph, ca. 1910. *Courtesy of The Mariners' Museum.*

USS *Virginia*, photograph, ca. 1910. *Courtesy of The Mariners' Museum.*

USS *Ozark*,
photograph, ca.
1910. *Courtesy
of The Mariners'
Museum.*

1910

The New Navy monitor *Nevada* was renamed USS *Tonopah* (BM-8).

23 April   USS *Puritan* (BM-1) was decommissioned.

14 November   Barnstorming pilot Eugene B. Ely successfully piloted the first aircraft from the deck of a warship (USS *Birmingham*) in Hampton Roads, Virginia, foreshadowing the role the aircraft carrier would eventually play in naval warfare.

1914

28 July   Austrian monitors *Koros* and *Leitha* fired the first shots against Serbia during World War I while operating in the Danube River.

5 September   German submarine U-21 sank the HMS *Pathfinder*. The *Pathfinder* was the first warship sunk by a submarine since the American Civil War.

1916

31 May   <u>Battle of Jutland</u>.

1917

13 June   USS *Amphitrite* (BM-2) collided with the steamship *Manchuria* while on submarine net duty. The *Manchuria* was abandoned and later beached.

1919

24 March   USS *Monadock* (BM-3) was decommissioned.

31 May   USS *Amphitrite* (BM-2) was decommissioned.

1920

3 January   USS *Amphitrite* was sold to A.L.D. Bucksten of Elizabeth City, North Carolina. Stripped of her turret and superstructure, the monitor was towed to Beaufort,

USS *Amphitrite*, photograph, ca. 1910. *Courtesy of The Mariners' Museum.*

South Carolina, where she was used as a floating hotel. The *Amphitrite* was then towed to Florida and it was rumored that "a certain amount of fashionable gambling was carried out on board."

1922

26 January — Monitors *Tonopah*, *Ozark*, *Miantonomoh* and *Puritan* were sold for scrap.

24 March — New Navy monitor the USS *Tallahassee* was decommissioned.

25 July — USS *Tallahassee* was sold.

1923

24 August — USS *Monadnock* (BM-3) was sold.

1926

1 June — The New Navy monitor USS *Cheyenne* (BM-10) was decommissioned.

1937

25 January — The New Navy monitor *Cheyenne* was the last monitor struck from the Naval Vessel Register.

1939

20 April — USS *Cheyenne* (BM-10) was sold for scrap.

1943 — The former USS *Amphitrite* was chartered by the United States government to provide housing for workmen building a new air station at Elizabeth City, North Carolina.

USS *Cheyenne*, photograph, ca. 1920. *Courtesy of The Mariners' Museum.*

Amphitrite Hotel, photograph, ca. 1950. *Courtesy of The Mariners' Museum.*

1950 The former *Amphitrite* was towed to the Chesapeake Bay and placed into a slip dredged into the bank at Sandy Point near where the new Chesapeake Bay Bridge was to be built. The floating restaurant business venture was unsuccessful.

1951 *Amphitrite* was towed to Baltimore, Maryland.

1952 *Amphitrite*, the last U.S. Navy monitor, was scrapped by Patapsco Steel Corporation, Fairfield, Maryland.

IRONCLAD RECOVERY

A S SOON AS THE WAR was over there was a general desire to memorialize the people, places, events and vessels associated with the Civil War at sea. The public wanted to learn more about the history and, as time went by, a feeling arose that significant people and events had to be commemorated. Of particular interest was the March 8–9, 1862 Battle of Hampton Roads. Everyone who had served in the battle or had been one of the thousands of individuals who had at least witnessed the engagement felt that they had been part of one of history's most meaningful events. Many shared written remembrances or told others how to paint a record of the great battle. A few participants were granted special medals or presentation swords. Others were lionized for their leadership, daring and courage. As these veterans passed on to greater reward, more and more importance was given to objects associated with the people. The physical connection of place and artifact enabled people fifty to one hundred years after the event to understand the event's meaning. Artifacts such as a sword or piece of iron became "holy relics" as links to a dramatic battle such as the USS *Monitor*–CSS *Virginia* engagement. An object provides a dimension to history that cannot be replicated by word or painting. You can read about the harrowing fate of the USS *Monitor*'s sinking off Cape Hatteras in the early morning hours of December 31, 1862, or you can view lithographs depicting the scene. Nothing, however, completes such a chilling connection with the event as does the red lantern recovered from the *Monitor* wreck site.

The process of collecting Civil War objects began before the war was over. While being repaired in the Washington Navy Yard, the USS *Monitor* became Washington's premier tourist attraction. The ironclad was visited daily by all manner of curiosity seekers, who often left with various souvenirs. "When we came up to clean that night," crew member Louis Stodder remembered, "there was not a key, doorknob, escutcheon—there wasn't a thing that hadn't been carried away." Likewise after Appomattox, people continued to seek artifacts to commemorate or interpret this naval battle. The CSS *Virginia* was still a wreck off Craney Island in 1865 and considered a hazard to navigation. Accordingly, several contracts were issued during the postwar era to remove the wreck. Some work was completed in 1867; however, the entire hull was not raised and towed into dry dock until 1875. Iron plate, cannon, the drive shaft and the replacement ram were recovered. Most of the material was sold for scrap; however, a few iron plate sections, as well as the anchor, wheel and drive shaft, were presented to museums. Numerous souvenirs were made from iron and wood portions of the vessel. These items found a ready market among Hampton Roads residents and visitors. The Old Dominion Iron and Nail Works of Richmond produced several tokens and horseshoes noting "Made From The Armor Plate The *Merrimac*— The First Ironclad 1862." Tredegar Iron Works also produced iron plate horseshoes for the 1907 Jamestown Exposition. Souvenirs were still in production, including a paperweight for the Edison

Illuminating Company's 1928 annual meeting held at Old Point Comfort, until the 1930s. Even though iron plate was unavailable to make *Monitor* trinkets, the ship was venerated in other ways. Statues were built honoring men associated with the *Monitor*, like John Ericsson, and references to the Union ironclad could be found everywhere. The Scandinavian Brotherhood of America used an image of the *Monitor* as part of their logo.

Public recognition of the importance of ironclads and the Battle of Hampton Roads continued to grow throughout the nineteenth and early twentieth centuries. A *Passaic*-class monitor was a featured display during the Philadelphia Centennial Exhibition. Similar to the famous panoramic painting of the Battle of Gettysburg, a "*Merrimac* and *Monitor* Naval Battle" cyclorama was created by French artist Theo Poilpot. This huge painting toured the nation in the 1880s and 1890s. The 1907 Jamestown Exposition held in Norfolk featured a reenactment of the battle between the *Monitor* and *Merrimack* along with the cyclorama painting. The *Monitor* and *Merrimac* panoramic painting has since disappeared; however, the public has turned its interest toward the discovery, conservation and interpretation of the actual ironclads.

The Civil War Centennial celebration heightened interest in the war. The identification of several wreck sites prompted efforts to raise, preserve and present ironclads like the CSS *Neuse* and the USS *Cairo*. Since the USS *Monitor* was considered iconic, a desire to locate the wreck off Cape Hatteras developed in the 1970s. The ironclad's discovery in 1973 caused the creation of the *Monitor* National Marine Sanctuary and the selection of The Mariners' Museum to house artifacts recovered from the wreck site. When NOAA archaeologists realized that the *Monitor* was rapidly deteriorating, efforts were undertaken to raise significant sections of the ironclad. In 2002 the turret was raised and moved to The Mariners' Museum. In turn, the turret, engine and other artifacts became the focal point of The Mariners' Museum's *Monitor* Center. The opening of the museum facility is scheduled for March 9, 2007, 145 years after the Battle of Hampton Roads. It will offer Civil War enthusiasts the opportunity to virtually touch one of the ironclads that changed naval warfare.

1940	The site of the CSS *Neuse* was discovered; however, the U.S. Army Corps of Engineers decided that it was not practical to salvage the ironclad's remains.
1945	The U.S. Navy, using the newly developed underwater object locator Mark IV, detected a submerged object off Cape Hatteras Light, North Carolina. It was speculated that the object could be the USS *Monitor*.
1952	Raynor McMullen organized the USS *Monitor* foundation and offered $1,000 to anyone who could locate the USS *Monitor*.
1954	High school students recovered 6.4-inch Brooke projectiles from the *Neuse* wreck site.
1955	Efforts were initiated to preserve and display the USS *Constellation* in Baltimore, Maryland.

1956	Local Kinston, North Carolina businessmen Henry Clay Casey and Lemuel Houston attempted to raise the *Neuse*. The effort was unsuccessful.
	National Park Service (NPS) historian Edwin L. Bearss discovered the USS *Cairo* wreck.
20 November	Despite being declared a "relic" by the U.S. Navy, Admiral David G. Farragut's flagship, the USS *Hartford*, sunk at her berth at the Norfolk Navy Yard. The wreck was salvaged and several items were saved.
1961	
28 October	The first sections of the CSS *Neuse* were raised.
1963	The CSS *Jackson* was raised near Columbus, Georgia.
	The CSS *Neuse* was raised near Kinston, North Carolina.
1964	The CSS *Neuse* was moved to Caswell–Neuse Park in Kinston, North Carolina.
	The USS *Cairo* was raised from the Yazoo River.
1965	The USS *Cairo* was placed on barges and towed to Ingalls Shipyard, Pascagoula, Mississippi. The *Cairo*'s armor plate was removed, cleaned and stored. The two engines were taken apart, cleaned and reassembled. The hull was braced.
1972	The U.S. Congress enacted legislation authorizing the NPS to accept title to the *Cairo* and restore the ironclad for display in Vicksburg National Military Park.
	The CSS *Neuse* Visitor Center was opened.
1973	
May	The USS *Monitor* foundation and underwater archaeological associates claimed to have found the *Monitor*'s turret using sonar.
27 August	Duke University, Massachusetts Institute of Technology, National Geographic and the North Carolina Department of Cultural Resources expedition aboard the *Eastward* side-scan sonar recorded a "long amorphous echo." Faulty cameras recorded fuzzy images of a flat surface and a "circular protrusion."
1974	
8 March	Duke University announced that it had located the wreck of the USS *Monitor*.
1977	A team from NOAA, Harbor Branch, the U.S. Navy and North Carolina Division of Archives and History completed an extensive photogrammetric survey of the wreck. A brass signal lantern was recovered forty feet north of the wreck.
1983	A team from NOAA, Harbor Branch and East Carolina University studied the feasibility of any major recovery operations. The *Monitor*'s unique four-fluked anchor was recovered.
1990	Teams from Harbor Branch and NOAA aboard the *R/V Seward-Johnson* made video and photographic images of the wreck using the *Johnson-Seahawk 1* submersible.

APPENDIX 1

1991	A team from NOAA and Harbor Branch carried out an emergency inspection of the *Monitor* wreck site in response to a U.S. Coast Guard report of unauthorized anchoring within the Sanctuary.
1993	Divers under the direction of Roderick Farb made high-quality photographic images of the *Monitor* wreck.
1995	Efforts made to recover the *Monitor*'s propeller were unsuccessful.
1996	The U.S. Congress issued a mandate to the Secretary of Commerce to produce a long-range plan for stabilization of the wreck site and the recovery of selected components of the USS *Monitor*.
	Hurricane Fran flooded the Caswell-*Neuse* site. The *Neuse* was moved away from the riverbank.
1998	Research expedition of the *Monitor* National Marine Sanctuary recovered the *Monitor*'s cast-iron propeller and a section of the drive shaft.
1999	NOAA and the U.S. Navy team aboard the USS *Grasp* surveyed the *Monitor* wreck.
	Hurricane Floyd flooded the CSS *Neuse* Visitor Center.
2000	Teams from NOAA, the Cambrian Foundation, National Undersea Research Center and East Carolina University completed the survey and small artifact recovery operations.
	Derrick barge *Weeks 526* operated over the *Monitor* wreck site. The Engine Recovery System was successfully lowered over the wreck. The rudder supper skeg, propeller shaft section and stuffing box were recovered.
	Port Columbus National Civil War Naval Museum was opened to the public. The CSS *Jackson* was displayed.
2001	Derrick barge *Wotan* with the U.S. Navy and NOAA personnel on board recovered the *Monitor*'s engine and a section of the armor belt.
2002	The Derrick barge *Wotan* with the U.S. Navy and NOAA personnel recovered the turret of the USS *Monitor*.
	The turret arrived at The Mariners' Museum in Newport News, Virginia.
2004	The Mariners' Museum initiated construction of the *Monitor* Center.
2005	The CSS *Neuse* was reopened to the public.
2007	The Mariners' Museum USS *Monitor* Center was opened to the public.

UNION IRONCLADS

Name	Laid Down	Launched/Acquired	Commission
Agamenticus	1862	19 March 1863	5 May 1865
Atlanta (ex-CSS *Atlanta*, ex-*Fingal*)		9 May 1861	2 February 1864
Benton	1861	November 1861	24 February 1862
Cairo	1861	October 1861	25 January 1862
Camanche	1862	14 November 1864	24 May 1865
Canonicus	1862	1 August 1863	16 April 1864
Carondelet	1861	22 October 1861	15 January 1862
Casco	1863	7 May 1864	4 December 1864
Catawba	1862	13 April 1864	10 June 1865
Catskill	1862	16 December 1862	24 February 1863
Chickasaw	1862	10 February 1864	14 May 1864
Chillicothe	1862	1862	5 September 1862
Chimo	1863	5 May 1864	20 January 1865
Choctaw		1856 / 27 September 1862	23 March 1863
Cincinnati	1861	1861	16 January 1862
Cohoes	1863	31 May 1865	19 January 1866
Dictator	16 August 1862	26 December 1863	11 November 1864
Dunderberg	4 October 1862	22 July 1865	Never
Eastport	1852	31 October 1861 / August 1862	9 January 1863
Essex	1856	1861	October 1861
Etlah	1863	3 July 1865	12 March 1866
Galena	1861	14 February 1862	21 April 1862
Indianola	1862	4 September 1862	14 January 1863
Kalamazoo	1863	Never	Never
Keokuk (ex-*Moodna*)	19 April 1862	6 December 1862	March 1863
Kickapoo	1862	12 March 1864	8 July 1864
Klamath	1863	10 April 1865	6 May 1866

Name	Laid Down	Launched/Acquired	Commission
Koka	1863	18 May 1865	18 November 1865
Lafayette	1848	14 September 1862	27 February 1863
Lehigh	1862	17 January 1863	15 April 1863
Louisville	1861	1861	16 January 1862
Mahopac	1862	17 May 1864	22 September 1864
Manayunk	1862	18 December 1864	27 September 1865
Manhattan	1862	14 October 1863	6 June 1864
Marietta	1862	4 January 1865	16 December 1865
Miantonomoh	1862	15 August 1863	18 September 1865
Milwaukee	27 May 1862	8 February 1864	27 August 1864
Modoc	1863	21 March 1865	23 June 1865
Monadnock	1862	23 March 1864	4 October 1864
Monitor	25 October 1861	30 January 1862	25 February 1862
Montauk	1862	9 October 1862	17 December 1862
Mound City	1861	1861	16 January 1862
Nahant	1862	7 October 1862	29 December 1862
Nantucket	1862	6 December 1862	26 February 1863
Napa	1863	26 November 1864	4 May 1865
Naubue	1863	19 October 1864	17 March 1865
Nausett	1863	26 April 1865	10 August 1865
Neosho	1862	18 February 1863	13 May 1863
New Ironsides	November 1862	10 May 1862	21 August 1862
Oneota	1862	21 May 1864	10 June 1865
Onondaga	1862	29 July 1863	24 March 1864
Osage	1862	13 January 1863	10 July 1863
Ozark	1862	18 February 1863	18 February 1864
Passaconaway	18 November 1863	Never	Never
Passaic	1862	30 August 1862	25 November 1862
Patapsco	1862	27 September 1862	2 January 1863
Pittsburg	1861	1861	16 January 1862
Puritan	1863	2 July 1864	Never
Quinsigamond	15 April 1864	Never	Never
Roanoke	1854	13 December 1855	29 June 1863
Sandusky	1862	20 January 1865	26 December 1865
Sangamon	1862	27 October 1862	9 February 1863
Saugus	1862	16 December 1863	7 April 1864
Shackamaxon	1863	Never	Never

Name	Laid Down	Launched/Acquired	Commission
Shawnee	1863	13 March 1865	18 August 1865
Shiloh	1863	14 July 1865	12 March 1865
Squando	1863	31 December 1864	6 June 1865
Stevens Battery	1854	Never	Never
St. Louis	27 September 1861	12 October 1861	31 January 1862
Suncook	1863	1 February 1865	17 July 1865
Tecumseh	1862	12 September 1863	19 April 1864
Tennessee (ex-CSS *Tennessee*)	October 1862	5 August 1864	19 August 1864
Tippecanoe	1862	22 December 1864	15 February 1866
Tonawanda	1863	6 May 1864	12 October 1865
Tunxis	1863	4 June 1864	12 July 1864
Tuscumbia	1862	12 December 1862	12 March 1863
Umpqua	1863	12 December 1864	7 May 1866
Wassuc	1863	25 July 1865	28 October 1865
Waxsaw	1863	4 May 1865	21 October 1865
Weehawken	17 June 1862	5 November 1862	18 January 1863
Winnebago	1862	4 July 1863	27 April 1864
Yazoo	1863	8 May 1865	15 December 1865
Yuma	1863	30 May 1865	6 May 1866

CONFEDERATE IRONCLADS

Name	Laid Down	Acquired	Launched/Acquired	Commission
Albemarle	April 1863		1 July 1863	17 April 1864
Arkansas	October 1861		25 April 1862	26 May 1862
Atlanta (ex-*Fingal*)		Spring 1862	9 May 1862	22 November 1862
Baltic		1862	1860	May 1862
Charleston	December 1862		1863	September 1863
Chicora	25 April 1862		23 August 1862	November 1862
Columbia			10 March 1864	1864
Eastport (ex-*C.E. Killman*)	1852	31 October 1861		Never
Fredericksburg	1863		30 November 1863	March 1864
Huntsville	1862		7 February 1863	1863
Jackson (*Muscogee*)	1862		22 December 1864	Never
Louisiana	15 October 1861		6 February 1862	Never
Manassas (ex-*Enoch Train*)	1855	1861	12 September 1861	December 1861
Milledgeville	February 1863		October 1864	Never
Mississippi (Laird Ram-*El Monassir*)	April 1862		29 August 1863	Never
Mississippi	14 October 1861		19 April 1862	Never
Missouri	December 1862		14 April 1863	12 September 1863
Nashville			1863	Never
Neuse	1863		November 1863	April 1864

Name	Laid Down	Acquired	Launched/Acquired	Commission
North Carolina (Laird Ram-*El Tousson*)	April 1862		4 July 1863	Never
North Carolina	Spring 1862		October 1863	December 1863
Palmetto State	January 1862		11 October 1862	November 1862
Raleigh	Spring 1862		Fall 1864	30 April 1864
Richmond	February 1862		6 May 1862	July 1862
Santa Maria (aka *Glasgow* and *Frigate No. 61*)	1863		23 February 1864	Never
Savannah	April 1862		4 February 1863	30 June 1863
Stonewall	1863		21 June 1864	January 1865
Tennessee I	October 1861		Never	Never
Tennessee II	October 1862		February 1863	16 February 1864
Texas			January 1865	Never
Tuscaloosa	1862		7 February 1863	1863
Virginia I (ex-*Merrimack*)	14 June 1855	20 April 1861	17 February 1862	17 February 1862
Virginia II	1863		June 1864	June 1864
Wilmington	1863		Never	Never

The Confederate navy laid down six additional ironclads, which were never named.

SELECT BIBLIOGRAPHY

Anderson, Bern. *By Sea and By River: The Naval History of the Civil War.* New York: Alfred A. Knopf Co., 1962.

Ballard, G.A. "British Battleships of the 1870s: The *Warrior* and *Black Prince*." *Mariner's Mirror*, April 1930, 168–86.

Barnard, J.G. *Notes on Sea Coast Defense.* New York: D. Van Nostrand, 1861.

Brooke, George M., Jr. *John M. Brooke, Naval Scientist and Educator.* Charlottesville: University Press of Virginia, 1980.

Browning, Robert M., Jr. *From Cape Charles to Cape Fear: The North Atlantic Blockading Squadron during the Civil War.* Tuscaloosa: The University of Alabama Press, 1993.

Coski, John M. *Capital Navy: The Men, Ships, and Operations of the James River Squadron.* Campbell, CA: Savas Woodbury Publishers, 1996.

Dahlgren, Madeline V. *Memoir of John A. Dahlgren.* Boston: J.R. Osgood and Company, 1882.

Daly, Robert W., ed. *Aboard the USS* Monitor*: 1862: the Letters of Acting Paymaster William Frederick Keeler, US Navy to his wife, Anna.* Annapolis: United States Naval Institute Press, 1964.

Daly, R.W. *How the* Merrimac *Won: The Strategic Story of the CSS* Virginia. New York: Thomas Y. Cromwell, 1957.

David, William C. *Duel Between the First Ironclads.* Garden City, NJ: Doubleday & Company, 1975.

Delafield, Richard, Alfred Mordecai and George McClellan. *Report Published by Secretary of War and Military Commission to Europe, 1854–1856.* 3 vols. Washington: Government Printing Office, 1857–60.

Dew, Charles B. *Ironmaker to the Confederacy: Joseph R. Anderson and the Tredegar Iron Works.* New Haven, CT: Yale University Press, 1966.

Durkin, Joseph T. *Stephen R. Mallory: Confederate Naval Chief.* Chapel Hill: University of North Carolina Press, 1954.

Elliott, Robert G. *Ironclad of the Roanoke.* Shippensburg, PA: White Mane Books, 1999.

Faust, Patricia L., ed. *Historical Times Illustrated Encyclopedia of the Civil War.* New York: Harper & Row, 1986.

Griffiths, Oliver W. "The New War Steamers." *The United States Nautical Magazine,* April 1855, 298–310.

Hagerman, George M. "Lord of the Turtle Boats." U.S. Naval Institute Proceedings 93 (December 1967): 66–75.

Hogg, Ian V. *A History of Artillery.* London: Hamlyn Publishing Group, 1974.

Jones, Virgil Carrington. *The Civil War at Sea.* 3 vols. New York: Holt, Pinehart, and Winston, 1960–62.

Luraghi, Raimondo. *A History of the Confederate Navy.* Translated by Paolo E. Coletta. Annapolis: United States Naval Institute Press, 1996.

Marvel, William, ed. *The Monitor Chronicles.* New York: Simon & Schuster, 2000.

Mosocco, Ronald A. *The Chronological Tracking of the American Civil War.* Williamsburg, VA: James River Publications, 1995.

Nash, Howard P., Jr. *A Naval History of the Civil War.* New York: A.S. Barnes and Company, 1972.

Nevin, John. *Gideon Welles, Lincoln's Secretary of the Navy.* New York: Oxford University Press, 1973.

Pemsel, Helmut. *Atlas of Naval Warfare.* London: Arms and Armour Press, 1977.

Pimlott, John, ed. *Atlas of Warfare.* New York: Gallery Books, 1988.

Quarstein, John V. *C.S.S. Virginia: Mistress of Hampton Roads.* Appomattox, VA: R.E. Howard, 2000.

Rogers, U.C.B. *A History of Artillery.* Secaucus, NJ: The Citadel Press, 1975.

Scharf, J. Thomas. *History of the Confederate States Navy from Its Organization to the Surrender of Its Last Vessel.* New York: Rogers & Sherwood, 1887. Reprint, New York: Gramercy Books, Random House Publishing, Inc. 1996.

Silverstone, Paul H. *Civil War Navies: 1855–1883.* Annapolis: Naval Institute Press, 2001.

Simson, Jay W. *Naval Strategies of the Civil War.* Nashville: Cumberland House, 2001.

Still, William N., Jr. *The Confederate Navy: The Ships, Men and Organization, 1861–65.* Annapolis: United States Naval Institute Press, 1997.

———. *Confederate Shipbuilding.* Columbia: University of South Carolina Press, 1987.

———. *Iron Afloat: The Story of Confederate Armorclads.* Nashville: Vanderbilt University Press, 1971.

Tucker, Spencer C. *Handbook of the 19th Century Naval Warfare.* Annapolis: Naval Institute Press, 2000.

U.S. Department of the Navy. *Civil War Chronology 1861–1865.* Washington: U.S. Government Printing Office, 1971.

———. *Dictionary of American Naval Fighting Ships.* 8 vols. Washington: U.S. Government Printing Office, 1959.

———. *Official Records of the Union and Confederate Navies in the War of Rebellion.* 30 vols. Washington: U.S. Government Printing Office, 1894–1922.

Warner, Oliver. *Great Sea Battles.* New York: Spring Books, 1963.

INDEX

A

Aaron Mercy 47
Aboukir Island 37
Absolute 126
Achille 39
Adriatic 76
Aegean Sea 15, 17
Aetna 46, 56
Affondatore 232
Agamenticus 164, 236
Age of Exploration 24
Age of Sail 26
Agrippa, Marcus 15, 18
Albany 39, 118
Albemarle 76, 93, 94, 125, 160, 170, 173, 177,
        178, 180, 182, 183, 184, 187, 188, 189,
        191, 192, 194, 196, 201, 206, 208, 217,
        232
Albemarle Sound 93
Alden, James 65, 66, 200
Alecto 42, 53
Alligator 126, 164
Almirante Cochrane 235
American Coaster 128
Amphitrite 228, 233, 234, 237, 238, 250, 251,
        254
Amy Warwick 74
Anaconda Plan 71, 222
Anderson, Robert 57, 66
Anglo-Dutch War 25
Arkansas 81, 87, 89, 126, 135, 137, 158, 195,
        240, 241
Armstrong, William G. 45, 55
Army of the Potomac 101, 117, 119, 121, 137

Aroostook 87, 128, 132
Atahualpa 232, 235
Atlanta 71, 144, 154, 168, 169, 192, 194, 228,
        233, 236
Attack on Veracruz, Mexico 49
Augusta 158
Azuma 220, 232

B

Bache, Alexander 73
Bacot, R.N. 188
Baltic 30, 83, 135, 178, 184, 220
Baltimore Riot 68
Bankhead, John 73, 76, 99, 100, 119, 148,
        149
Banks, Nathaniel 183
Barca, Hanikar 17
Barnard, John Gross 73, 117, 119
Barney, Joseph 121
Baron De Kalb 145, 156, 161, 164, 172
Barron, Samuel 38, 77, 216
Barton 84
Bassett, Henry D. 160
Battery Parsons 214
Battle of Actium 15, 16, 18
Battle of Albemarle Sound 192
Battle of Baltimore 41
Battle of Chin Do Island 28
Battle of Copenhagen 38
Battle of Craney Island 118
Battle of Cumae 15, 18
Battle of Dover 19
Battle of Ecnomus 15, 17
Battle of Fair Oaks 135

Battle of Gabbard Bank 25, 29

Battle of Galveston 155

Battle of Hampton Roads 6, 7, 9, 10, 11, 88, 144, 153, 224, 228, 255, 256

Battle of Kentist Knock 29

Battle of Lake Champlain 41

Battle of Lemnos 17

Battle of Lepanto 17, 22, 24

Battle of Manassas 74

Battle of Manila Bay 238

Battle of Minorca 30

Battle of Mylae 18

Battle of Myonnesus 15, 17

Battle of Naulochus 15, 18

Battle of Navarino Bay 48

Battle of Noryang 28

Battle of Okpo 28

Battle of Palermo 30

Battle of Pusan 28

Battle of Quiberon Bay 17

Battle of Salamis 17

Battle of Shiloh 119

Battle of Sinope 54, 55

Battle of Sluys 20

Battle of the Capes 26

Battle of the Chesapeake Capes 32

Battle of the Hellespont 18

Battle of the Masts 16, 18

Battle of the Nile 37

Battle of the Saintes 26, 34

Battle of Trafalgar 38

Battle of Tsushima 240

Battle of Williamsburg 127

Battle of Yalu River 237

Battle of Yellow Sea 240

Battle of Zierikzee 20

Bayou City 155

Bearss, Edwin L. 257

Beaufort 86, 89, 90, 95, 97, 101, 106, 109, 117, 120, 124, 213

Beaufort, North Carolina 86, 89, 117, 145

Beauregard 82, 127, 175

Beauregard, P.G.T. 66, 74, 154, 155, 158, 167, 168, 172, 173, 175, 176, 188

Bellerophon 230

Bengal Marine 49

Benjamin, Judah 116

Bentham, Samuel 34

Benton 83, 96, 145, 168, 183

Bessemer, Henry 56

Big Tybee Island 86

Birmingham 250

Black Prince 46

Black Sea 34, 46, 56

Blake, Robert 29, 30

Blanco En Calada 235

Blockade Strategy Board 73

Blomefield, Thomas 34

Bloodgood, Albert 39

Bombardment of Copenhagen 39

Bombardment of Kinburn 55

Bombshell 189, 191

bomb ketch 30

Bomford, George 39, 45

Bonhomme 32

Booth, John Wilkes 219

Boscawen, Edward 26

Boston 39, 55, 93, 140, 144, 172, 184, 189, 216, 217, 219, 228, 236

Boulogne, France 39

Bouvet 233

Bragg, Braxton 188, 217

Breckinridge 126

Brent, Thomas W. 208

Brest, France 43

Britannia 192

British Isles 16, 26, 28

Broke, Philip 39

Brooke, John Mercer 60, 62, 72, 73, 76, 77, 98, 116, 117, 119, 136, 175, 192

Brooke gun 62, 113, 134, 158

Brooklyn 196

Brooklyn Navy Yard 65, 100, 229

Brown, Isaac Newton 87, 135

Brown, J. Thompson 71

Brown Shipyard 139

Bucentaure 39

Buchanan, Franklin 69, 77, 84, 94, 95, 97, 98, 99, 101, 106, 109, 139, 176, 179, 181, 196

Buchanan, Thomas McKean 156

Bug River 56

Bulloch, James D. 71, 170

Bull Run 74, 85

Burgh, Hubert de 19

Burnside, Ambrose E. 85, 90, 91, 117

Burwell's Bay 70, 128

Bushnell, Cornelius 61, 77, 79

Butler, Benjamin Franklin 72, 76, 77, 179, 188, 209

Butts, Francis 149

Byng, John 30

Byzantium 16, 18

C

C.P. Williams 159

Cadiz 39

Caesar, Julius 15, 17

Cairo 62, 79, 93, 144, 153, 256, 257

Calais 27

Calhoun 156

Callinicus 16

Cambrian Foundation 258

Camp Butler 72, 77, 109, 110

Camp Hamilton 72

Canada 26

Cannon, Le Grand B. 110

Cano, Sebastian del 20

Canonicus 9, 172, 173, 186, 201, 207, 211, 228, 230, 232, 235, 240, 241

Canonicus-class 172, 176, 186, 194, 195, 201, 208, 230, 237, 240, 241

Cape Ecnomus 17

Cape Hatteras, North Carolina 76, 233, 255

Cape Henry, Virginia 93, 107, 109

Cape of Good Hope 24

Captain 233

Capture of Dublin 19

Carondelet 79, 82, 87, 92, 94, 95, 135, 137, 168, 183, 194, 207

carronade 24, 32

Carron Company 32

Carter, Robert Randolph 73

Carthage 15

Casco-class 189, 195, 201, 207, 213, 216, 217, 219, 220, 221, 229, 230

Catawba 186, 232, 235

Catskill 139, 144, 161, 164, 166, 172, 173, 196, 238, 240

Cavalli, Giovanni 45, 53

Cerberus 232, 233, 234

Ceres 188, 189

Chambers, Ben 54

Champion 127

Charleston 57, 66, 83, 126, 139, 141, 154, 155, 158, 159, 160, 164, 166, 167, 172, 173, 177, 194, 210, 212, 216, 217

Charleston Mercury 168

Charleston Navy Yard 55, 56, 184

Charlotte Dumas 34

Chesapeake 39

Chesapeake-Shannon Duel 39

Chesapeake Bay 107

Cheyenne 228, 241, 251

Chicago 228, 236

Chickasaw 181, 194, 195, 196, 201

Chicora 126, 139, 154, 155, 158, 172, 173, 180, 217

Chillicothe 139, 161, 164, 183, 184, 194, 195

Chilton, William P. 63

Chimo 189, 213

China War 49

Chippewa 126

Choctaw 140, 164, 183

Chucera 128

Cincinnati 79, 92, 94, 118, 130, 139, 145, 156, 168

Cinque Port 19

City-class 62, 76, 79, 85, 87, 90, 92, 93, 94, 136

City of Richmond 215

City Point Yard 172

Clerk, John 26

Clermont 39

Cockspur Island 86

Cockspur Roads 83

Codrington, Edward 48

Cohoes 230

Coles, Cowper 55, 57, 233

Collingwood 236

Collingwood, Cuthbert 38

Columbia 68, 183, 195, 211

columbiad 39, 45, 127, 134

Columbus 68

Columbus, Christopher 20, 24

Columbus Navy Yard 208

Comanche 139, 207, 220

Committee on Naval Affairs 63, 64, 71

Commodore 119

Commodore Barney 91, 172, 213

Commodore Hull 189, 192

Commodore Jones 192

Commodore Morris 156

Commodore Perry 91

Commonwealth of Virginia 38, 63, 67, 68, 71

Comte de Grasse 26, 32, 34

Conestoga 72, 76, 141

Confederate Congress 71

Confederate North Carolina Squadron 79

Confederate States 58, 63, 70, 73, 98

Confederate States Marine Corps 84

Congress 52, 81, 85, 91, 93, 107, 109, 110, 112, 121, 137, 138, 139, 236

Congreve, William 39, 41

Connecticut 240

Constantine 18, 235

Constantine, Thaddeus Sobieski 83

Constantinople 16, 18, 19

Constellation 55, 256

Continental Iron Works 62, 82, 83, 94, 184, 195

Cooke, James W. 177, 180, 189, 201

Copenhagen 26, 211

coppering 32

Cotton Plant 189

Craney Island 68, 106

Craven, Tunis A.M. 195

Crimean War 45, 46, 55

Cumberland 52, 65, 67, 68, 69, 70, 71, 81, 85, 91, 94, 101, 106, 107, 109, 110, 112, 137, 139, 224

Cumberland River 85

Curlew 79

Currituck 100, 128

Cushing, William 178, 195, 196, 206

Cyprus 22

D

Dacotah 93, 128

Dahlgren, John 45, 54, 63, 71, 98, 113, 116, 170, 175, 180, 181, 194

Dahlgren gun 45, 63, 93, 110, 114, 136, 139, 154, 167, 168, 170, 186, 194, 196, 214, 215, 229

Dale, Richard 34

David 175

Davidson, Hunter 113, 141, 184

Davis, Charles Henry 61, 73, 74, 87, 136

Davis, Jefferson 63, 64, 70, 83, 118, 119, 137, 180, 188

Dawn 161

Daylight 80, 126, 213

Deckerman, Allan 80

Declaration of Independence 69

Delafield, Richard 46

Delafield Report 46

Delameter, Cornelius S. 77

Delameter Iron Works 77

Delaware 68, 72, 91, 176

Democratic Party 65

Demologos 26, 41

Devastation 45, 56, 234

deWith, Witte 29

Diablo 234

Diana 156

Dictator 176, 207, 235, 237

Dismal Swamp Canal 124

Dix, John 110

Dnieper River 56

Dolphin 67, 68

Don Juan of Austria 17, 22

Doubleday, Abner 66

Douglas, Charles 32

Dragon 81, 91, 115

Drake, Francis 27

Dreadnought 237, 240

Drewry 213, 214

Drewry's Bluff 6, 10, 87, 89, 117, 118, 132, 134, 219

Drumgold's Bluff 145

Duke of York 25

Dunderberg 140, 229

Dunkirk 27

DuPont, Samuel Francis 69, 73, 82, 139, 141, 155, 156, 164, 165, 166, 167, 170, 221

DuQuesne, Abraham 30

E

Eads, James 62, 71, 76, 79, 88, 92, 135, 160, 181

Early, Jubal A. 119

Eason Shipyard 139

Eastport 82, 183, 184, 186, 189

Eastward 257

East Carolina University 258

East India Company 49

Edward III 20

Eggleston, John Randolph 70, 84, 107, 213

Elizabeth River 32, 72, 85, 98, 106, 115, 120, 129, 132

Ellet, Charles 87, 118

Eltham's Landing 128

Ely, Eugene B. 250

El Monassir 170, 230

El Tousson 173, 230

Emily Ann 72

Emperor Leo II 16

English Channel 27

Enoch Train 77

Enrico Dandolo 234

Erebus 46, 56

Ergherzog Ferdinand Max 232

Ericsson 112

Ericsson, John 42, 48, 51, 52, 53, 55, 61, 77, 79, 80, 82, 83, 93, 116, 139, 153, 167, 175, 237, 256

Ericsson Battery 61, 79

Essay on Naval Tactics 26

Essex 81, 88, 90, 91, 94, 97, 137, 139, 180, 183

Estrella 156

Etiwan 173

Etlah 230

Eutaw 213

Experiences faites sur une arme nouvelle 43, 47

F

Fairfax, A.B. 77

Fanny 76, 80, 95

Farmer 72

Farragut, David Glasgow 86, 90, 94, 126, 137, 194, 196, 201, 257

Farrand, Ebenezer 132, 210, 219, 220

Fighting Instructions 25, 29, 30, 32, 34

Fingal 71, 83, 144, 154

First Punic War 15

First Vermont Regiment 72

Fleet In Fighting 25

Florida 63, 65, 74, 130, 228, 240, 251

Flusser, Charles 125, 187

Foote, Andrew Hull 85, 90, 117, 119, 170

Forrest, French 70, 72, 74, 93, 96, 98, 118

Forsyth, Alexander 39

Fort Barrancas 63, 130

Fort Beauregard 82

Fort Blakely 219

Fort Boykin 128, 132, 135

Fort Calhoun 73, 117

Fort Carroll 110

Fort Clark 77
Fort Darling 144
Fort Donelson 85, 90, 95, 170
Fort Fisher 177, 208, 209, 210, 211, 212, 222
Fort Hatteras 77
Fort Heiman 164
Fort Henry 85
Fort Hindman 156
Fort Huger 128, 132, 135
Fort Jackson 86, 124
Fort Kinburn 56
Fort Macon 86, 90, 126, 153
Fort McAllister 156, 159, 161
Fort McHenry 41
Fort Monroe 71, 72, 74, 76, 84, 87, 90, 91, 96, 101, 109, 110, 116, 117, 120, 127, 128, 129
Fort Morgan 63, 179, 196, 200, 201
Fort Moultrie 57, 166, 173, 175, 180, 207, 211
Fort Pemberton 161, 164
Fort Pickens 63, 65, 66
Fort Pitt Foundry 54
Fort Pulaski 83, 86, 93, 119, 120, 153
Fort St. Phillip 86
Fort Sumter 57, 63, 65, 66, 155, 164, 165, 166, 173, 175
Fort Wagner 172, 173
Fort Walker 82
Fougeaux 39
Fox, Gustavus 90, 93, 94, 115, 117, 141, 144
France 46
Francis B. Ogden 48
Franco-Prussian War 233
Franklin, William Buell 128
Fredericksburg 175, 180, 195, 201, 213, 214, 219
French and Indian War 25
Frobisher, Martin 27
Fry, Joseph 234
Fulton 26, 41, 42, 48, 130
Fulton, Robert 39, 41

G

G.W. Parke Custis 83
Gaines 200
Galena 61, 77, 79, 87, 95, 124, 126, 128, 130, 132, 134, 137, 196
Garnett, Algernon S. 83
Geer, George 101, 135, 137, 138, 141, 148, 149
Gemsbok 126
General Beauregard 130
General Bragg 130
General Earl Van Dorn 130
General Lovell 126, 130
General M. Jeff Thompson 130
General Quitman 126
General Scott 127
General Sterling Price 130
General Sumter 130
George G. Baker 76
George M. Smith 70
George W. Lawrence Yard 230
Georgia 74, 167, 208
Germantown 67, 68, 69, 72, 98
Gillespie, Andrew 38
Gillis, James H. 156
Gilmer, Thomas 53
Gilmore, Quincy Adams 86, 119, 172
Glatton 56
Globe Iron Works 229
Gloire 46, 57
Gloucester Point 71, 117, 119, 127
Goldsborough, L.M. 79, 81, 85, 87, 90, 91, 92, 93, 94, 117, 119, 128
Gosport Navy Yard 32, 34, 37, 38, 47, 49, 54, 56, 57, 58, 62, 65, 66, 67, 68, 69, 70, 72, 77, 83, 84, 91, 94, 96, 98, 100, 116, 118, 120, 121, 127, 129, 130, 132, 165, 232
Governor Moore 126
Grand Era 168
Grant, Ulysses S. 85, 95, 155, 209, 212
Grasp 258

Gravelines 27
Graves, Thomas 26, 32
Great Britain 26, 32, 34, 46, 52
Great Dismal Swamp 76, 95
Greek fire 16, 18, 19
Green, Thomas 186
Greene, Samuel Dana 89, 93, 100, 115, 145
Greenpoint Ship Yard 80
Griswold, John A. 77, 79
Guadeloupe 34, 51
Guieysse, Pierre Armand 45
Gulf of Ambracia 18
Gulf of Patras 22

H

H.L. Hunley 161, 172, 173, 175, 176, 182
Halleck, Henry 90, 118
Halligen, J.P. 215
Hampton 214
Hampton Flats 110
Hampton Roads 106, 110, 113
Hanno 17
Harmony 77
Harriet Lane 72, 155
Hartford 88, 94, 125, 196, 200, 257
Hartford-class 46
Hastings, Frank 26, 42, 47
Hatteras Inlet, North Carolina 76, 77, 90, 91
Hawke, Edward 26, 32, 42
Hawkins, Richard 27
Head of the Passes 10, 62, 80
Heihachiro, Togo 240
Heintzelman, Samuel Peter 117
Henry Brinker 91
Hideyoshi, Shogun 28
Hill, Frederick 80
Hoke, Richard 177, 186
Hollins, George 73, 74, 80
Hood, John Bell 207
Hornet 213, 214
Housatonic 158, 182

Howe, Richard 34
Howlett's Battery 207
Howquah 192
Huascar 235
Hudson River 39
Huger, Benjamin 93
Huger, Thomas B. 92
Hunchback 91, 213, 214
Huntsville 160, 201, 210, 219
Huntsville-class 160

I

I.N. Seymour 90
Iceland 19
Ida 84
Indiana 228
Indianola 139, 156, 160, 161, 176, 211
Indian Chief 175
Infanta 184
Inflexible 234
Ingraham, Duncan 72, 158, 164
Ionian Sea 18
Iowa 238
Ironclad Board 61, 74, 76, 79
Ironsides 88
Isherwood, Benjamin Franklin 66, 67
Island No. 10 117, 119
Isondiza 169
Itasca 196
Ivy 80

J

Jack, Eugenius Alexander 84
Jackson 182, 208, 219, 257
Jackson, Andrew 65
Jamestown 120, 121, 127
Jamestown Island 71, 73, 77, 80, 87, 130
James Eason Shipyard 183
James L. Day 80
Jeffers, William N. 117
Johnson-Seahawk 1 257

Johnston, James D. 201

Johnston, Joseph Eggleston 74, 100, 121, 127

John C. Calhoun 156

Jones, Catesby ap Roger 67, 71, 77, 80, 83, 95, 96, 98, 109, 110, 132, 173, 176, 181, 182, 184

Jones, John Paul 32, 34

Jones, Thomas 71

Jordan, Marshall P. 84

Junaluska 80

K

Kaiser 232

Kalamazoo 230

Kalamazoo-class 175, 186, 230

Kansas 192

Karteria 26, 42, 47

Kearny, Philip 127

Kearsarge 195, 238

Keeler, William 100, 112, 120, 121, 126, 128, 129, 137, 140, 141, 145, 149

Kennebec 196

Kentucky 228, 238

Keokuk 144, 155, 166, 167, 168, 173

Kevill, Thomas 99, 124

Keystone State 158

Key West 64

Kickapoo 183, 196

Kinburn 46

Kinsman 156

Klamath 219, 230

Koka 230

Korea 24, 28

Koros 250

L

L'Orient 37

Lackawanna 196, 200

Lafayette 140, 161

Laird Shipyard 49

Lake Champlain 26

Lake Erie 26

Lake Ontario 65

Lamb, William 209, 212, 222

LaMountain, John 74, 76

Lancaster 54, 88, 137

Landis 126

Langhorne's (Causey) Mill 119

Lave 45, 46, 56

Lave-class 56

Lawrence, James 39

Lee, Robert E. 70, 135

Lee's Mill 119

Lehigh 139, 156, 168, 175, 180, 195, 216, 238, 240

Leitha 250

Lenthall, John 140, 164, 184, 229

Letcher, John 67

Letters of Marque 71

Lexington 72, 76, 90

Le Havre 26, 27

Le Pacificateur 43, 47

Licinius 18

Lincoln, Abraham 57, 65, 68, 76, 77, 79, 87, 101, 117, 127, 128, 129, 130, 132, 144, 155, 219

Littlepage, Hardin 106

Little Rebel 130

Liverpool 47, 51, 175

Lockwood 90, 125

Lome, Stanislas Charles Henri Laurent Dupuy de 46

London Times 88

Lord Cornwallis 32

Lord Rodney 34

Louisiana 63, 79, 80, 81, 86, 89, 90, 94, 121, 124, 126, 137, 139, 155, 156, 167, 172, 180, 183, 184, 186, 188, 189, 194, 195, 208, 220

Louisville 79, 92, 95, 145, 156, 183, 194, 195

Lovell, Mansfield 92

Lynch, William 79, 84, 93, 95, 165

Lynnhaven 32

Lynnhaven Roads, Virginia 80

M

Macdonough, Thomas 41

Macomb, William N. 216

Magellan, Ferdinand 20

Magruder, John Bankhead 73, 76, 99, 100, 119, 155

Mahopac 194, 201, 207, 211, 240

Maine 228, 237

Majestic 237

Mallory, Charles King 72

Mallory, Stephen Russell 58, 64, 72, 74, 80, 83, 89, 95, 99, 112, 119, 127, 138, 155, 160, 165, 168, 175, 181, 182, 196, 207, 210, 212, 213, 215, 219, 223, 228

Manassas 62, 76, 77, 80, 86, 100, 126

Manayunk 208, 230, 240

Manchuria 250

Manco Capac 232, 235

Manhattan 195, 196

Mansfield, Joseph King Fenno 109

Maratanza 132, 137

Marblehead 127

Margaret 74

Maria 233

Maria J. Carlton 124

Marietta 211

Marietta-class 213

Marmaduke, Henry Hungerford 84

Marquis de Jouffroy 34

Marston, John 93, 96, 110

Marstrand 30

Mary and Virginia 71

Mary Pierce 74

Mary Willis 72

Massassoit 213, 214

Mattabesett 191, 194

Maury, Matthew Fontaine 62, 136

McCauley, Charles Stewart 65

McClellan, George Brinton 10, 46, 82, 85, 86, 90, 101, 117, 119

McDowell, Irvin 74

McGowan, John 63

Medina Sidonia 27

Mediterranean Sea 15, 18

Meigs, Montgomery 62

Memphis 158, 183

Memphis, Tennessee 53, 76, 81, 87, 118, 126, 136

Mercedita 158

Merrimac 110, 113, 115, 256

Merrimac's Prow 144

Merrimack 7, 9, 46, 55, 56, 57, 58, 60, 65, 66, 67, 68, 71, 72, 73, 74, 81, 83, 84, 88, 91, 93, 94, 95, 96, 107, 116, 118, 129, 158, 180, 192, 224, 237, 256

Merrimack-class 56, 57

Merrimack II 139

Mersey Iron Works 51

Meteor 233

Mexican War 45, 65

Miami 127, 177, 187, 188, 192, 213

Miantonomoh 228, 229, 233, 234, 236, 238, 241, 251

Miantonomoh-class 228

Michigan 52

Middle Ground Shoal 109

Milledgeville 208

Miller, Patrick 34

Milwaukee 135, 181, 183, 196, 201, 218

Milwaukee-class 181, 189, 194

Minnesota 56, 72, 73, 74, 96, 109, 110, 112, 113, 114, 115, 144, 184

Minor, Robert Dabney 109, 117, 136, 181, 182, 194

Mississippi 45, 51, 54, 79, 80, 86, 91, 124, 125, 126, 135, 137, 139, 155, 160, 164, 168, 173, 177, 230

Mississippi River 62, 71, 76, 80, 155

Missouri 51, 52, 135, 167, 173, 180, 210, 220, 221

Mithridates III 17

Mobile Bay 10, 63, 73, 135, 161, 172, 173, 176, 179, 180, 196, 201, 215

Modoc 217

Mohammed 18

Monadnock 164, 184, 192, 201, 211, 232, 234, 237, 238, 251

Monadnock-class 164, 184, 192

Monarch 232

Monitor 7, 9, 10, 61, 77, 79, 82, 85, 86, 87, 88, 89, 90, 93, 94, 96, 98, 99, 100, 101, 107, 109, 110, 112, 113, 114, 115, 116, 117, 118, 119, 120, 121, 126, 128, 129, 130, 132, 134, 135, 137, 138, 139, 140, 141, 144, 145, 148, 149, 152, 153, 156, 184, 224, 228, 255, 256, 257, 258

Monitor-class 189

Monitor National Marine Sanctuary 256, 258

Monongahela 196, 200

Montauk 139, 141, 144, 156, 159, 161, 166, 172, 173, 195, 219, 240

Monticello 72, 74, 195

Mordecai, Alfred 46

Morris, Upham 109

Morse 91

Mosquito Fleet 79

Mosquito Flotilla 54

Mound City 71, 79, 83, 92, 130, 136, 183, 194

Mount Vernon 192

Mulberry Island Point 95, 119, 124

Murray, E.C. 79

Muscogee 182, 208

Music 156

N

Nahant 139, 140, 145, 154, 161, 166, 169, 172, 173, 175, 180, 238, 240

Nakhimov, Pavel Stepanovich 45, 54

Nansemond 192, 213

Nansemond River 72

Nantucket 139, 144, 161, 166, 172

Napoleon 39, 55

Napoleonic Wars 42

Narragansett-class 46

Nashville 117, 161, 184, 201, 210, 219, 220

National Undersea Research Center 258

Naubuc 217

Naugatuck 87, 120, 121, 128, 132, 134

Nausett 219, 229

Naval Bureau of Provisions and Clothing 65

Naval Observatory 66

Naval Submarine Battery Service 141

Navarino Bay 26, 42

Neafie Shipyard 126

Nelson, Horatio 26, 38

Nemesis 49

Neosho 156, 160, 168, 183, 184, 189, 195, 207

Neosho-class 156, 160

Neptune 155

Neuse 165, 177, 180, 181, 183, 188, 217, 256, 257, 258

Nevada 240, 250

Newport News Point 72, 77, 83, 85, 99, 101, 106, 110, 121

New Era 81

New Falls City 186

New Ironsides 61, 79, 130, 139, 140, 141, 155, 156, 164, 166, 168, 172, 173, 175, 209, 211, 232

New Orleans 63, 72, 73, 76, 79, 80, 81, 86, 89, 92, 118, 124, 126, 137, 223

New York 32, 39, 53, 66, 68, 79, 85, 90, 92, 96, 98, 99, 100, 139, 140, 141, 144, 184, 195, 206, 229

Niagara 216, 217, 218

Nicholson, Somerville 127

Nicklis, Jacob 141, 145, 156

Nightingale 80

Nikolaou Harbor 56

Nile 26

Nimitz-class 10

Nina 20

NOAA 256, 257, 258

Norfolk, Virginia 67, 68, 72, 76, 87, 90, 93, 94, 95, 121, 124, 127, 128, 130, 256

Normandy 16, 20

Norris, William 106

North Atlantic Blockading Squadron 79, 168, 213

North Carolina 70, 77, 79, 85, 90, 91, 93, 94,
    95, 98, 117, 121, 124, 126, 127, 141,
    145, 155, 164, 165, 170, 177, 178, 189,
    192, 196, 206, 230
North Carolina Sounds 77
Nouvelle Force Maritime et Artillerie 43, 47
Nuestra Senora de Rosa 27

O

O'Neil, Charles 107
Ocean View 129, 130
Ocracoke Inlet, North Carolina 79
Octavian 15, 18
Octorna 196
Ogeechee River 156
Ohio 79
Ohio River 76
Olmstead, Charles 119
Oneida 196, 200
One hundred fifteenth Virginia Militia 72
Onondaga 172, 184, 195, 196, 207, 210, 213,
    214, 215, 216, 232
Orator 51
Oregon 51
Osage 156, 172, 183, 184, 186, 218
Ossipee 196
Ottawa 82
Ottoman Turks 22, 24
Ouachita 221
Ozark 160, 182, 183, 194, 229, 241, 251

P

Page, Thomas Jefferson 127, 211
Paixhans, Henri-Joseph 43, 47
Palestro 232
Palmetto State 141, 154, 155, 158, 172, 173,
    217
Pamlico Sound 76, 80, 93
Pamunkey River 128, 132, 136
Parke, John G. 126
Parker, Hyde 38

Parker, William 106, 213, 216
Parrott, Robert Parker 45, 62
Parrott gun 62
Pasha, Ali 22
Pasha, Ibrahim 48
Pasha, Osman 54
Passaconaway 175, 230
Passaic 88, 136, 139, 141, 144, 148, 156, 161,
    166, 172, 173, 180, 186, 195, 220, 238
Passaic-class 88, 136, 139, 140, 141, 144, 145,
    154, 155, 156, 160, 161, 166, 168, 172,
    186, 196, 208, 220, 240, 256
Patapsco 139, 140, 155, 161, 164, 166, 172,
    173, 175, 181, 207, 212, 254
Pathfinder 250
Patrick Henry 77, 83, 84, 94, 97, 113, 120, 124,
    127
Paul, Francois Joseph 26
Paulding, Hiram 61, 68, 70, 74
Pawnee 65, 68, 69, 70, 77, 79, 82
Peacemaker 53
Pegram, Robert 67
Pembina 82, 95
Pendergrast, Austin 109
Pendergrast, Garrett J. 67
Peninsula Campaign 10, 86, 89
Pennsylvania 49, 68, 130, 220, 230, 234
Pensacola Navy Yard 63
Perry, Matthew Calbraith 48, 51, 55, 164
Persano,Carlo Pellion di 230
Perseverance 47
Persian War 15
Pettit-Smith, Francis 42
Phelps, L.S. 90
Philadelphia 91
Philadelphia Navy Yard 49, 51, 192
Phillips, Dinwiddie 106
Phoenix Foundry 53
Pierce, Ebenezer 72
Pig Point 72, 84
Pinta 20
Pitt, William 26
Pittsburg 79, 92, 168, 183, 194

Planter 128

Platypus II 234

Plymouth 27, 67, 68, 72

Plymouth, North Carolina 177, 178, 183, 184, 186, 187, 188, 207, 216

Pompey, Sextus 18

Pook, Samuel 62, 76, 95

Pook's Turtles 62, 76

Pope Pius 22

Popham, Home 38

Porter, David Dixon 90, 124, 210

Porter, John Luke 53, 60, 73, 89, 170, 184, 189

Portsmouth, Virginia 32, 47, 67, 127, 130, 232

Portsmouth Navy Yard 175

Port Arthur 240

Port Hudson 139, 155, 164, 172

Port Royal 63, 82, 87, 89, 128, 132, 196

Port Royal Sound 63, 82, 89, 156, 158, 223

Potomac River 53, 73, 74

Powhatan 53, 118, 194

Preble 80

Presto 180

Princeton 45, 52

Prince Albert 196

Prince Henry the Navigator 24

Protector 237

Psyttaleia 17

Punic Wars 15

Puritan 195, 228, 251

Putnam 125

Pyroscaphe 34

Q

Quackenbush, Stephen P. 212

Quaker State 158

Queen of the West 87, 137, 160

Queen Victoria 72

Quiberon Bay 15, 26, 32, 215

Quinsigamond 186, 230

R

R/V Seward-Johnson 257

Rains, Gabriel 127

Raleigh 79, 95, 97, 101, 106, 109, 120, 121, 165, 177, 189, 192, 195

Raleigh, Walter 24

Ramsay, Ashton 101, 107, 114, 132, 192

Ramses III 15, 17

Raritan 68, 70

Rattler 42, 52, 53

Rattlesnake 161

Redoubtable 39

Renshaw, William B. 155

Republican Party 65

Resolute 74, 84, 169

Ressel, Joseph 42

Re d'Italia 232

Re diPorto Gallo 232

Rhodes 22

Rhode Island 145, 148, 149, 152

Richmond, Virginia 72, 80, 85, 87, 89, 94, 118, 119, 126, 127, 128, 130, 132, 134, 135, 136, 137, 158, 175, 179, 180, 184, 192, 194, 196, 200, 201, 207, 209, 210, 213, 214, 215, 216, 219, 223, 255

Richmond-class 126, 127, 160, 189

Richmond Howitzers 71

Rip Raps Battery 73, 117

Roanoke 88, 93, 109, 110, 170, 237

Roanoke Island 85

Rochambeau 140, 229

Rochelle, James Henry 61, 113

Rocketts Navy Yard 127

Rodgers, John 68, 72, 126, 132, 134, 165, 166, 168, 170

Rodman, Thomas Jackson 45, 53

Rodney, Sir George 26

Roe, Francis 192

Rosseau, Lawrence 71

Rowan, Stephen C. 65

Rowland, Thomas 82, 83

Royal George 42
Royal Sovereign 38, 230

S

Sabine 65
Sacramento 217
Salamis 15
Sally Magee 73
Sally Mears 74
Sampson 84
Sandusky 213
Sangamon 141, 160, 217, 238
Sangus 207
Santa Anna 27
Santa Cruz 30
Santa Maria 20
Santa Rosa Island 63
Santissima Trinidad 39
San Jacinto 53, 128
San Juan d'Ulua 49, 54
Saranac 53
Sassacus 178, 191, 192
Saugus 176, 207, 211, 219, 235, 237
Savannah 47, 77, 84, 95, 119, 154, 159, 160, 170, 207, 208
Savannah, Georgia 47, 160
Scheldt estuary 20
Schroeder, Charles 117
Scorpion 45, 214, 230
Scott, Winfield 71, 72, 127, 222, 238
Scourge 45
Sea Bird 84
Sebago 128
Second Punic War 15
Secor Shipyard 136, 194
Selfridge, Thomas O. 71, 116, 144, 186
Seminole 64, 79, 128, 196
Seminole War 64, 79
Semmes, Raphael 217
Senate Committee on Naval Affairs 64
Seneca 82, 161
Senora de Rosaria 27

Serapis 32
Seth Low 100, 101, 107
Sevastopol 45, 54, 55
Seven-Day's Battles 137
Seven Years' War 25
Seward, William 77
Sewell's Point 10, 67, 72, 73, 76, 110, 113, 115, 120, 121, 124, 128, 130, 132
Shackamaxon 230
Shannon 39, 234
Shawnee 217, 229
Shawseen 90
Shelfridge, Thomas O. 68
Sherman, William Tecumseh 179, 207, 210
Shiloh 230
Ship Island 63
Sicily 16, 17
Sidonia, Medina 27
Signal Book for the Ships of War 34
Simms, Charles Carroll 83, 184
Sinope 45
Sixth Massachusetts Regiment 68
Smith, Joseph 61, 74, 109
Smith, Melancton 178, 189, 191
Smith, Petit 48
Smith, William 91
Southfield 91, 177, 187, 188, 206
South Atlantic Blockading Squadron 82, 154, 155, 156, 170, 175, 180, 194
South Carolina 57, 63, 74, 126, 139, 141, 154, 156, 158, 164, 172, 173, 175, 180, 194, 207, 211, 216, 228, 241, 251
Spain 20, 28, 215, 216, 217, 238
Spanish-American War 228, 238
Spanish Armada 24, 27
Spanish Fort 219
Sphinx 195, 210
Spitfire 45
Spotswood, Charles F.M. 167
Sprowle, Andrew 32
Sputen Duyvil 214
Squib 184, 186
St. Lawrence 110

St. Louis 76, 79, 81, 91, 94, 95
St. Nicholas 73, 74
St. Patrick 215
St. Philip 125, 126
Staerkodder 195, 210
Stanton, Edwin 96, 113, 118, 173
Star 72
State of Georgia 126, 148
Stevens, Henry 88, 137
Stevens, Robert L. 51, 64
Stevens, Thomas 138
Stevens Battery 46, 128, 132
Stevenson, John A. 72
Stevens Battery 51, 87, 120
Stimers, Alban 80, 83, 84, 88, 96, 98, 116, 117, 189
Stockton, Robert 52, 53
Stodder, Louis 109, 140, 255
Stonewall 195, 211, 215, 216, 218
Stonewall Jackson 126
Stringham, Silas Horton 76
Sullivan's Island 207
Sumter 66, 88, 137, 166, 173
Sun-sin, Yi 28
Suncook 216, 229
Susan Jane 77
Susquehanna 53, 69, 128
Symington, William 34

T

Talcott, Andrew 70
Taliaferro, William Booth 67
Tallahassee 251
Tallahatchie River 161, 164
Tattnall, Josiah 54, 82, 83, 84, 93, 118, 121, 129, 130, 137, 170
Taylor, Zachary 83
Teaser 73, 77, 97, 109, 120, 121, 136, 137
Tecumseh 179, 196
Tegetthoff, Wilhelm Von 232
Telegraphic Signals or Marine Vocabulary 38
Temeraire 39

Tennessee 178, 196
Tennessee II 181
Terror 46, 234, 236, 238, 241
Terry, Alfred 209, 210, 211
Texas 219
Themistocles 17
Theresa C. 71
The Mariners' Museum 7, 9, 256, 258
The Star of the West 63
Third Massachusetts Volunteers 68
Thomas Freeborn 72
Thomson Shipyard 71
Thunderbolt 46
Thunderer 234
Tift Brothers 79, 124
Timberclads 72
Timby, Theodore 49
Tippecanoe 208, 230, 233, 238, 240
Tombigbee River 219, 220
Tonawanda 192, 233
Tonnante 45, 56
Tonopah 250, 251
Torch 173
Torpedo 213, 214
torpedoes 62, 74, 89, 95, 126, 127, 136, 141, 144, 145, 153, 155, 165, 177, 179, 181, 182, 200, 206, 208, 216, 222, 223, 224, 240
Toulon 26
Trafalgar 26
Treadwell, Daniel 43
Treaty of London 48
Trechard, Stephen 152
Tredegar Iron Works 74, 81, 126, 255
Trinidad 64
triremes 15
Triumph 233
Tucker, John Randolph 83, 94, 158, 164, 217
Tunxis 195
turtleships 28
Tuscaloosa 210, 219
Tuscumbia 144, 164, 168
Tybee Island 119

Tyler 72, 76, 87, 90, 137
Tyler, John 51, 53

U

U.S. Naval Academy 69
U.S. Navy Corps of Engineers 66
U.S. Navy Ordnance Bureau 71
Umpqua 230
Underwriter 180
Union 76
Union Department of Virginia 72, 76
United States 26, 46, 51, 52, 57, 58, 63, 68, 70, 98, 127, 234
Upshur, Abel 53

V

Van Brunt, G.J.H. 112
Varuna 126
Veracruz 45, 54, 69
Vicksburg National Military Park 257
Victory 30, 32, 38, 39
Viking 16
Vikings 19
Villeneuve, Pierre Charles de 39
Villeroy, Brutus de 126
Ville de Paris 34
Vincennes 80
Virginia 7, 9, 10, 32, 60, 79, 85, 86, 88, 89, 95, 96, 97, 98, 99, 100, 101, 106, 107, 109, 110, 112, 113, 114, 115, 116, 117, 118, 119, 120, 121, 127, 128, 129, 130, 132, 137, 140, 153, 181, 192, 196, 201, 215, 219, 224, 228, 229, 240, 241, 255
Virginia II 194, 195, 201, 213, 214, 215, 219
Virginia Militia 67
Virginia State Engineers 70
Virginia State Navy 67
Virginius 224, 234
Vixen 45
Vulcan 47

W

W. Burton 126
Wachusett 127, 128
Wainwright, Jonathan M. 155
Warley, Alexander F. 201
Warrington Navy Yard 130
Warrior 46, 57, 88, 95, 126
Warwick 83, 87, 119, 121, 127
Warwick River 83
War of 1812 26, 39, 49, 65, 71
War of Independence 26, 42
War of Spanish Succession 25
Washington, D.C. 79, 85, 110
Washington Navy Yard 54, 56, 63, 65, 68, 69, 71, 140, 141, 219, 255
Wassau 230
Wassau Sound 10, 93, 154, 169
Water Witch 80
Watt, James 32
Waxsaw 220, 230
Webb, William 109, 154, 160, 169
Weehawken 136, 141, 154, 156, 165, 166, 168, 169, 172, 173, 176
Weeks, Greenville 145
Weitzel, Godfrey 209
Welles, Gideon 60, 65, 71, 73, 74, 77, 79, 81, 93, 96, 100, 110, 113, 139, 141, 154, 159, 164, 168, 173, 175, 189, 194, 196, 216, 218, 222
Wessels, Henry W. 188
Western Gulf Blockading Squadron 90
Westfield 155
West Point 62, 128
Whistling Dick 168
White, Moses J. 126
Whitehall 90, 116, 165
Whitehead 125, 182, 188, 189
Whitworth, Joseph 45
Wigfall, Louis T. 66
Williamson, William Price 60, 73
William H. Webb 140, 160
William N. Webb Yard 229

William Putnam 213

Willink, Henry F. 160

Winfred 72

Winnebago 189, 195, 196, 201

Winona 137

Winslow, John 77, 79, 90

Wise, Henry W. 117

Wissahickon 161

Wivern 173, 230

Wood, John Taylor 83, 109, 115, 134, 180

Wool, John Ellis 76, 117, 128

Worden, John L. 65, 66, 83, 92, 96, 98, 110, 156

World War I 228, 250

Wotan 258

Wright, Horatio Gouverneur 68

Wyalusins 191

Wyandotte 233, 238, 240

Wyoming 228, 240, 241

X

Xerxes 17

Y

Yankee 69, 71

Yazoo 230

Yazoo City 135, 172

Yazoo River 87

York 76

Yorktown 32, 77, 87, 96, 117, 119, 121, 127

York River 71, 87, 117, 119, 128, 136

Young's Mill 119

Young America 70

Yuma 230

Z

Zouave 81, 91, 109

The
Mariners' Museum

ONE OF THE LARGEST MARITIME museums in the world, The Mariners' Museum of Newport News, Virginia, opened in 1930 and houses an astonishing collection of thirty-five thousand artifacts relating to the ocean and its ongoing relationship with humankind. In 2007 The Mariners' Museum will open the USS *Monitor* Center. Visit www.mariner.org for more information.

JOHN V. QUARSTEIN IS AN award-winning historian and has written and published over three hundred journal articles, appeared in many documentaries for PBS, The History Channel and BBC. He is historian for the USS *Monitor* Center at The Mariners' Museum and has been curator or consultant to many other museums and historical institutions. In his spare time, he is an avid duckhunter and collector of decoys and antique shotguns.

Visit us at
www.historypress.net

Asheville Eye Clinic
Earl Sunderhaus M.D., PA
119 Tunnel Rd.
Asheville, NC. 28805